Grandson of a Ghost

GRANDSON OF A GHOST

SCOTT DEPALMA

Gago Press
grandsonofaghost.com

Copyright © 2016 by Scott Depalma

All rights reserved

No part of this book may be reproduced or transmitted in any form or by any means, without permission in writing from the author.

Cover and book interior design by Scott Depalma
Edited by Edit911. Marc D. Baldwin, Ph.D., Edit911.com

Library of Congress Control Number: 2016951078

ISBN: 978-0-9979449-0-7 (Paperback)
ISBN: 978-0-9979449-1-4 (Ebook)

Grandson of a Ghost

Published by Gago Press

www.grandsonofaghost.com

While historic events, organization names and prominent figures from the time periods are real, main character names and some locations have been changed.

Dedicated to
Jacob Ham, Ph.D.

CONTENTS

PROLOGUE / **2015**   11

CHAPTER 1 / **1968**   15

CHAPTER 2 / **1973**   45

CHAPTER 3 / **1978**   73

CHAPTER 4 / **1981**   105

CHAPTER 5 / **1985**   137

CHAPTER 6 / **1988**   165

CHAPTER 7 / **2000**   189

CHAPTER 8 / **2013**   209

CHAPTER 9 / **2014**   235

AUTHOR'S AFTERWORD   263

> "It is a joy to be hidden,
> and disaster not to be found."
>
> Donald Woods Winnicott,
> English pediatrician and psychoanalyst
> (April 7, 1896 – January 28, 1971)

PROLOGUE
2015

Anything Scott knew about his grandfather started with a whisper from his older cousin.

"I have a secret," Deirdre said, leaning in close to his ear. "David told me."

"What is it?" Scott asked.

They were at his grandmother's house for Easter. Exactly when he couldn't remember, but they were teenagers. They'd been out back weeding their grandmother's flower garden for a few hours in the afternoon, and decided to take a break and walk around the block.

"You can't tell anyone," she said as they approached the sidewalk and got further away from everyone in the house. "You have to swear."

"I swear."

They continued down the sidewalk for a while without speaking.

"You know how no one talks about our grandfather?"

"My mom's dad? Your dad's dad?" Scott asked to help keep it straight. He had no mental picture or reference for his grandfather. Deirdre's question took him by surprise. "Yes. It's weird. We know nothing about him."

"Because he killed himself."

Scott suddenly tensed and stopped walking. He looked at Deirdre.

"How do you know?"

"My dad told David," she said. "Think about it. Grandma was always alone. Grandpa was never mentioned. We don't even get to see pictures. No one wants to remember him. Like they're hiding something. It makes sense."

In a scary way, it *did* make sense.

"Did your brother say what happened?" Scott asked.

"Not exactly. But something about the basement and maybe a belt. I think that's what he found out. I'm afraid to ask more. Don't tell anyone I told you."

"I won't. I promise."

They continued walking. Scott listened as Deirdre changed the subject and made a joke, but he couldn't concentrate. The secret unnerved him. Why had his parents never told him?

Years would pass before they ever mentioned it to each other again. They lived in different states, and after this visit, would only see each other a few times as they grew older. They lived separate lives, and communications between Scott and his relatives were formal, measured and infrequent. Scott's mother, Ava, had kept tight control of family interactions with them.

Even now as a full-grown man, Scott felt the act of searching the Internet for details of his grandfather's death was an act of disobedience. Ava would see it as an invasion and forbid it. Scott felt nervous as he researched his book and found a listing in the Death Indexes of the Pennsylvania Historical and Museum Commission website.

He searched via his mother's maiden name, and deduced the year of his grandfather's death from the date of his mother's birth. It was an unusual detail, and the one piece of information he actually knew: Scott's grandfather killed himself before Ava was born.

Scott finally learned his grandfather's first name. It matched his uncle's, but Scott had never made the connection. Now it made sense because eldest sons were often namesakes.

Scott was excited by his discovery, salvaged from more than seven decades, recorded in pixels for eternity: A first and last name (Dimitri Adamov), his age at time of death (35), and date of his passing (July 8, 1938) — exactly three months and twelve days before Ava's birth.

The story was true. He'd uncovered the proof.

Scott surmised he was the only living member of the extended family to know the age of his grandfather when he killed himself. It was a much younger age than he had imagined.

How could it have happened? It was an impenetrable secret. And like most horrific tragedies, it was better to forget and move forward in an attempt to heal than to recount or discuss in an attempt to find meaning. There was no meaning. Nothing good or comforting could be said. No lesson or wisdom could be gleaned from its exploration, only pain and damage.

And so no one talked about it.

And the ghost crept in unnoticed.

CHAPTER ONE
1968

As they drove northward from Maryland, Ava began to feel a sense of isolation. The rolling hills and cloud-capped mountains were beautiful, but as the miles turned to hours, the reality of leaving everything and everyone she knew became real and unsettling.

Ava's husband Robert had accepted a professional, career-track engineering job at a regional manufacturing plant of IBM. The life they dreamed of and worked hard for was just beginning. Vermont seemed like a great place to raise their two children, far from dangers and fresh and clean.

For now, her five-year-old son Scott was sleeping quietly in the back seat with his older sister, Pamela. Ava turned in the front seat to survey them, and reached to adjust the pillow they both shared, so it wouldn't slip off the seat. Satisfied, she turned back and looked out the front window.

The two lane road wound on, and traffic sometimes backed up behind slow-moving trucks that needed to switch to a lower gear in order to climb the steep hills. It was tricky to pass them because of blind curves and a spotty mist that made it difficult to see oncoming cars.

Ava and Robert had grown up outside of Baltimore, in a town settled by a mix of European immigrants, primarily from Poland, Russia and Italy. Robert's father had been a carpenter who worked in a coal mine and died young of black lung disease. The family was poor, each member resigned, ultimately, to face the world with no backup plan. They learned to save, ration, and squirrel away anything that might later be reused.

Robert was great with math. It became clear in high school he tested in the top percentile and was encouraged to apply for scholarships. The University of Maryland offered him nearly a free-ride based on need. He excelled at there, and later got into a Syracuse University master's degree program, also on a scholarship. He was an example of the American Dream when it worked: an Italian-American coal miner's son, using intelligence and hard work to make his life better. The system rewarded his talent, and even helped to pay.

Now he was making the most significant change of his career, uprooting his family to start a new life. Ava was supportive and knew it was the right path to take. Though, as the drive wore on and darkness settled in, the long gaps between houses or lack of any sort of activity worried her.

"Funny how dark it is," she said. "Don't they use street lights?"

"Not enough people, I guess." Richard answered. "Really in the country now."

"Not even a place to get gas, or stop if you had to."

Robert looked at the dash board and checked the meter.

"Don't worry. We're fine, honey."

This was the fourth time in three months they had made the trip north to Vermont, but now there was no turning back. First came interview trips, awash with possibility, and tours of the area to get a taste of what could be. When the job was offered and accepted, they found a small ranch-style house in a cul-de-sac, so the kids could play outside without much car traffic.

With many details to attend to and adrenaline-fueled decisions to make in the process up to this moment — driving in the station wagon and nearly to their final destination — it suddenly felt quiet and unreal and scary to Ava.

"Wonder how my mother feels about us moving away?" Ava asked, not expecting a response, but thinking aloud. "Now that we're gone."

Chapter 1 / 1968

Ava's mother lived alone, and was fiercely self-sufficient. She had kept her family going after the death of her husband; there was no one else, there was no other choice.

As the only girl and the youngest child, Ava had always been treated as "the baby" growing up. Her brothers — and especially her mother — felt a strong obligation to protect her since she had never met her father. She knew she was "supposed" to have a father, but didn't know what it was like to have one.

They shielded and kept things from her like the book *Goldilocks*, because they had no Papa Bear. She felt shame because others pitied her, and at an early age picked up on the taboo nature of her absent father's death since no one ever discussed it.

Her brothers bore the burden of having a father, and then waking up one morning without one. They would never return to who they were.

On the morning after the suicide, they had walked into the kitchen, one by one, like always, ready for breakfast, but their mother was sitting at the table, staring at a small, ceramic ashtray. In it were the remains of some of her husband's cigarettes. She didn't seem to notice the boys as they entered, and didn't speak for a long while.

Ava was almost five before she figured out by seeing other families that there was supposed to be a man or a father in charge of the house, not three older brothers. They did their best to fill in, and paid heavily for that responsibility. Ava saw the trouble her brothers got into when they did something wrong. She heard screams and watched beatings. Their mother responded to the profound family loss with a strict set of rules, and harsh physical punishment for mistakes or misbehavior. It was a matter of survival. Life was not kind. Stakes were high. Obedience was required. Breaking rules meant disrespect for their mother and a failure to grasp the terrible burden that had been thrust upon her.

The suicide brought shame. Looks of pity. People talking and wondering about details. And worst of all: the unavoidable conclusion that their family wasn't worth staying alive for. None of them. Not their mother. Not the sons. Not Ava.

Over the years, when sitting alone, thinking about things, wondering what her father might have been like and what could have happened, she came to blame herself for being the last drop, the final burden, the tidal surge that ushers in a deadly flood with enough force to make a dam break.

"Honey, you awake?" Robert asked.

"Almost dozed off. Sorry," Ava said. "You're doing the hard part. I'm supposed to be keeping you company."

"Don't worry. We're almost there," he said. "Definitely getting close, now."

"Do you think we passed the movers?"

"Trucks drive so fast I think they got ahead," Robert said. "We're gonna meet up at the motel and unpack in the morning, anyway. Doesn't really matter if they get there first."

"What do you want do about dinner? There's not even a McDonald's."

"We can ask at the motel. Don't worry."

Ava did worry. The final leg of the trip suddenly felt loaded with potential problems. Did the motel still have their reservation? Would the movers be able to park the truck in the lot? Would their belongings be safe overnight? Where would they take the kids for dinner? What if Pamela and Scott couldn't sleep? It would be their first night ever in a motel room.

She kept her thoughts to herself and watched the road. She recognized the sign for their exit as it came into view, and felt an unwelcome sensation they were out on their own with no safety net. But, as was usually the case, none of her fears came to pass. They arrived to the motel without incident. A restaurant nearby was open. And when it was time for bed, the kids slept soundly.

The next morning, the moving truck had already left the motel parking lot when they vacated their room to check out. Ava wondered if they should skip breakfast and head directly to the house to supervise the movers, but the kids needed to eat.

They found a Howard Johnson's and settled into a booth. She began to feel out of control because the movers had started without them. Her stress level rose as she watched Pamela playfully flip through the big, colorful, plastic-coated menu.

"Let's just order pancakes," Ava said. "You love those, Pamela."

"I want waffles," she answered. "Look at these with strawberries."

"Can't we just order? Where's the waitress?"

Anxious, Ava looked around the orange dining room. She waved her hand and finally caught the server's attention.

"We're ready to order," Ava said.

The waitress pulled out a notepad from an apron pocket. "Sure. Who's first?"

"Pamela? Go ahead. You wanted waffles, right?"

"Yes. These ones with strawberries." Pamela pointed to the menu photo.

"Me too," Scott said.

Ava ordered coffee for Robert and herself, and they each ordered country omelets. "We're kinda in a hurry," Ava said as the waitress finished writing and turned toward the kitchen.

Robert sat across the booth with Scott who tried to rip the paper place mat in front of him. Pamela hummed and alternated between looking around the room and out the big window. Ava managed a smile when the coffee came, and focused on the cup and her thoughts. Did the movers lose the key? What if they ignore the labels on the boxes or don't understand which room is which? There is no way they could know which is Pamela's room and which is Scott's, and which is the master, because they were all about the same size. Are they more apt to drop or break something if they work unsupervised? Would they be careful with the boxes marked "fragile" — the ones with the antique stemware and china her mother had given her? What if the sofa doesn't fit in the front door? They will need to make assembling the beds and the kitchen table a priority.

The breakfast came and Ava forced herself to cut the waffle for Pamela into small bites. It was difficult to focus, with the anxiety she felt with each passing minute knowing the move was going on without her.

"Are we almost finished? Scott, stop drowning your plate in syrup."

Ava watched from outside herself as the waitress, in slow motion, arrived to clear the table, leave the check, disappear, reappear, take the check with the cash Robert placed on the table. She watched as they got up from the table and shuffled out to the car, Scott holding Robert's hand, Pamela following. When Robert turned the key and started the engine, Ava exhaled.

As they approached the driveway of their new home, Ava was relieved to see a collection of boxes on the front lawn, the front door to the house open, the back of the moving truck open, two workers carrying the sofa.

As soon as Robert pulled alongside the truck and stopped the car, Ava rushed over to the workers.

"How's it going? Is everything okay?"

"It's all fine, Ma'am."

"Can you show me what's going on?"

Ava looked toward the car and saw Robert taking the kids out. She followed the mover through the front door into the house. She immediately focused on the pile of boxes strewn about the living room.

"Can we get these moved into the right rooms?"

By the day's end, somehow it all got done. Everything unloaded from the truck, nothing broken. Boxes in the correct rooms, some even unpacked. Furniture assembled. Beds made. A new homestead established. When the movers left and the truck pulled out of the driveway, Ava felt amazed. Somehow things had worked out. In the morning, it had seemed impossible

Scott and Pamela excitedly ran around the house, at times stopping to make use of empty boxes as forts and hiding places. Robert left to find a place to bring back pizza for dinner.

The next afternoon, Ava walked Scott and Pamela down the driveway to check the mailbox. She had arranged to have mail forwarded in advance, and wanted to see if anything had arrived. As they reached the base of the driveway, Ava noticed a woman on the front steps of the house next door. She wore a long, paisley-patterned dress, and a thin leather headband. She waved and began to walk toward them.

"Hi, I'm Sandra," she said as she approached the mailbox and smiled. "It's nice to meet you."

Sandra and Ava shook hands.

"I'm Ava. This is Pamela and this is Scott." Ava motioned toward each of them. "My husband's inside. His name's Robert."

Sandra greeted Pamela and Scott with a smile and extended her hand. "Such cuties. How old are you?"

"Scott's five, and Pamela's seven," Ava said.

"That's perfect. Pamela's the same age as my daughter, Jennifer. There're lots of kids in the neighborhood. You'll all make friends," Sandra said.

She looked back to Ava. "How did the move go?"

"It was nerve-racking, but went as well as it could. We're still digging out," Ava answered.

"Where did you move from?"

"Maryland. Outside of Baltimore."

"Oh, far away."

"Yes, kind of. It's about eight hours drive."

"That's very far for us. My husband and I are from here. Born and raised." Sandra paused. "What brings you here?"

"My husband got a job at IBM."

"Oh, another one. That's nice. Mr. Sommers works there too. He's in that red house over there."

Sandra slid her finger across the side of the mailbox.

"What's the name gonna say?"

"The name?"

"On the mailbox."

"Oh, right," Ava said. "Depalma."

Sandra smiled. "That's pretty."

"It's Italian."

"Sounds fancy."

"It means 'from the palm,'" Ava said. "My side comes from the Ukraine."

"Wow, not quite sure where that is."

"It's part of the Soviet Union. Borders on Poland."

"Communists?" Sandra asked.

"No, my grandparents arrived here before they took over. Anyway, we're all Americans now."

"That's what's important," Sandra said. "We're all coming together. Becoming one interconnected family, regardless of where our journey began. Welcome to the neighborhood. Lovely to have you and great to meet you." She touched Scott's nose and shook one of Pamela's fingers. "You, too."

Ava smiled. "Very nice to meet you, too."

"Is there anything you need? Anything I can bring over?"

"No, I think we're all set for now. Just gotta get settled. But, thanks." Sandra took one step backward.

"Sure. Give a holler if you need any help. And see you soon!" She turned and walked toward her house.

"Look, Pamela. We got some mail."

Ava lifted her up and Pamela reached inside to pull out the letters. Scott grabbed Ava's leg to try to climb up. Ava put Pamela down and picked up Scott to peek inside, but he was more interested in the red flag on the side of the box. He reached out. She shuffled around to let him move it up and down.

"What's that do?" Pamela asked.

"It's for the mailman," Ava answered. "When we put in letters for him to take, we put the flag up. Then when he takes the mail, he puts the flag down. It's a signal."

"Oh, cool. Can I try it?"

She let them both fiddle with the flag on the side of the box, then gathered them up, along with the mail, and walked back to the house.

"Daddy, we already got mail," Pamela announced as they entered.

"Let me see," Robert said. He was standing at the kitchen table, unpacking dishes from a box and making piles.

"I met a neighbor," Ava said. "From the beige house next door. Her name is Sandra."

"Oh, that's great. Was she nice?"

"I guess so. It's hard to tell." Ava said. She paused. "She's kind of a hippie."

"Really?"

"She wears a headband. Walks around barefoot. Wears kind of a crazy dress."

"Has she lived here long?" Robert asked.

"She's from around here. Born and raised."

"Good. She'll know where everything is."

"Guess so," Ava said. "It feels odd being in a new place. Like we're strangers."

"Guess we are. At least for now."

Robert went back to unpacking, Ava joined him and the kids played in the living room. Each box that got emptied, broken-down, and folded became a small victory. They continued through the day, and into the evening. They all turned in early, after a hard day's work.

A few days passed, then a week or two, and they began to feel settled and established a routine. Ava was in charge of the household and caring for the children while Robert went to work. His job was demanding, and Ava did whatever she could to support his career.

She kept the house clean, did the grocery shopping, and always had supper ready when he got home a little before six. She kept organized by making lists of what needed to be done each day. Chores like laundry, dusting and vacuuming were spread out across the week, in between the cycle of dressing, feeding, resting and playing with the kids.

Pamela was a huge help to Ava from an early age. She followed her mother around the house, bringing Scott along with her, and dressing and playing with him when Ava asked her to do so.

Ava especially liked having help in the kitchen. She taught Pamela and Scott to set the table and sat them on the counter as she made pancakes for breakfast, or prepared the dough and fillings for Russian *Pirozhki* that would be baked later for supper.

"My mother taught me to make these. Now I'm showing you," Ava told Pamela as she chopped and shredded a head of cabbage.

"I don't like that," Pamela said pointing to the bowl.

"You just think you don't," Ava said. She opened the refrigerator, pulled a package of ground beef from the lower drawer, and brought it to the counter.

"Why can't we just have burgers?" Pamela asked.

"Because I want you to learn about other foods. Things my mother made for me."

She seasoned the meat and began to brown it in a skillet. As the aroma filled the kitchen and Pamela helped Ava stir and break up the beef, Scott edged over to the window to take a look outside. The backyard was neatly mowed and surrounded on three sides by small shrub pines that formed a border along the property line. A single, large maple tree stood in the center. There was a garden area tilled in the back, and to the left was a square sandbox with wood beams on each side to sit on.

"I wanna go outside," Scott said.

Ava looked over at him from the stove. "We're cooking now."

"Please? I don't want to cook."

"Pamela, do you want to go outside with your brother or cook with me?"

"Cook with you."

Ava looked at Scott. "Okay, you can go outside, but stay where I can see you through the window." She wiped her hands on a dish towel and got Scott down from the counter. "Keep stirring, Pamela."

Scott ran to the kitchen door that led to the garage. It opened to the yard through the back door.

"Stay where I can see you from the window," Ava called after Scott as the door closed behind him. She went back to the skillet and surveyed the beef Pamela continued to stir. She took Pamela's hand and helped her finish stirring. The meat was done and Ava used a slotted spoon to drain it and transfer it to the bowl of cabbage. They stirred the mixture and seasoned the combination. Ava paused to glance out the window to see what Scott was up to. He was standing beneath the maple tree, using a fallen stick to poke at a knot on the side of the trunk.

"Now we're going to make the dough," Ava said as she got butter, salt and flour, and moved to set up a work station on the kitchen table. She mixed the ingredients together, added water, and began to knead the dough with her hands. Pamela reached into the bowl and squeezed the dough between her fingers. With a sticky hand, Ava grasped a measuring cup and dipped into the bag of flour, then gently sifted and scattered it in a light layer across the surface of the table top.

With her hands still covered in dough, she took a step backward to take a peek out the window.

Scott was sitting now on the grass beneath the tree, waving the stick like a magic wand. As Ava turned to return to kneading the dough, a movement caught her eye at the far end of the back yard. Into a gap between the pine shrubs, a huge black-and-white-spotted head emerged: a cow had wandered into the yard. Ava stood in disbelief as the animal continued to lumber toward the center of the lawn.

"My God!" She ran to the door. "You stay here," Ava shouted from across the room as Pamela looked up from the bowl.

Ava's doughy hand slipped on the door knob as she pulled the door open to cut through the garage and exit the back door to the yard. Scott's back was to the cow, and he didn't notice as it walked behind him.

The bottom of the back door stuck, and Ava kicked to open it as she rushed outside. The cow watched her as she entered the yard. She walked quickly but delicately to not startle her, and headed toward Scott. With one fluid motion, she scooped him up and held him on her hip.

She immediately turned toward the cow and was relieved to see it bend its head to graze as it nonchalantly continued wandering across the lawn. Scott shrieked with delight when he saw it. Ava moved slowly toward the door to the garage, walking backwards while holding Scott and watching the cow.

"Wow. Look at that," Pamela said as she walked out the garage door into the yard.

"I told you to stay inside," Ava said. She continued walking backwards until she stood alongside Pamela with Scott held tight. The dough batter from her hands smeared onto his shorts and thigh.

"Where did she come from?" Pamela asked.

"No idea. But she's not supposed to be here."

The cow continued its aimless journey and crossed into the yard next door.

"Can we follow him?" Scott asked. "Please!"

Ava paused for a moment, watching the cow and how it seemed to care little about them. "For a bit. But walk slowly and stay by me."

As the cow continued along, they found themselves half way across Sandra's backyard. The cow stopped to graze. They watched as his tail flicked away flies that landed on his back. They stepped closer to get a better look, but kept back about ten feet. A screen door slammed behind them and Ava turned to see Sandra coming toward them.

"I see you met one of the neighbors," she said as she caught up to them.

"Neighbors?" Ava asked.

"Every now and again she gets out from Bundy's farm. Cows can walk over the fence when a post goes down," Sandra said. "I'll call Todd and let him know one got out, if he doesn't know already."

"Can they be dangerous? Territorial?"

"No, very gentle. Dairy cows."

"Oh, good to know," Sandra said as she put Scott down next to her. She reached to take Pamela's hand, but stopped and showed her doughy palm to Sandra.

"I got scared. Scott was outside and we were inside cooking when I noticed the cow in our yard walking towards him. I rushed out because I thought it was dangerous. I just made a mess of things. Got dough all over Scott. Plus, I think I left the stove on. And the dough is just sitting out and with the move I guess I'm still feeling unsettled...."

Ava's voice broke and she started to tear up. "And I wanted to have it in the oven already." She looked at her watch. "I guess we should head back."

"I can help, if you'd like," Sandra said.

"No, it's fine. We'll just get cleaned up and pick up where we left off."

"I'll make sure Todd's cow makes it back to the pasture," Sandra said, and turned to Pamela. "And you, honey, how would you like to come to a birthday party tomorrow? My daughter Jennifer turns seven."

"Same as me," Pamela said, and nodded her head enthusiastically.

"It would be fun to see some new neighbors," Ava said.

"Of course it would! There will be lots of kids from around the neighborhood. Plus their Moms. You can meet everyone. The party starts at two."

"But what about Scott? I can't leave him alone."

"He can come, too," Sandra said. "It'll be good to have at least one boy at the party. Anyway, they're all close enough in age."

Scott smiled and took Ava's hand. They started walking back toward the house. "Okay, that's great, then. We'll see you tomorrow at two. And thanks for explaining about the cow," Ava said. She turned briefly to watch it, and Sandra returned to her house.

"Well, that was interesting," Ava said as they approached the back door. "Turn the knob, please, Pamela. I'm still all doughy."

Once inside, Ava washed her hands, then sat Scott on the counter next to the sink. She took off his shorts and wiped his legs with a wet paper towel to remove the dough. "Let's get you some fresh clothes," she said as she put him back on the floor and they walked to his bedroom. She opened his third drawer and picked out a new pair of shorts. "I'll meet you back in the kitchen."

Pamela was already washed and ready to get back to kneading the dough. She sat at the table waiting for her mother.

"Can we start again?" she asked.

"Yes, let's see where we left off."

They finished preparing the *Pirozhki*. Later, when Robert returned from work, they ate supper together and told him about the cow adventure. Scott and Pamela were cajoled to get ready for bed early to be rested for the big day ahead: the birthday party next door.

As Ava cleaned up the kitchen, Robert read to the children *Green Eggs and Ham* and *One Fish, Two Fish, Red Fish, Blue Fish*, then tucked them into bed. Ava came in to kiss them goodnight.

Ava woke up the next morning feeling excited.

"Gotta get myself moving," she said to Robert as she got out of bed. "Lots to do today."

"The party, right?" Robert asked.

"Yes. Want the children to look good. They're gonna meet new neighbors. Kids the same age."

"Great for them to meet before school starts," Robert said. "You'll meet the moms. Feel more settled."

Ava was eager to make friends of her own. She knew it was natural to feel lonely after moving to a new state, but was bothered by how isolated she felt. There was so much to do in the house while Robert was at work, and the pressure of raising two children left little time for anything beyond the necessities of her role.

She remembered her mother's selfless dedication to the daily demands of raising four children alone: a non-stop cycle of shopping, preparing for meals, cooking, cleaning, and tending to three sons and a daughter who needed to be clothed, educated and guided so they could grow to be successful in an indifferent world.

She wanted to follow her mother's example. Ava would do her part to honor the sacrifices of her mother by making something of herself, and raising well-behaved children. She needed to ensure they had advantages she never enjoyed herself: a loving father who provided for the family, and a safe, suburban "American" upbringing unencumbered by ties to extended family who, by their doting presence alone, would never let her forget about the father she never met.

Chapter 1 / 1968

After breakfast, Ava left Pamela and Scott to play in the living room while she rushed to complete chores that needed to get finished before the party. She felt stressed, not only to get things done early, but by the prospect of meeting new people. She wanted to fit in, but worried the neighbors would be measuring them up and down and making their judgments.

She chose outfits for Pamela and Scott and laid the clothes on their beds to be ready for them to change into after lunch. She gave them both baths, and added waves to Pamela's hair with a few curlers. She had seen her brothers use hair tonic to create a neat side part, and she used it on Scott to slick down his hair.

By 1:45 they were dressed and ready for the party.

"I want you to be on your best behavior," Ava told them as they left the house for the short walk across the lawn. "There will be lots of new people, and it's a great chance to make friends."

The front door to Sandra's house was open, and *The Beatles'* "Hello Goodbye" poured into the yard. Ava reached out and rang the doorbell as Pamela and Scott climbed the three front steps behind her. It only took a moment for Sandra to appear.

"Welcome! Come in," she said as she pushed the screen door open. Her hair was curly and teased out higher and wider than Ava had ever seen before. "Everyone's here, between the kitchen and the backyard. Make yourselves at home."

A record player was set up on the kitchen counter with a stack of 45-rpm records scattered around it, and a plastic crate full of albums. Five girls were excitedly organizing and creating a stack of records to be played in order. A group of six women were standing together over hors d'oeuvres arranged on the kitchen table. Others were standing in the backyard with a group of girls blowing up balloons in the exact same spot as the cow had stood the day before.

Sandra led Ava to the table, with Pamela and Scott holding hands and following like small train cars. "This is our new neighbor, Ava," Sandra told the women, and smiled. "They moved in next door a few weeks ago. And this is Pamela and Scott."

They all exchanged greetings and Ava was relieved to see the neighborhood had at least a dozen children in the same age range as hers. Sandra called her daughter Jennifer over, and introduced her to Pamela and Scott. They exchanged whispers, and soon started making their way toward the record player.

"That's okay. I'll be right here," Ava said as Jennifer led Pamela and Scott over to the group of girls by the counter. "All You Need Is Love" was at the top of the stack, placed on the turntable, and as the song began to play they turned up the volume and sang along.

"Your kids are adorable," Sandra said. "You said Scott would be starting kindergarten in September?"

"Yes, and Pamela's in second grade."

"Mrs. Baxter has a wonderful kindergarten set up in the back of her home. It's just a short walk from here, and I bet there's still time to get him in to register."

"That's great news, thanks for telling me," Ava said. "I knew how the elementary schools worked, but wasn't sure about kindergarten. Especially without a recommendation."

The conversation moved to the women's other children who weren't at the party, their husbands and what they did for a living. Sandra introduced Ava one by one to the women around the table. Many of the husbands worked professional jobs in engineering like Richard, at either IBM or General Electric. One owned a country store that sold everything from bread to canned goods, milk and alcohol to garden hoses and screwdrivers.

Ava learned not all her neighbors were locals. Some had moved from other states, with European-born grandparents like her own. She felt relieved to not feel like an *Other*, as she had feared. One of the mothers with stick-straight blonde hair named Karen revealed that both her parents were Polish and they sometimes had Polka dances in their living room, complete with an accordion player.

"Sounds like fun," Ava said. "We had a bunch of Polish friends back in Maryland. Everyone was from somewhere else. Do you make *Pierogis*?"

Chapter 1 / 1968

"Yes, the kids love them," Karen answered. "Also *Kielbasa*."

"Of course! I love it. I wouldn't have the first idea where to buy it here, though."

"You can't, really," Karen said. "I always bring back a supply when we visit my parents in Pennsylvania."

"I miss having lots of little stores around," Ava said. "There's not many places to shop. And none of the foods we grew up with."

"I know," Karen said. "You're in the country, now. Hopefully, things will get better when more people move here. We're growing fast." She pulled out a pack of Virginia Slims and offered it to Ava. "Do you smoke?"

"No, I never really started."

"Mind if I have one?"

"Not at all." Ava looked at the packaging. "Looks pretty."

"Made for women," Karen said. "Imagine that, our own cigarettes." She lit up and delicately blew the smoke away from the table.

"Can I ask you something?" Ava said.

"Of course."

"Do you ever get lonely during the day? I mean, while your husband — Peter, was it? — is at work?"

"Yes, it's Peter," Karen said. "What do you mean, lonely? Your kids are with you, right?"

"Yes, of course. Keeping me company. And busy. They're great. But I never leave the house. Except to go grocery shopping."

"Oh, that kind of lonely. I know what you mean," Karen said. She paused to drag on her cigarette. "Don't forget, it's summer vacation. Kids are home. It'll all change in a few weeks when you're running to the bus stop, running to school, picking them up from activities, meeting teachers. Plus, you're new here. You'll make friends in the neighborhood. We keep each other company. Lunches, getting hair done, *conspiring*."

"I don't even know where to go."

"That's what I mean. We'll show you."

Ava reached for a carrot stick and grazed the top of the blue cheese dip on the table. She looked outside and watched Sandra helping the girls with balloons in the backyard. The group of mothers outside were laughing and drinking iced tea. "Let It Be" was playing, loudly, and the children in the kitchen sang along with the chorus.

"Is there a place you like to go to?" Ava asked.

"Yes, a salon in the town center near the railroad station," Karen said. "I'm going next week, if you'd like to come along."

There was a scream, followed by a loud, long scratching sound from the record player.

Everyone in the kitchen looked toward the sound.

The noise continued, and Jennifer screamed "Stop it!" as she pushed Scott away from her. As he fell backward, his arm hit the stack of records, and they fell from the counter top and scattered on the floor.

"What happened?" Ava asked as she ran over to the commotion.

"He pulled my hair," Jennifer said, and started crying.

"She pushed me!" Scott said.

"It wasn't your turn!" Jennifer protested.

"I wanted to try it," Scott said.

Ava grabbed Scott by the arm and pulled him away. "Pamela, help Jennifer pick up the records. I'm bringing Scott home."

"No!" Scott screamed. "I didn't do *anything*."

"You're not behaving nicely."

Ava grasped Scott's hand and led him away from the kitchen and toward the entrance to the living room. He resisted, leaning backward, but she continued ahead until they reached the front door.

The screen door slammed behind them as they left the house and walked home, Scott continuing to pull backward while Ava led him forcefully along. What had just happened? How could Scott have created such a scene? It was the exact impression she *didn't* want her family to make on the new neighbors. They would be judged. She walked with long strides, her right arm extended behind her, pulling Scott by one hand. He stumbled, but the strength of the forward momentum lifted him up and he regained his footing.

They reached the front steps of their house, and Ava extended her left hand to the screen door handle, pulled it open and lifted Scott up the top two steps by his arm, and pulled him inside.

She closed the heavy front door behind them.

Then she slapped Scott across the face. It was the the first time she had hit him the same way her mother had hit her brothers when they were little.

"You embarrassed me. You embarrassed *us*," Ava shouted.

Scott fell backward and started crying. Ava picked him up from the floor, and hit him again. He started to fall backward, but she grabbed his shoulder, then grasped him on both sides and squeezed his upper arms with her fingers.

"I told you to be on your best behavior," she said looking at him square in the eyes. She shook him and his head bobbed back and forth.

"We're trying to meet our neighbors and make friends, *and this is how you act?*"

He shrieked and she pushed him to the floor. She reached down and grabbed his wrist and dragged him down the hallway toward the door to the kitchen.

"You're going to your room, to think about what you did."

He kicked his legs as he was pulled on his back by his arm through the kitchen to the base of the stairs.

"You're just making this worse. Stop kicking!" Ava shouted again.

She grasped the rail with one hand and pulled him up the stairs with the other.

"Stop it!" Ava shouted and lifted him up from the floor, dragging him the rest of the way up by one arm.

"Stop crying, or I'll give you something to cry about!"

She continued to pull him down the hallway and into his bedroom. She knelt on the floor and raised one knee with her leg planted firmly down. She grabbed Scott from behind his neck and bent him over, pulled down his shorts, and hit him repeatedly on his bare buttocks with sharp, loud whacks.

He wailed with sudden, silent breaks while he gasped for air. Ava stood up and Scott dropped to the floor.

"Now, pull your pants up and think about what you did," Ava said.

She walked to the bedroom door and slammed it behind her. She realized she was shaking and went to the living room to calm down.

Ava listened to Scott's crying and remembered the cries of her brothers through their bedroom doors. She heard her mother's voice, clearly, strongly: "I give up. You *make me* do this. It's the only thing you'll listen to. First, your father shames us. Now, you're making it worse." Her mother had hated when they did something really bad like embarrass the family. And that was exactly what Scott had done.

Ava started crying. Quietly at first, but then the tears came forcefully.

She had disciplined Scott before, but more like small spankings. This went beyond. It had all happened so quickly.

She got up from the chair and walked to Scott's bedroom. She stood outside the door momentarily and listened to his sobbing and quick, shallow breaths. She wiped her eyes, opened the door, and was surprised to see him on the floor, leaning against the bed with his shorts still pulled down.

He didn't notice the door opening and Ava rushed over to him, bent down, and picked him up.

"I'm sorry," she said.

"I didn't mean it," he answered, crying louder as she hugged him.

"I know. We're the new people. You have to play nicely or people will think you don't know how to behave. That I didn't teach you."

She held him tight for a moment, then gently laid him down on the bed. She lifted him slightly as she pulled up his shorts, then smoothed out his shirt. She settled next to him on the bed.

"I'll stay here with you, but it's time to stop crying."

She wiped his cheeks with her finger. She didn't know how much time passed until he started to quiet down.

She thought of her mother, and how she would wait until the cries of one of her brothers stopped before returning to his bedroom to make up with him. She remembered her mother explaining to her: "It's important to give them time to think about what they did before letting them know everything will be okay."

Chapter 1 / 1968

"Now, just lie here quietly and rest," Ava said, continuing to stroke Scott's face. "I'm going back to Sandra's house to get Pamela."

Scott's breathing slowed. He lay on his back and stared at the ceiling.

Ava got up from the bed, and quietly closed the bedroom door. She returned to the party, found Pamela, and brought her home.

Four months passed, and a new routine was established during the week: most mornings Ava, Pamela and Scott walked to the bus stop and waited for it to arrive, standing in line with the other mothers and their kids in the neighborhood headed for the elementary school.

Pamela would wave through the bus window when she found her seat, and Ava and Scott would continue up the street to his kindergarten, where she would drop him off with Mrs. Baxter. Ava would then return home to complete the day's chores as efficiently as she could, to free up a block of time to spend with the kids later in the afternoon, talking about school and looking at their creations, maybe hanging some on the refrigerator door.

It was not yet cold, but rather crisp, and cloudier than the summer months. The sun sat low in the sky and set noticeably early. Ava didn't like dusk approaching in late afternoon. She felt a pressure to get started early on errands while there was still daylight.

She looked forward to the weekends when Robert was home and they could get things done and enjoy activities as a family.

It was Ava's birthday weekend, and to help make it special, she made plans to go to the hairdresser with Karen on Saturday morning. Ava liked Karen's conservative disposition more than some of her other neighbors' embrace of a *cultural revolution* that was supposedly happening all around them. Robert planned to drop Ava off at the salon to join Karen, and then he would spend alone time with the kids to shop for a birthday present.

With Pamela and Scott in the back seat, they drove to the center of town and pulled up in front of the salon. Karen was already there, standing in front, smoking a Virginia Slim. Ava waved through the car window.

"See you guys in a bit," Ava said as she opened the car door. "Give me about an hour. Maybe a little more. Have fun, love you."

She waved to them through the window, turned and walked toward Karen.

Robert pulled away from the curb. "Let's find Mommy a present," he said. "We'll try Ben Franklin. There's tons of stuff."

Pamela clapped her hands, and she and Scott excitedly fidgeted in their seats. "And you can pick out a toy, too."

They continued through the center of town, turned right, and about a mile later pulled into the parking lot of a strip mall of about a dozen stores, including a pizza place, a dry cleaner, florist, laundromat, an Aubuchon Hardware and a Grand Union grocery store.

Robert parked the car and the kids hopped out the back doors. They made their way to the store entrance and pulled open the glass front doors. They walked the first aisle and Pamela and Scott ran ahead to examine the items on the lower shelves.

"What about this?" Scott asked and lifted a wicker basket filled with dried flowers.

"It's okay, but let's keep looking," Pamela said.

They turned to the next aisle and found themselves in an area with candles and glassware. Robert watched as they rushed about comparing different options. They smelled candles and held a glass vase up to the light. They continued down the aisle and both stopped on a ruby red blown glass candy dish.

"Wow. What about this?" Pamela asked. It had an elongated stem base, similar to a martini glass, but with a wide bowl and glass lid on top. "It's beautiful."

"Yeah," Scott said.

Robert approached and picked up the dish.

"You're right. Looks like something Mommy will really like."

He lifted the lid by the small knob on top and looked for any cracks or imperfections.

"What's it for?" Scott asked.

"You put candy inside," Robert said. "It's a candy dish."

"Can we get it?" Pamela asked.

"Yes," Robert said. "Great choice. I'll hold it. Now pick out toys for yourselves."

They quickly walked ahead to turn the corner to the next aisle. Robert followed behind, watching them instinctively find their way to the toy section. Pamela breezed past the dolls and started exploring the crafts and games. Scott stopped at the Matchbox cars, tested a few on the front shelf, made a selection, then got on the floor in front of a wire comic book rack that revolved around a circular base. He spun it slowly as he looked at the covers visible from the floor while driving the cars in a circle to keep up with the turning of the rack. Pamela studied the front of the game box for Twister, placed it on the floor and wandered slowly down the aisle, stopping at the Play-Doh Fun Factory.

Robert walked between them, and placed the candy dish down on an empty spot on the top shelf. He sat down next to Scott. "What did you pick out?"

"Cars," Scott said. "And a comic book." He pointed to the cover of *The Amazing Spider-Man,* Mission: Crush the Kingpin!

Pamela wandered over, her arms full with the Twister box, the Fun Factory, and a three-pack of Play-Doh.

"Look what I got," she said.

Scott turned and marveled at her selections.

"Great stuff! " Robert said. "All set?"

Robert stood up and Scott followed, balancing three cars on the front of the comic book. Pamela stacked her toys and walked to follow Robert, who brought the candy dish. They made their way to the front of the store to find the cash register, paid and walked to the car.

"We gotta pick up a cake then go back and get Mommy," Robert said. "Remember her present is a secret. You'll help me wrap it when we get home."

The next morning, Robert got up early to surprise Ava with breakfast in bed for her birthday. He quietly made his way to the kitchen to start the coffee, and it didn't take long before Pamela and Scott appeared next to him. When breakfast was ready, he carefully lifted the tray, and walked slowly up the stairs to their bedroom with Pamela and Scott following behind, trying to contain their excitement. The door was cracked open, and Robert pushed it wider with his foot as he entered the room.

Ava was awake, lying in bed and smiling broadly.

"Surprise!" Robert and the kids shouted as they entered. Pamela and Scott ran past Robert to the bed and jumped up next to Ava and hugged her as she laid back and held them both, Pamela on her left and Scott on the right.

Robert gently placed the tray down near the foot of his side of the bed.

"This is wonderful," Ava said. "I'm really living."

When everyone finished, Robert made quick trips between the bed and the kitchen until the dishes were cleared and the tray was empty except for a last sip of coffee. From the doorway Robert motioned with his finger to Pamela and Scott who came running. He bent over and whispered in their ears.

Scott turned and ran back to the bed and jumped up. "We have a present for you!" he said and jumped back down. He and Pamela then quickly followed Robert downstairs.

In a moment they returned, both of them carrying their present, and Robert followed with two packages of his own. They placed the gifts on the bed for Ava to open. She started with the one from Pamela and Scott. They were silent as she carefully unwrapped it.

She removed the lid from the box and the tissue paper padding the inside. "I wonder what this can be?" Ava asked and revealed the base of the brightly colored glass.

"It's a candy dish," Pamela said.

"It's beautiful," Ava said, and unwrapped the lid and placed it on top of the fluted base. "Did you guys pick this out yourselves?"

"Yes," Scott said proudly.

She stood up and admired it.

"Come with me," she said, and walked toward the door. "I know the perfect spot."

Everyone followed as she headed downstairs and to the living room. She placed the candy dish directly in the center on the mantel above the fireplace.

"I love it," she said and took a step back to check out its positioning.

They decided to get dressed and to set the day's activities in motion: first church, followed by a stop back home to prepare for a drive up a mountain road to Stowe to see the fall foliage. From there they would go out for dinner, and then return home to have birthday cake.

At day's end, they sang "Happy Birthday" and watched Ava blow out the candles on her cake. "Thank you for a wonderful day," Ava said. Before long, it was time for bed.

The next morning, Robert went to work and Ava, Pamela and Scott began their Monday routine. At the end of the school day, Ava met Scott at his kindergarten and walked him home. He described some of his projects and showed her two finger paintings, which Ava hung on the refrigerator when they returned.

Ava set out some cheddar cheese, grapes and Ritz crackers for Scott, and left to fold the laundry that was waiting in the bedroom. He finished his snack and as usual went to the playroom to wait for Pamela to come home. A metal dart board hung on the wall, and Scott had a spring-loaded pistol that shot plastic darts that stuck especially well after he licked the suction-cupped rubber tips.

Scott heard the kitchen door close when Pamela got home. Ava called out to her, and she went to the bedroom. After showing Ava the drawing she made of a birthday cake, replete with the story of her mother's birthday celebration, Pamela got herself a snack and went to the playroom. She sat on the floor and opened her Twister game.

Scott watched closely as she unfolded the plastic mat and spread it across the floor. She set the spinner next to the mat and started to play. Scott went back to his dart board. Pamela tried spinning with her left hand while aligning her feet and her right hand according to her spins. She fell, and tried it again.

Scott turned and found Pamela with legs spread on opposite sides of the mat and bent over with one hand on red and the other trying to spin the spinner. He aimed at her rear end and fired a dart, hitting her. She screamed and fell to the mat, laughing and rolling over.

"Ouch!" she said, giggling and continuing to roll on the mat.

He picked up another dart and reloaded. Pamela saw him aim at her and shrieked with laughter as she scrambled to escape the playroom and made for the door. She ran into the hallway and Scott fired a dart but missed and it bounced off the wall.

Pamela's laughs continued as she ran to the living room and hid behind the sofa. Scott grabbed another dart and chased after her. As he entered the living room, Pamela jumped up from her hiding spot, stuck her tongue out and crouched back down. She jumped up again and Scott fired a dart. It flew over her head and struck above the fireplace, hitting a corner of the candy dish. It tipped over, rolled off the mantel and shattered on the stone below.

They stood in stunned silence.

Ava heard the crash from the bedroom, and rushed to the living room. She saw Pamela and Scott standing, staring at the glass shards scattered on the floor.

"I'm sorry!" Scott cried out.

"What happened?" Ava asked.

"He shot at me," Pamela said.

Ava saw the dart gun in Scott's hand.

"Go to your room, Pamela," Ava said. Pamela left and went upstairs.

Ava walked over to Scott and slapped him. He lurched backward, dropped the gun and started crying.

"How could you do this?" Ava asked.

She grabbed his arm and pulled him toward the fireplace.

"Look at what you did."

He struggled instinctively to get away, so Ava struck repeatedly with an open hand, wherever she could make contact. Scott fell down and she continued to strike as he curled into a ball on the floor.

"You shot a dart at your sister?" She looked at the shattered glass. "You don't care about *anything*."

Scott rolled sideways, his head coming near the glass. Ava tried to grab his arms, but they were crossed in front of his chest so she grabbed his left leg and pulled him away from the fireplace. He started screaming and kicked as she dragged him from the living room to the kitchen, away from the glass.

He managed to get free and pulled himself with this elbows across the floor to the space between the legs of the bar stools and the wooden cabinet doors below the counter top. Ava reached down and grabbed his hair and his head banged into the side of the cabinet.

"You're not getting off so easy. Get up off the floor and take your punishment."

She pulled the barstool backward and lifted Scott from the floor.

"Why do you *make me* do this?"

She shook him, turned him around, pulled down his pants and spanked him. They were both crying loudly. She stood up and Scott collapsed on the floor, hiding his face with the palm of his hand.

"Go to your room and don't come out until I come and get you."

Scott slowly stood, trying to cover himself by pulling up his underpants at the same time. He started walking, holding his pants up at the waist with both hands, and made his way up the stairs.

Ava went to the closet and got a dust pan and a broom. She wept as she walked to the living room and swept up the shattered glass.

The candy dish meant nothing. She was foolish to have liked it in the first place. She dumped its remains in the kitchen waste basket, and pulled out the Hoover to vacuum up glass shards in the carpet around the fireplace.

Shaking, she went to the bathroom to wash her face.

After about an hour Ava went upstairs and quietly opened the door to Pamela's room.

"I'm sorry we broke your present," Pamela said, putting down the book she was looking at.

Ava walked over to the bed and hugged her.

"What happened?" Ava asked.

"We were just playing. It was my fault, too. Scott didn't mean it."

"He can't shoot darts at you. That crosses the line," Ava said. "I hate that he makes me scream like that. And you have to hear it. I'm going to talk to him."

She crossed the hallway to Scott's bedroom, slowly opened the door and found him sitting on the bed.

"I'm sorry, Mommy," he said as she walked toward him.

"I know," Ava said and hugged him. "But, you're selfish. And you don't listen. *That's* what's bad. *That's* what I'm trying to correct. It was my birthday present. Do you even care?"

Scott nodded slowly.

"You're going to have to tell your father what you did when he comes home."

Scott stiffened and Ava stood up and walked to the door.

"I have to start dinner. You can come down when you're ready."

Ava went to the kitchen. The sounds and smells of preparations for dinner brought Pamela downstairs, and after a few minutes Scott slinked slowly down the stairs.

Ava worked silently over the stove and Pamela started setting the table. Scott stood against the wall watching them, then he joined Pamela folding napkins and putting out the silverware.

When Robert got home from work, dinner was ready. They sat at the table and as usual, Robert asked the kids about their day.

Ava looked at Scott. "Tell him what you did."

Scott hesitated, looked down at his plate, and said, "I broke the candy dish."

"How did *that* happen?" Robert asked.

"A dart shot at Pamela," Scott said quietly.

"He was out of control," Ava said.

"Can we glue it back together?" Robert asked.

"No, it's completely shattered," Ava said. "He shot it off the mantel.

Chapter 1 / 1968

Does he have any idea how that makes me feel? My birthday present. From both of you. Smashed a day later. Like it means *nothing*."

Ava burst into tears.

Robert got up from his seat and put his arm around Ava. "We'll have to get another one. I'm pretty sure they had more. I'll check tomorrow."

Ava became despondent and didn't speak for the rest of the meal. Robert asked Pamela about school and she answered flatly. Scott stared into his plate. When they finished dinner, Ava silently washed the dishes and Robert read *The Burlington Free Press*. Pamela and Scott quietly crept to the couch in the back room to watch *Bewitched*.

When it got close to bed time, Ava told Pamela and Scott they had to take a bath, since they had skipped the night before. They went to the upstairs bathroom and Ava ran the water to fill the tub and added Mr. Bubble.

Pamela and Scott got undressed and climbed into the tub, splashing in the water and putting bubbles on their faces to make fake beards.

"I'll be back in a few minutes to wash your hair," Ava said, and left to get their pajamas.

She wondered if they were getting too old to be bathing together even though she'd read it would probably be fine for at least another year. Making an issue out of separating them would invite confusion.

She picked out clean pajamas from their drawers, and was just crossing the hallway to enter Scott's bedroom when she heard Pamela scream.

Ava dropped the pajamas on the bed and ran to the bathroom.

Inside, she found Pamela standing in the bath tub, looking down warily at the water's surface. Scott sat with knees bent up in front of him, both arms wrapped tightly around his legs.

A small poop floated on the water's surface, close to Pamela's leg.

She screamed again and lifted her leg to get out of the tub. Ava grabbed her arm as she climbed out, and pulled a towel around her.

"I tried to hold it in," Scott said.

"You did it on purpose," Pamela said. "He was laughing!"

"Go get into your PJs," Ava said and sent Pamela out of the bathroom wrapped in the towel.

Ava closed the bathroom door and walked over to Scott.

She bent over and slapped him. He slipped backward and hit his head on the back of the tub with a resonant thud and started crying loudly as he lost control and slid low into the water. Ava grabbed his arm and abruptly pulled him to a standing position.

With one hand holding his arm raised above his head, she turned him around and hit him with the other. His legs buckled and water and bubbles splashed over the side of the tub. She pulled him back up and lifted him out of the tub. He fell to the floor and she grabbed him from behind the neck and lifted his head above the edge of the bath tub with his face toward the surface of the water.

"Look what you did! You are an animal! People don't poop in a bath tub."

She stood up, grabbed one of his arms and dragged him to the toilet.

She slammed the seat down and sat him on it.

"You've got to go so bad you can't hold it? Do it now."

Scott shivered as water dripped off his body and down the sides of the toilet bowl.

"Don't get up, and don't come out until you're sorry for what you've done."

Ava took a step back. She heard her mother's voice, this time her own.

"After everything you've done today? You *make me* do this."

Ava walked out and started crying. She crossed the hallway to her bedroom and collapsed on the bed.

From behind a closed door, Pamela trembled as she listened.

CHAPTER TWO
1973

Robert was a good employee and dedicated to his career. He was promoted and given more responsibility, requiring travel to Seoul every few months to ensure the proper installation of the mainframe computer components purchased from his company by the South Korean government. His travels would take him away for a week or 10 days. On Saturday mornings before a trip, Ava planned his outfits and packed his suitcase. She would later prepare a big lunch that they would share together before the drive to the airport.

Pamela and Scott always came along for the ride, and loved going to the lookout tower on the upper floor of the airport to watch the planes. Robert would stay with them for as long as possible before leaving to board his flight, and always told Pamela and Scott to be on their best behavior for Ava, because she would be alone. Scott hated when Robert kissed them and walked away.

It was the first week of December, and Robert's last trip of the year. Ava drove them home from the airport, slowly and carefully because it was snowy and roads were slippery. She was dispirited, so no one talked much in the car. Pamela and Scott immediately recognized her downcast mood and knew when they needed to keep quiet.

When they got home and settled, Pamela and Scott decided to get dressed to go sledding. The perfect hill was just a seven-minute walk from their house, in the pasture of Bundy's farm. The cows spent the winter in an adjacent field, separated by a creek they could not cross. Kids from the neighborhood were permitted to jump the fence to use the hill for sledding.

Getting dressed was a difficult process that required snow pants, thermal socks, tall winter boots, a scarf, parka, hat and mittens. Ava inspected them before allowing Pamela and Scott into the garage to get their sleds. She lifted up the door to let them out, and told them to be home before it got dark.

They walked to Bundy's farm and found a dozen kids from the neighborhood already over the fence with a collection of toboggans, discs and wooden steel runner sleds. They joined their friends at the top of the hill and lined up for their turn to ride. Scott went first, and Pamela followed on an aluminum flying saucer. It turned into a race and they both laughed on the way down.

The terrain leveled off at the bottom of the hill, with a straight expanse that led to a creek with only a few patches of ice on top, because the water flowed too rapidly to freeze. Sledders inevitably tried to jump the creek or intentionally crashed just before falling in because it was dramatic and fun. At the bottom of the hill, Pamela and Scott got out of their sleds and pulled them along behind them as they headed back up. They made dozens of runs, sometimes doubling up in one sled, or trading sleds with their friends and piling on a toboggan with five others.

The sun was low in the sky.

"Mom said we gotta be home before dark," Pamela said.

"Let's play 'Jump the Creek,'" Scott said, pointing down the hill to the group of friends who made it to the other side.

"No way," Pamela said.

"Come on. Just one more time," Scott said and sat in the back of the sled.

He motioned for Pamela to get in front. She climbed in and they pushed with their arms to start down the slope. As they headed toward the steepest drop near the bottom, Pamela put her hands out to try to slow down, but Scott pulled them back in and they both started laughing.

"Don't do it!" Pamela shouted as they sped toward the creek. Pamela kicked her legs out to try to stop the sled, but it wasn't enough and the front of the sled crashed into the bank on the far side of the creek. Pamela screamed and tumbled out. As she stood up, her boot broke through a patch of ice on the creek's surface, and got stuck in the water below.

"I can't get it out," Pamela shouted and Scott leaned over and tried to wriggle her boot out. The other kids came running over and gathered around them.

"I'm stuck! Go get Mom!" Pamela said and continued to try to dislodge her boot. She sat on the edge of the creek and pulled her foot out of the boot that had filled with water, wiggling her toes inside the wet sock. She stuck her foot out in front of her, leaving the boot in the water.

"I'll be right back," Scott said and ran up the hill to get Ava. He was nervous and knew he would be in trouble, but had to go fast because Pamela needed help and couldn't get home with just one boot. It was getting dark. He was out of breath when he made it to the front door and ran inside.

"Mom! Come quick. Pamela needs help. She fell in the creek," he said.

Ava appeared in the living room. "What? What happened?"

"She slipped on the ice and her boot's in the creek."

"What was she doing? She knows better."

"Don't know. But she needs a new sock and a boot."

Ava ran to Pamela's room and grabbed a pair of wool socks and hiking boots. She pulled on her parka and ran with Scott toward Bundy's farm. At the top of the hill they saw the group of kids gathered around Pamela by the edge of the creek. Ava and Scott made their way down the hill, holding their arms out to keep their balance. Ava rushed over to Pamela.

"Honey, you okay?"

"Yes, but my boot's stuck. My foot's soaking wet," Pamela said and pointed. Ava grabbed her leg, removed the wet sock, and rubbed her foot between both her hands to warm it. She pulled the fresh socks out of her pocket. Pamela put one on, and changed into the hiking boots.

"You could've gotten frostbite," Ava said. She looked at the boot in the water. "What's it stuck on?"

She reached down and grasped the top of the boot. It was difficult to see because the broken ice on top was in multiple layers and obscured the bottom. She wiggled the boot and felt something give. She pulled up harder and a branch broke through the ice along with the boot. She dumped the water out and tried to rinse off some of the mud sticking to the sole.

"You got it!" Pamela said.

"Can you walk home?" Ava asked.

"My foot tingles, but I can do it," Pamela said, and they started the walk up the hill. Scott pulled the sled along behind them, and took the wet boot from Ava.

"I'll carry it up," he said. At the top of the hill they got the other sled, and climbed over the fence to continue home. It was dark now, and they walked quickly.

"I'll get a fire going," Ava said. "We need to warm you both up."

Back inside the house, Pamela and Scott changed into their pajamas and put on slippers. Ava started the fire, then put out pillows and blankets for Pamela and Scott to cuddle up.

Ava went to the kitchen to make hot chocolate. Since Robert was away, she decided to set up dinner in front of the fire instead of at the table like usual. She warmed up SpaghettiOs, heated some dinner rolls, put dishes on a serving tray and brought everything out to the living room where they ate leisurely on the floor in front of the fire.

"How's your foot?" Ava asked.

"It stung before, but now it's good," Pamela answered.

When they finished dinner, Ava let Pamela and Scott go to the back room to watch TV while she cleaned the dishes, then surprised them with some popcorn. They watched shows together until it was Scott's bedtime, and Ava brought him upstairs to tuck him in. She pulled up the covers, kissed him goodnight, turned out the lights, and closed the door.

Ava walked back to the TV room. Pamela laid on the couch with a blanket and her feet propped up on a pillow. Ava sat next to her and rubbed her foot.

"Still okay? No burning?" Ava asked.

"Yes, all better."

"That's good," Ava said. "Now you see what happens by the creek. It isn't safe. Next time could be worse. Your whole body could go in. It's very dangerous in winter."

Pamela nodded and continued to look at the television.

"I'm surprised you were walking there. It's not like you," Ava said.

Pamela turned toward Ava. "I wasn't walking."

"No?" Ava asked and hesitated. "Scott said you slipped on the ice."

"I didn't slip."

"Then, what happened?"

"We were in a sled together. Scott crashed it into the creek."

Ava was silent.

"I was in front. Lots of kids were doing it — I mean — trying to jump the creek," Pamela continued.

"Did he do it on purpose?" Ava asked.

"I don't think so."

"He lied about it," Ava said, and the look on her face changed. "I'm not letting this go. You could've gotten frostbite."

She got up from the couch. Pamela's heart raced as Ava left the room. She knew Scott would be in trouble and she had caused it, but she didn't mean to. It was an accident. It just slipped out. She hid under the blanket and closed her eyes.

Ava went up the stairs and stood outside the door to Scott's bedroom. She couldn't believe that he had steered the sled into the creek, and lied that Pamela slipped, as if he had nothing to do with it. Why couldn't she raise him correctly? He was nothing like Pamela. Disciplining him had become a full time job. He was in trouble nearly every day, and the worst part was, he remained stubborn and didn't learn from his mistakes. No, actually, he was getting progressively worse with his lack of respect — lying to her face — and endangering his sister.

She opened the door to his bedroom and turned on the light. He didn't wake up, so she walked to his bed, pulled down the blankets, and shook him awake. He abruptly sat up with a panicked look and peered through half-closed eyelids while his eyes adjusted to the light.

"What? What?"

"Pamela told me you crashed the sled," Ava said. "You *lied* to me."

His heart started pounding. She grabbed his arm and pulled him up. He screamed and jumped to the floor and tried to roll partially under the bed, covering his face with his hand.

"You can't hide. Get up! We're going downstairs."

She pulled him out from under the bed and up to a standing position, and led him down the hallway by one hand. He cried, but didn't resist, because he knew what was coming, and there was no escaping it.

"I'm sorry!" Scott called out.

They continued down the stairs, Ava in front with one hand on the rail, and one hand behind her pulling him.

In the kitchen, Ava opened the door of a large closet, dug behind the coats hanging on hooks on each side, and bent to grasp a wooden paddle propped up in the corner behind them. It was half an inch thick and three inches wide. She picked it up and turned toward Scott.

"Pull down your pants."

He continued to cry and unbuttoned his pajama bottoms. She turned him around and bent him over. He screamed with each crack of the paddle, the last strokes leaving red bands on his skin. Suddenly, Ava stopped, stood up, and slammed the paddle down on the counter top.

"I raised you to tell the truth. Especially to your father and me!"

Through his tears Scott nodded and pulled up his pajamas. "I'm sorry."

"You've got to learn," Ava said and grabbed him by the arm. "You should've told me you crashed the sled. Pamela had nothing to do with

Chapter 2 / 1973

it. Now go back to bed and think about what you did. You're always so difficult. Your father told you to be good while he's away. I'm going to tell him."

Ava burst out crying.

Scott slowly walked up the stairs to his room. He closed the door, turned out the light and walked in the dark to his bed. He climbed in, pulled the covers up, and realized he was trembling. He gradually stopped crying but couldn't fall asleep for a long while. He listened to Ava's sobs from the kitchen and wished it would stop. He wondered if she would come back to punish him some more.

The next morning he crept to the kitchen. No one was awake, so he quietly ate a bowl of cereal. He put the dish in the sink. As carefully as he could, he opened the door in the kitchen, closed it behind him and entered the garage.

To the left was a stairway to the basement. It was underground, with an unfinished concrete floor and six narrow horizontal windows that let light in from outside, just above ground level. He liked the dark spookiness of the room, and didn't put on any lights. It felt safe and private and no one could look in from outside without getting down on the ground.

There was a laundry station with a washer and dryer against the far wall, and Robert had a tool bench and work area in the left back corner. There was also a large shelf of toys for him and Pamela, with a carpet and a blanket in front for them to play on. Scott kept a small pile of comic books on the shelf. He brought them over to the carpet and laid down on the blanket. He looked through two of them, and then skipped to the middle of his old favorite, *The Amazing Spider-Man*, Mission: Crush the Kingpin!

He laid on his stomach on top the blanket and rubbed himself as he looked at the story opened in front of him. He didn't know why or even how, but the sensation he felt was soothing, calming, exciting, and extremely pleasurable.

He carefully studied the story. The powerful Kingpin went from dominance over his captive, Spider-Man — even over-powering him in a fist fight — only to have the tables turn on him and end up defeated by his nemesis who turned out to be the better fighter. How could this happen? The Kingpin was in control and was the aggressor at the start. Watching an arrogant villain gradually lose control and then be defeated aroused him and had been a point of interest to him for years, for as long as he could remember.

He had learned that rubbing on a blanket or pillow or the bottom sheet in his bed would turn into some kind of all-controlling experience, an adventure he could become a part of and escape to. And at the end of the fight came a huge rush of pleasure and his body would collapse with an elated, peaceful feeling and he would sometimes fall asleep.

The bodies and tight suits of the characters somehow attracted him, and he also liked the fights on many shows on TV, not just comic books. Any show with good guys against bad guys. If a show came on and he was alone he would rub against the inside of his pajamas or pants on top of the sofa or the carpet, waiting for the good guy to fight the bad guy at the end.

He remembered one time at his grandmother's house there was a room full of people near the television and one of his fight shows came on. He watched from under a side table with a lamp on top, rubbing on the floor. He figured the rubbing was not allowed or was somehow bad because he never saw anyone else doing it, and everything that had to do with a penis or going to the bathroom was awkward and private. But the compulsion was so strong the idea of not rubbing when a fight came on never occurred to him. It was a natural, automatic reaction and he was unable to resist it.

He studied the long, drawn-out struggle of Spider-Man and the Kingpin, enjoying the feeling of transformation and transportation and energy in his body. He tried to keep the feeling going for as long as he could, because it took him far away, to another world. A wave of pleasure surged through his body. He then collapsed, turned to his side and curled into a ball on the blanket. As the good feeling slowly faded, a sense of shame and dread descended on him. He had to go back upstairs.

Chapter 2 / 1973

A week passed, and Robert returned home from South Korea. It was the weekend, and Ava planned to bake cookies and they would put up the Christmas tree. Pamela and Scott went with Robert to a tree farm, to select and cut one down. Ava stayed home, preparing cookie dough so it would be ready for the kids to decorate when they got home.

At the farm, Pamela and Scott ran excitedly through the rows of trees on a snow-packed trail that carved a crooked path through the drifts and wove through the different varieties of pines. They loved each one they passed. Robert selected a Balsam Fir and pulled out a tape measure to verify the height. The attendant cut down the tree, tied it to contain the branches, and Robert pulled it to the car.

When they got home, they raced inside to show Ava their prize, which was tied to the rack on the roof of the car. They all helped to get the tree inside, and Robert adjusted its position in the base to get it straight. Ava stood back and looked at it from several vantage points while he tightened the stand screws.

"Perfect," she said, and they cut the ties that held the branches. "It'll need a few hours to open up. In the meantime, we can do the cookies."

Ava had already unpacked the boxes of Christmas ornaments and lights and arranged them on tables around the room and on top of the sofa. Robert moved the tree carefully to its position in front of the picture window in the living room and rotated it several times to find the best fit.

The kids followed Ava to the kitchen to start decorating the cookies. They sat at the kitchen table and marveled at the set up: six small bowls with different colored confectioner's sugar icing were set up with small spoons on the left side, and an assortment of sprinkles, red hots, and colored sugars on the right. In between them was a wax-papered work area where Ava placed the sheet pans loaded with cookies to be decorated.

They started with the easiest, the pinwheels that needed only colored sugar. Next came sugar cookies molded to shapes of Christmas trees, candy canes, stars and elves. Pamela and Scott carefully painted the cookies with egg whites before delicately decorating with the colored sugars and sprinkles. Scott watched with frustration as Pamela precisely mixed multi-colors to create an outfit on an elf. He struggled with a single color, and failed to keep the pants separated from the shirt. Pamela worked with him on the next one, and it turned out better. They finished the last sugar cookie sheet pan, and prepared for the next batch.

The gingerbread men arrived to the decorating table. Pamela explained they were all identical, so the challenge was in decorating each distinctively. Scott grew nervous and tried to copy Pamela as she spooned the red icing on to create a shirt and pants, but switched to white and green to create buttons, boots, a belt, a face and a hat.

"Mine's not working," Scott said as the icing from the hat bled down into the face of the gingerbread man.

Pamela laughed and told him to try another one. He painted on icing, using the back of the spoon, and admired his creation — until he looked over at Pamela's, and saw the suspenders and polka-dotted shirt. He decided to shift tactics and painted his next one solid green, and added a face in white and a spot in the middle in blue.

"What's that?" Pamela asked.

"A belly button," he said.

"That's ugly."

They continued to work, Scott icing his next one with a thick layer of solid blue, with white trim around the edges. Pamela watched his heavy hand with the icing and decided to do the opposite. She used only a fine line of white to outline her new one.

"That's not enough," Scott said. He reached over with a heaping spoonful of blue icing and plopped it down in the center of her cookie.

"Mom, look what Scott did!" Pamela called out.

Ava came over, saw the mess on Pamela's side and pulled Scott away from the table by the neck of his pullover shirt. In a spasm of rage, he made a fist and slammed the bottom corner of the sheet pan that hung over the edge of the table. It flew upward, knocked over the sugars and pushed a bowl of icing off the table with a crash.

"Do you have to ruin *everything*?" Ava lifted him from the chair and slapped him. He fell and started crying. "Go to your room! We're decorating the Christmas tree without you."

Scott got up from the floor, walked to the stairs, and through his tears slowly made his way to his room and sat on the bed.

Ava picked up the bowl of icing and got a new spoon. "Can you finish these yourself?" she asked Pamela, and pointed to the tray with Scott's undecorated cookies. Pamela nodded and straightened the small bottles of sugar. She decorated in silence and Ava left the kitchen.

"What happened?" Robert asked as Ava entered the living room.

"It's Scott again," Ava said. "I sent him to his room."

She walked to the sofa and carried the box containing the strings of Christmas lights to the tree.

"Are we ready to start?"

Robert untangled each string of lights and extended them into straight lines across the living room floor. He plugged them in, and replaced the bulbs that didn't light. He started at the base of the tree and worked his way up. Ava passed the light strings to Robert as he moved around the tree in a circle.

When they finished, they turned on the lights, stood back to look, and made small adjustments.

Ava went to the kitchen to check on Pamela. She was putting final touches on the last of the gingerbread men. Ava began to clean up the mess of sheet pans, spilled sprinkles and empty bowls of icing.

When they both finished, they arranged the cookies inside Tupperware containers in neat rows separated by sheets of wax paper, put them in the freezer, and went to the living room.

Robert moved the empty boxes that stored the lights out of the way, opened a step stool and set it next to the tree. Pamela walked around to admire the opened boxes of ornaments.

"Can we start now?" she asked, and reached for one.

She carefully walked to the tree and chose a spot for the first ornament. She went back to get another, climbed the step stool, and reached as high as she could. Robert helped her steady the branch as she squeezed the hook into place. Ava came in from the kitchen. She picked an ornament, and added it to the tree.

Scott looked in the mirror hanging above the bureau in his bedroom. His turtleneck collar was stretched and falling down from where Ava had pulled it. He tried to make it stand up tight against his neck by pulling in the edges and making a fold, but it slumped back down.

He gave up and sat on the bed. He hated the waiting part. He listened carefully for footsteps that might come up the stairs. He desperately wanted to decorate the Christmas tree, and the longer he sat, the deeper his shame grew at being excluded. Why was he so bad and always in trouble? Why did he ruin things? Why did he make his mother so angry? Why wasn't he good? Why did he make his mother cry?

That was the worst of all: when a beating stopped and Ava left him and went to her room and cried uncontrollably for what seemed like hours. He would cringe, holding himself, knowing he was the cause of it. His shame was more painful than the beating itself. He would strain to listen for the point when the sobbing would start to diminish. Then a fear would take hold, because it would only be a matter of time before his mother came back into the room.

He hoped she would come back to make up, but sometimes the door would open to a second round of screaming and a punishment like being grounded, or excluded from an upcoming activity. Or sometimes another beating. It was impossible to know while trapped in a tense limbo, waiting for the cries of his mother to stop.

The sound of footsteps on the stairs brought him back to the present, and his heart started to race. He listened as the steps came down the hallway and approached his bedroom. The door opened and Ava entered.

"I'm sorry, Mommy," Scott said immediately as she walked toward him.

"Are you ready to come down now?" she asked. "We've started decorating the tree."

She turned and walked out the door. Scott got up from the bed and slowly followed. By the time he made it to the living room, Ava was hanging ornaments with Pamela and Robert. Scott peeked around the corner and was crestfallen when he saw the tree half decorated.

He quietly walked to the sofa, surveyed the remaining ornaments scattered about in half-empty boxes. He selected one. With an overwhelming sense of shame, walked to the tree and hung it.

Pamela smiled at him and pointed to a red and gold glass ball garland weaving around the tree. Ava and Robert nodded and responded to what she said, but Scott did not hear. In silence he walked back to the boxes of ornaments, picked one, and carefully hung it. He repeated the routine, searching out spaces on the tree still open. He did not notice Ava had left the room until she returned with four small wrapped boxes.

"You don't deserve this, but here's one for you," she said and handed a box to Scott.

He took the present and sat on a corner of the sofa. He was afraid to open it. He watched as Pamela unwrapped and opened her box, revealing a gold-plated star ornament with her name engraved on it.

Scott picked at the paper on the corner of his box. Ava would not have given it to him if he couldn't have it, he decided, so he unwrapped the paper. Inside was a gold-plated ornament in the shape of a Christmas tree with his name engraved on the front.

He stared at it and listened as Pamela thanked Ava and Robert and walked to the tree to find a perfect spot for her star. He felt undeserving of the present and guilty about being in trouble and shame for missing the first half of the tree decorating.

What remained was joyless. He meekly thanked Ava and Robert, walked to the tree, and searched out a spot on an inside branch where no one would see his ornament.

Six months passed. It was the beginning of June, and Scott remembered dreaming he was swimming. When he awoke, he realized with horror he had wet the bed. He immediately kicked back the covers and jumped to the floor. He started shaking. Could he somehow hide it? What was Ava going to do? A sense of dread descended upon him, as he realized the trouble that was sure to come when she found out.

He pulled off his wet pajama bottoms and underpants and threw them on the bed. Would everything dry if he just left it uncovered? He went to his bureau and changed into fresh clothes. If he pulled off the sheets and sneaked to the basement, could he figure out how to wash them and no one would find out? It would take a long time to wash and if Ava caught him it would be even worse. He had no choice but to tell her. He remembered he had tried an experiment once before, and maybe it would work again: he had made her promise in advance not to get mad before he told her something and she'd agreed. She hadn't hit him. He had no choice but to try again.

He heard Ava in the kitchen preparing breakfast, and he slowly walked down the hallway to the top of the stairs. He was trembling. What if his plan didn't work? He was sure to get a beating, because this was really bad. He hated the spanking paddle in the closet and it was so close and easy for her to grab from the kitchen. He walked down the stairs, passed the closet and stopped behind Ava, who was standing in front of the stove. She turned around.

"Good morning," Ava said, and smiled.

"Morning."

"Ready for breakfast?" Ava asked. When he didn't answer she turned again.

Scott held back tears. "Promise you won't get mad?"

Ava put down the spatula and turned off the burner.

"Yes. What is it?"

"I wet the bed," Scott said and stood absolutely still as tears filled his eyes.

Ava walked over and hugged him. "That's okay, honey. Let's go upstairs." She held his hand as they went up. They entered his bedroom and Ava got a laundry basket from the closet. Scott pointed to his pajamas in the center of his bed. She gathered them and stripped the sheets off the bed, including the mattress pad below.

"It's not bad. It happens sometimes to everyone," Ava said.

A wave of relief washed over him. He didn't understand why he wasn't in trouble. Perhaps it was the promise. He followed Ava as she walked with the laundry basket through the hallway, down the stairs, and exited through the kitchen door to the garage, then down to the basement. He watched silently as she loaded the washing machine, added a scoop of detergent, and closed the lid.

"We'll come back down in an hour and put them in the dryer," she said, and touched Scott's hair. "Then, you can help me make the bed."

Scott smiled and held her hand as they walked back upstairs.

The next morning Scott found himself sitting on the front steps next to the milk box, trying to stop crying before leaving to catch the school bus. He had been beaten again, this time for spilling something at breakfast and for a small red scab on the bridge of his nose that Ava said he picked at. It looked bad because people would see it. But Scott never touched it.

He had to compose himself quickly, or he would miss the bus, and he was already late. He was ashamed to be caught crying at the bus stop, so he flipped the lid of the milk box open and peeked inside and pretended to be a giant who was about the smash the villagers he found inside. They pleaded for mercy, so he closed the lid, waited a moment, then peeked again inside to make sure they were grateful. They had happily returned to their daily duties. So the giant gathered himself up and put on his backpack to free his hands, because today he had music class and had to carry his violin with him.

It was the last week of school until summer vacation, and this would be his last violin lesson until the first week in September. As he approached the street corner, he saw the yellow school bus flashing its lights and loading passengers, so he ran to catch it. He made it up the steep stairs of the bus entryway, holding his violin case with his right hand angled behind his back.

He quickly surveyed the inside of the bus, looking for a friend or an empty seat that wasn't near Bucky, the Bus Bully. He spotted an empty seat, but it was dangerously close to Bucky, only three or four rows away. The bus was mostly full so instead of squeezing in next to someone, he decide to risk it and take the empty seat.

He put his backpack next to him and stood the violin case on the floor between his legs to keep it steady. The bus finished loading and the door closed. It pulled away from the curb and started on its route toward school.

Before long a voice spoke from behind him.

"The violin's for sissies," Bucky said loudly. Scott's heart pounded and he pretended not to hear as the voice continued.

"I'm talking to you," Bucky said. The bus was moving and Bucky now stood in the aisle just behind Scott's seat. He leaned over and slapped Scott in the back of his head.

Scott turned, gave Bucky a disgusted look, and said, "Stop it." His heart raced and he quickly turned his head to look toward the front of the bus.

"You gonna make me?" Bucky asked, and smacked him again.

"No, just stop," Scott said as sternly as he could muster.

The bus rambled along. Was Bucky still lurking? Scott turned his head slightly and tried to look behind him. It seemed that Bucky had moved back to his seat. Scott exhaled and turned his attention to the voices coming from the back of the bus. He strained to hear if the threat had passed — if he was again anonymous, invisible next to the window — or if he was still a target. It seemed Bucky had moved onto someone else, so Scott drifted away and watched the cars go by as the bus continued toward the school.

He stared out the window and thought about the villagers in the milk box. They lived in a hostile place where, at any moment, the lid could be snatched off and their lives shattered by the forces outside. They lived with a sense of dread, always on alert, always in danger. And now Scott was a villager and Bucky was the giant. A villager was never safe. Today the giant spared him, but it wouldn't be for long.

When the bus arrived at school, Scott found two friends and they walked together to their classroom. They sat at their desks, waited for roll call, and stood to say the Pledge of Allegiance.

Later that afternoon, after social studies, math, English, recess and his violin lesson in the music room, Scott's teacher announced they would be getting their report cards early, because they had completed the year's requirements. Outdoor games, a crafts competition and field trips were planned for the last few days. Thursday's trip would be to the Shelburne Museum and she made clear permission slips needed to be signed by each student's parents and brought to class by Wednesday. The students grew excited with the prospect of summer vacation upon them, and days of fun ahead. The volume in the room rose as the teacher walked to each student's desk and handed out the permission slips and report cards.

Scott got his and carefully opened the envelope. He quickly scanned the columns to see where the check marks fell. They were Above Average or Excellent, except for one at the bottom. Under the Behavior section, "Assertiveness" was marked "Needs Improvement." He grew very nervous and wondered what it meant. Ava had made clear he and Pamela were not to receive any check marks in "Needs Improvement."

He continued to study the report card and tried to fathom what "Assertiveness" meant. He didn't dare ask the teacher; he was ashamed to, because obviously she thought he was bad at it. With resignation, he stuffed the report card back into the envelope and put it in his backpack. His teacher released class for the day, and the students quickly scattered and descended on the row of school buses waiting in the parking lot outside. Scott walked past his bus, scanning the windows for any sign of Bucky. It seemed safe, so Scott circled back and climbed inside.

Pondering his report card, Scott knew he would be in trouble, and the fear inside him grew unbearable as the school bus drove closer and closer to home. He was afraid of a beating, but also of the possibility of missing out on the field trip if Ava, as punishment, refused to sign the permission slip.

The bus pulled into the stop on the corner and Scott got out with the rest of the kids from the neighborhood. He walked slowly home, terrified to show the report card and not knowing what to do. Maybe he could get her to sign the permission slip first, and then later show the report card, and she would forget she signed the slip. Or maybe he could try to make her promise not to get mad, like he did with the wet bed, and then show the report card, but there was no guarantee she would sign the slip.

He reached the driveway, taking each step as slowly as he could toward the kitchen door. He entered the garage and slowly opened it. Ava was sitting at the table waiting for him. He studied her face closely, looking for any clue that would reveal her mood.

Scott immediately recognized a sadness and grew nervous. He knew he had to tread carefully when Ava looked downcast and distant. He didn't want to make her feel worse. He recognized the music coming from the living room as *The Carpenters*. Ava had sometimes shared with him and Pamela that the pretty voice made her feel better when she had *the blues*.

"Hi, Honey. How was your day?" she asked quietly, and softly smiled. Lifting her head and looking up from the table appeared to require some effort.

"Hi, Mommy. It was good."

"How was your violin lesson?"

"Good. I think I got better."

"Of course. I hear it when you practice."

"Now, I'm done. Almost summer vacation."

"You'll have to practice over the summer or you'll go backwards." There was silence for a moment. "Do you want a snack?"

Ava slowly walked to the refrigerator and got some pudding she had prepared. Scott put his violin case down and opened his backpack. He pulled out the permission slip.

"We have a trip Thursday, to the Shelburne Museum," he said.

"Oh, that's wonderful," Ava said and smiled.

Scott still sensed she was sad, but she had smiled, so that was a good signal.

"Can you please sign this so I can go?" Scott asked and gently pushed the paper forward.

She looked it over, got up, and slowly walked to the counter to get a pen. "Looks like a great field trip," she said and signed the paper.

Scott took it back, put it in his backpack, and zipped it shut.

Chapter 2 / 1973

"Thanks, Mommy."

He ate his bowl of pudding. Ava had *the blues* so the report card would have to wait until tomorrow. He couldn't risk it. He didn't dare. He brought the dirty dish to the sink, then headed to his room to put away his backpack and violin. He went back downstairs to the playroom while Ava quietly started prepping for dinner, standing over the kitchen sink and gazing out the window as the water ran from the faucet.

Scott turned the large plastic screw bolt to fasten the orange clamp for his Hot Wheels track to the lip of the wooden windowsill in the playroom. He put together several lengths of track that ended with a 360-degree loop, and began to race cars down the course. He continued to play even as he could make out the voices of Pamela and Ava talking in the kitchen. He scurried between the clamp and the loop as he tested how cars of different weights fared with the upside-down curve at the end. About fifteen minutes passed. He launched another car down the track and Ava suddenly appeared in the doorway to the playroom.

"Did you get your report card today?" Ava asked.

Scott's heart started pounding and he froze standing in place as he looked up.

"No," he said. "I think tomorrow."

"Pamela said the whole school got them today. She has hers," Ava said. "Are you sure?"

Scott hesitated. He was caught. "No," he said.

"What do you mean, 'no'?"

"I mean yes."

"You have it? Your report card?"

Scott nodded slowly. Ava walked over and slapped him. He fell backward and into the clamp holding the track below the window. The clamp snapped free and he collapsed with the track onto the floor.

"How could you lie?" Ava demanded. "How could you hide it from me?"

She walked over to him as he lay on the floor, hiding his face in his arms amid the dislodged pieces of track. Ava hit him as he lay on the floor and he tried to squirm toward the loop across the room. She reached down, grabbed him by the hair and shook him as she lifted him upwards, the weight of his body swiveling below his neck as his head thrust from side to side.

He cried out and tried to focus, but the playroom descended into a chaotic, spinning blur with no up, no down and no escape. He felt a burning pain on top of his head where Ava grasped a handful of hair and continued to shake him.

"*Where is it?*"

Scott tried to answer through his tears, but couldn't form words as his body was suddenly thrust forward and flew into a large set of wooden shelves standing against the wall and stacked with toys. His face caught a corner of the lower edge of one of the shelves and he felt a stabbing pain above his right eye, just below the eyebrow. Toys all around crashed down on him and he collapsed with them, curling into a ball and hoping it would stop.

"Where is it?" Ava asked again, sobbing loudly.

"In my backpack," Scott whispered and scrambled up with his back pushed against the shelf and his knees pulled in front of him. He covered his eye.

"Why do you *make me* do this?" Ava screamed. "This is how your sister is going to remember me."

Ava walked toward him and knelt above him.

"*I hate you!*" She paused a moment, as if shaken by her own words. "Right this minute, I hate you."

With a burst of tears, she stood and left the room.

Scott felt shattered and a strange panic surged through him. His heart pounded and his eyes wildly canvassed the room.

He continued to sit without moving, unable to fathom what to do next. He listened intently, trying to get clues from the sounds around him. From far away, he heard Ava's sobs coming from upstairs. The cries terrified him and filled him with shame.

Little by little he became aware he wanted to get up and move away from the mess of toys and boxes that lay scattered about him on the floor. He stood slowly and felt a throbbing sensation above his right eye. He crept to the doorway, looked around, and listened.

The house was silent except for Ava's sobs. He continued across the hallway to the bathroom. He quietly closed the door, turned on the light, and went to the mirror to look at his eye. It wasn't bleeding, but there was a red indentation about a half inch long on the skin above his eye socket.

He turned on the faucet to wet his finger to touch the wound. When he bent his head down, he was startled to see several hairs drop down into the sink. He reached up with his hand and gently rubbed the top of his head. With horror, he watched as clumps of hair fell into the sink.

He panicked and again started crying. What was happening? There was nothing he could do about his eye. He stopped touching his hair and left the bathroom. In the hallway again he paused to listen. Still, Ava cried. It would be terrifying to walk by her room to get to his, but he had to do it.

How long would she hate him? Forever? He made his way through the kitchen and to the stairs. One by one he ascended, trying to avoid any creaks that would give his position away. He made it to his bedroom, closed the door, and sat on the floor.

He started to tremble. What did it mean to be hated? Was it too late to do anything? Only an awful person could be hated by his own mother. The shame, terror and revulsion he felt froze him in place, as he listened to the sobs in the room next door.

He didn't know how much time had passed when the house began to quiet. He desperately wanted Ava to come into his room, but at the same time dreaded what was to come. He heard a door open. Some footsteps, then a door closing. The bathroom door. Silence, then water running in the basin. Silence again. Now, footsteps in the hallway. His heart quickened. Where were they going? He heard a stair creak and felt a rush of relief even though at the same time he wished the footsteps were coming in his direction.

He tensed and strained to hear more. Silence again and the agonizing wait. Still he sat on the floor, afraid to move. He disappeared inside the milk box. He was again one of the villagers, terrified of the giant who was going to drop down from the sky at any moment and kill him. Footsteps on the stairs brought him back to the terrifying realization Ava was returning. She was in the hallway and just outside his door. His teeth chattered and he started shaking when the door opened and Ava walked in. Her face was red from crying. She took a few steps in, knelt down in front of him, and looked Scott in the eye.

"I love you, because I have to, because I'm your mother," Ava said, and hugged him loosely and briefly.

Then, she pulled back and looked at him directly in the eye again.

"*But I don't like you.*"

She stood up, walked to the doorway, and turned.

"Bring your report card when you're ready to come downstairs," she said as she closed the door and went down to the kitchen.

Scott froze. What did that mean? It wasn't better. He wanted to be liked.

Numb, he laid backward on the floor, unable to absorb what was happening. He was crying softly, his breathing spasmodic.

Some time passed and he watched as the door cracked open, and Pamela silently entered. She closed the door behind her, walked over to Scott and sat down next to him, Indian-style. She gently lifted his head and rested it on her leg. She caressed his face, and quietly began to sing.

"*Nobody likes me.*

Everybody hates me.

Guess I'll go eat worms.

Big, fat juicy ones.

Eensy-teensy squeamy ones.

I hope they don't have germs."

Scott recoiled. "That's not funny."

"It's okay," Pamela said. "It's *supposed* to be."

"It's mean."

"Don't feel sorry for yourself."

She repeated the verse again, this time singing with a funny voice and tickling him.

Scott sat up and she hugged him. They sat quietly.

"Let's get up," Pamela said.

After a few minutes, Pamela stood and took Scott's hand. She led him across the hallway to her bedroom. She sat down alongside her Johnny and Jane West dolls, plus a horse and covered wagon she had set up on the floor in the middle of her room. She pushed the horse as if it were galloping toward Scott and tapped his foot. He smiled and followed the horse as she made it gallop back toward the covered wagon. Together they sat and played without talking.

A bit later Scott found himself back in his room, sitting on his bed with his report card beside him. He was terrified to go downstairs. But it was late enough now that his father would be home for dinner any minute, so he would wait. He never got in bad trouble from his mother when his father was home, and his father still probably liked him, even if his mother didn't. He turned and knelt on the bed, staring out the window down at the road with his elbows propped up on the window sill. It was almost six p.m. and would remain light out until almost 9 p.m., because it was just weeks before the summer solstice.

His heart quickened when he saw his father's car pull into the driveway. He didn't know what would happen, but at least now he would dare to go downstairs. He swiveled to the front of the bed and listened intently for voices in the kitchen. Finally some talking started when Robert entered the kitchen. He strained to hear if the voices sounded calm or angry. They seemed normal, so Scott crept to the door with report card in hand. He cracked the door open and took slow steps to the top of the stairs. He went down one by one and saw Ava, Robert and Pamela gathered around the kitchen table, looking at her report card.

He quietly slunk into the room, slowly approaching the outer edge of the kitchen table, hoping no one would be aware of his arrival.

Robert looked up from the table. "Hi, Scott."

"Hi, Daddy."

"What happened to your eye?" Robert asked, and walked over to him.

"I banged it."

"We should put some ice on it," Ava said and walked to the sink. She grabbed a small dish towel from below the sink, went to the freezer, and wrapped three ice cubes. She brought the ice pack to Scott and held it on his eyebrow above his right eye.

"I see you've got your report card," Ava said. She turned to Robert. "He hid it from me after school. Lied about it. Can you believe it?"

"Why would you do that?" Robert asked him.

"I was afraid," Scott said.

"Of what?"

"There's something bad in it," Scott said quietly.

"You take this," Ava said, placing the ice in Scott's right hand, and positioning it above his eye. "Just hold it there. I'll take the report card."

She brought it to the table and took it out of the envelope, placing it flat on the table. She and Robert studied it.

"This looks great," Robert said. "What's bad about it?"

"That," Scott said. He pointed toward a check mark.

Robert looked again. "It's on Behavior. 'Assertiveness.' It just means you need to work on speaking up. Being less shy. That's all."

"The rest is 'Above Average', or 'Excellent'," Ava said. "It's really good. You didn't need to hide this. Do you see how wrong that was?" she asked and walked over to him. She put her arm around him.

"Yes, Mommy," Scott said. "I'm sorry." A wave of relief washed over him. She was touching him. Maybe she liked him again.

"You've always got to tell the truth. I hope you've learned that now," Ava said. She pulled his hand with the ice away from his eye and looked at it. "It's less swollen. Just hold it there until dinner. It's almost ready. You can go watch TV."

Scott was happy to leave the kitchen and retreat to the safety of the back room. He switched on the TV and turned the knob to channel 5. His favorite show was on, *The Wild Wild West*. He started to watch while sitting on the couch. But he could tell there was going to be a fight because the hero was closing in on the villain. James West was handsome and a great fighter, but so was the bad guy.

Scott dropped the ice on the couch, moved to his spot below the side table, and rubbed himself on the floor as he watched. He couldn't stop himself. The sensation was calming, yet exciting, and made him feel good. He forgot about everything. All that mattered was watching the circus strongman thinking he was going to win, but getting stopped and beaten up by James West. He would do anything to watch it. Anything was worth it. The risk of getting caught or being late for dinner didn't matter.

The strongman was defeated after an intense struggle, and Scott felt himself transported as he disappeared into a world of physical pleasure, adventure and excitement. He had no idea why, or even how this was happening. It was uncontrollable. An escape. And somehow the fighters triggered it. He remained under the table, feeling removed from the house and thrilled he caught the fistfight in time, even as it ended and Pamela entered the room.

"What are you doing?" she asked as she spied Scott laying on his stomach with his head peeking out from under the front of the coffee table.

"Just watching TV," he answered.

"It's time for dinner," Pamela said and returned to the kitchen.

Scott crawled out from under the table, adjusted his pants, grabbed the ice from the couch and walked to the kitchen.

While he sat at the dinner table, he was aware of his mother, his father and Pamela talking but he was still thinking about the fight back at the circus. How could the strongman lose? He was much bigger than James West. Maybe the karate moves and skill were more powerful and important than brute strength. He didn't want to join in or talk about his report card or his day or share anything about being terrified of Bucky the Bus Bully who always made fun of his violin.

"Did you hear me, Scott?" Ava asked him.

"No, sorry," Scott answered.

"Tell your father where you're going Thursday."

"The Shelburne Museum," Scott said quietly. "It's a field trip."

Robert was excited for him and they talked about the last few days of school and the start of summer vacation.

Scott again lost focus. Did his mother like him yet?

After dinner, Pamela and Scott helped to clear the table and wash the dishes. When they finished, they went outside to join the other kids from the neighborhood who played in the street riding bikes, jumping rope and playing tag. Pamela found two friends and brought them to the driveway in front of their house. The garage door was open, so she went in, got some chalk, and they drew colored hopscotch squares on the fresh blacktop.

Scott saw them playing, and brought two friends to the garage. Inside, he had a large collection of wood pieces cut into different shapes that Robert had made for him, plus nails, screws, a small triangular saw, a hammer and a screwdriver. They selected pieces of wood and sat down on the floor in a circle with the supplies in the middle.

They began to work and joke and after some time his friend Mark asked, "What happened to your eye?"

"It's nothing," Scott said.

"But, how'd you do it?"

"With a Coke can."

"What? How?"

Scott paused a moment. "With a catapult that launched it up."

"What? Show me."

Scott took a long piece of wood and placed it over a two-by-four cut into a triangular shape. He positioned the long board like a teeter-totter, and slammed his fist down on one side.

"Let's test it," Mark said. He stood up and got a can of Coke from a shelf in the back of the garage. "Show me."

Scott took the can and balanced it on one side of the board. He slammed his fist down, and the can flew up a few inches and flopped over backwards.

"How'd it go up?" Mark asked.

"Dunno," Scott answered. "It worked before."

"Don't believe it."

"Maybe I was bent down more," Scott said.

He couldn't tell anyone what happened. He would never say it was his mother.

"Let's build something else," Scott said.

Scott mixed the two pieces of the catapult in with the rest of the pile. They used the saw to customize some pieces, and hammered boards together to make a barn with an angled roof. Pamela and her friends continued to play hopscotch in the driveway.

It was almost nightfall, and the sky lit up with colors of orange and purple.

"Wow, look at the sunset," Pamela called out from the driveway.

Scott and his friends went to her and looked up. They watched for a while and began to go their separate ways to get home before it got too dark.

Pamela walked into the garage to put her chalk away.

In a loud whisper, she turned to Scott who still stood in the driveway, and said, "You better clean this or you'll get in trouble."

She pointed at the wood and tools on the floor and went inside.

Scott stood a moment longer, then wandered to the front step. He sat next to the milk box and watched the colored sky turn to night. A bit later, in the starlight, he made his way to the garage to pick up his mess.

CHAPTER THREE
1978

The alarm rang at 5 a.m. with a loud clanging bell that made Scott's heart race as he groped about in the dark to find the metal button to make it stop. The sun wouldn't rise for another hour. It was September, and chilly outside. He only had a few more days to cover his friend's paper route, and wanted it to be over. He got out of bed, turned on the light and quickly pulled on the clothes he had set out on a chair the night before.

He went to the kitchen, ate a bowl of cereal, and pulled his coat and shoulder bag out the closet. The spanking paddle still leaned against the wall in a back corner behind some unused boots, and hadn't been used in years. Perhaps his mother had forgotten it was there. He closed the closet door, put on his coat, and went through the garage to get outside.

He walked in the middle of the empty street, past the school bus stop and continued to the main road to Bartlet's Store, where he spied the bundle of undelivered papers waiting for him outside the front door. He bent to retrieve the delivery list on top, with everyone's name and address who was getting the day's edition of *The Burlington Free Press*. He counted out the number of papers he would need for the first round of deliveries and loaded them into his shoulder pack. They were very heavy, and he struggled to lift the bag over his shoulder. He started on his way.

It was still dark out, and he followed the glow of street lights that illuminated the sidewalk, passing through one pool of light as it faded to black and searching out the next. He checked his list and began to deliver the papers, approaching each house and leaving one behind the storm door or on the front step. Half way through the first batch he crossed paths with a skunk near the front of Campbell's house. It turned and raised its tail, but Scott froze and the skunk ran harmlessly away. Scott exhaled and distributed the rest of the papers in his bag. He returned to the stack of papers in front of the store to get another batch, keeping a wary eye out for other skunks or aggressive dogs that sometimes sprang out.

He loaded his bag, threw away the twine and plastic wrap that had been covering the bundle, and left the store in the opposite direction. It was a lonely job. No one was awake and only an occasional car or truck would pass by the main road. At least now the sun had started to rise, and there was enough light in the sky to see without streetlights.

He took a right turn into a neighborhood he liked because the houses were closer together and he could empty his heavy load more quickly. When he finished, he returned to the main road and made his way toward a large parking lot in front of a wooden furniture store as a short cut toward the last neighborhood on his list.

As he was halfway across the parking lot, he watched as a car pulled in from the main road. Its wheels straightened and it accelerated as it barreled from the entrance of the parking lot directly toward where he was standing in the middle. Was it trying to run him down? With a surge of adrenaline, Scott bolted to the right and ran to the edge of the lot as the car raced by. He watched as the car continued past the furniture store where the lane continued on the right side.

Scott ran off the parking lot and quickly jumped over a small bank on the side, where he laid down on the grass to hide. He knew the car would be turning around. Who was trying to kill him? It looked like two guys in the car. His heart pounded as he heard the car make another approach. It drove slowly across the parking lot. Were they looking for him? He peeked over the edge of the grassy bank, but couldn't see who was driving. He laid back down so the driver wouldn't see him, then peeked up again when he heard the car continue beyond and watched as it pulled onto the main road and drove away.

He was shaking and couldn't believe what had happened. If he hadn't jumped and ran, he would have been run down. Who would do that to him? Why? He could only surmise someone hated him. He stayed down on the ground for at least five minutes, afraid the car would circle back and look for him again.

It got brighter outside as the sun continued to rise, and traffic got busier on the main road. He looked around and didn't see any sign of the car, so he stood up and cut through the grass of people's lawns to get to the last neighborhood on his list. He avoided the main road.

He finished his deliveries, still astonished at what had happened. It was like a dream. Who would believe him? If the driver was trying to scare him for fun, it had worked. But he knew if he had just stood there, the car could not have stopped and he would have been run over.

He made his way home, and quietly re-entered the house because everyone was still sleeping. He went to his room, undressed and got back into bed. He felt safe under the covers. Flushed with relief, he fell asleep.

When he got up, he went to the kitchen and Ava, Robert and Pamela were having breakfast. He sat at the table.

"How did the paper route go?" Ava asked.

"Pretty good," Scott said. He paused. "I almost got sprayed by a skunk."

They all started laughing. "Really?" Ava said. "Thank goodness you didn't."

They started talking and passed Scott a stack of pancakes. He kept thinking about the car in the parking lot and tried to figure out what had happened, replaying the scene over and over in his mind.

Should he tell his parents? He wanted to say something. It was a serious incident. He tried to speak.

"What is it, Scott?" Robert asked.

He became panicked and couldn't say a word. He never shared personal information because it made him sound weak and stupid. To admit he was scared and astonished by the morning's events would be too intense. Too needy. Even with his parents and sister. It was proof someone didn't like him. He had to keep it secret. They might wonder what he could have done wrong and he would look like an idiot.

"Any more bacon?" Scott asked.

The high school was walking distance from home, closer than driving if the shopping center was used as a shortcut. Pamela walked with Scott to school and showed him the way toward a footbridge that passed over a creek and led to a far corner of the high school parking lot. The bridge was lined with a half dozen older students and Scott instinctively tensed and hardened himself, because they looked tough. As they passed over it, Scott strained to listen to whatever voices he could hear to assess the danger.

He heard Pamela say 'Hi' to a few of them.

"Who's the wimp with Pam?" He heard one ask.

"It's cool. Her younger brother," another answered.

Scott felt lucky he was with Pamela, because she was one of the smartest in her class and still somehow popular with many of the different subgroups in the high school because she didn't fit any one stereotype. Brainy, a teachers' favorite, but she also smoked pot with some of the tough crowd. If he were on his own, he would be doomed. He knew it. He was skinny, uneasy, and looked very young for his age.

Sometimes in class sitting at his desk he would push up the tip of his nose so it didn't point down. He tried to reshape it. He had learned from the other students it was best to have a 'ski jump' shape, and he would push up the tip until over time a line formed in the skin on top.

In his freshman class, all the students were white, except for one Asian girl, who everyone called Chinese, even though her heritage was Japanese. Blacks didn't live here, because they didn't like cold weather. No one knew about Latinos. There were Mexicans in Mexico, and that was it. Scott was asked continually if he were Jewish. He didn't yet know anyone who was, but he deduced it was somehow lesser and he explained he was half Italian and that accounted for his Roman nose. It was a passable answer.

Scott was a good student and enrolled in the College Preparatory curriculum. He had high standards to live up to, because Pamela had scored in the top percentile on the PSAT exam and was already a National Merit Scholarship Finalist. As his first two years unfolded, he found himself doing well, with a consistent A-minus or B-plus average, but he fell far short of Pamela's near-perfect academic achievements.

Ava and Robert were fine with his performance, and didn't expect him to do as well as Pamela, because it was clear he wasn't as academically gifted. Perhaps, they reasoned, his talents lay elsewhere because he had become a good violinist and had already made first violin in the high school orchestra. But academically, they made clear their expectations: he had to get good enough grades to ensure entrance to a four-year, accredited university. A 4.0 average would not be expected, achievable or necessary.

Scott took it as confirmation he was dumb. His natural abilities took him to a high enough level that when faced with an obstacle he gave up easily and assumed he was too stupid to figure it out. He wasn't aware the resistance he faced when trying to grasp new, difficult concepts was normal and something others also faced. It didn't mean failure. But he believed it did, and saw most things as much more difficult than they actually were.

He remembered he had once explained to a classmate that a second in time was so quick, that it could not be measured with consecutive hand claps. Similarly, tests and auditions were impossibly difficult, designed to fool him, and the instruments through which teachers would find he was actually stupid or just average.

When facing a multiple-choice test, Scott would often flip flop his answer, unwilling to accept what he came up with was correct because it seemed too easy and he was falling into a trap. He didn't like to accept formulas or Phi or Pi or using tricks to determine mathematical problems like square roots; he wanted to know why exactly something was as it was, not use tools someone else came up with that he was told to accept blindly, so he wasted valuable test time. He would not score impressively on important exams like the PSAT and the SAT.

He found he could not concentrate or remain focused while teachers spoke and he daydreamed through important lessons and dialog in movies and television shows. Once he was caught by the History teacher with his head turned, staring at a globe on a side counter instead of looking at the chalk board, and he was asked to leave the classroom. Yet the same teacher didn't mind when Scott stared at him, apparently listening, but was instead imagining an elaborate fist fight that the teacher ultimately lost and ended with an uppercut and his humiliation in front of the class.

Years later, Scott would realize he had missed half of the history of World War II. He knew about the German part, but hadn't the slightest inclination the Japanese part was equally significant and horrific. He wasn't sure if he had daydreamed through the lesson, or if the Japanese saga had been skipped by the teacher, due to time constraints. Scott eventually discovered that scenes in movies were deliberately placed for a reason, and the pieces would come together to make sense. His habit of drifting away made him miss important dialog and characters. By the end of a film he would have no clear idea how it came to its conclusion or why. The whole of things seemed random — from mathematics to history to movies.

On his violin, he reached a B-Plus or A-Minus level without really trying. It came naturally. But the amount of effort and practice it took to rise to the next level, to master a difficult passage in a concerto eluded him. Obviously he wasn't talented enough, or it wouldn't be so difficult to improve. He would have moments of inspiration in his bedroom practicing when he would make significant progress, but later if he was nervous or the slightest bit distracted or self-critical he would regress. He found he played his best as part of the first violin section in an orchestra. He was hidden within the sea of players around him. He played loudly and confidently and would attack and sail through difficult runs and soaring high notes.

The high school orchestra was small, and in a year he became the concertmaster. He also played for the Vermont Youth Orchestra, which rehearsed on Saturday mornings in the Burlington High School gymnasium. To gain entry he had to audition, but never performed as well as he knew he could play. Still, he managed a seat in the middle of the first violin section.

He loved being a member. It was the first place he discovered the power of playing within a full, 80-member ensemble. He loved the way the sheet music was a mystery at the start of the season when it was selected and distributed by the conductor. But after three months of rehearsals, the music would reveal itself to the players in ways that most in the audience would only come to partially grasp. He loved long, pressure-cooker crescendos that raced toward fortissimo, towering, difficult symphonic climaxes that sent the violins to the stratosphere while the rest of the orchestra thundered below with a power that unleashed all the pain, beauty, struggle and poignancy of life. Somehow the composers captured it. And the players set it free. And he was one of them.

The wide mix of students from all over the state who played in the orchestra appealed to Scott. Perhaps it was because they were all musicians, but he found them smarter, more open-minded and less threatening than those in his own high school. He got a sense there was something more to life to be found. He liked his stand-partner, Carrie. She was pretty and carried herself with a poise that seemed exotic to him, especially since she was from the school everyone referred to as Cow Valley Union. He was surprised she was nice to him.

"How's it going?" Scott asked her one day, as they tuned up before rehearsal.

"Pretty good," she answered. "You?"

"Same. Excited for next week," Scott said.

"Why's that?"

"Senior Week. Crazy themes every day. Everyone dresses up."

"We just had that," Carrie said. "Yesterday was 'Greaser Day'. I had a whole look. My Mom helped me."

"Monday we have 'Current Events'".

"Sounds hard. Any ideas?" Carrie asked.

"I was thinking Ayatollah Khomeini."

"Creative," Carrie said. "I would think Jimmy Carter. Or Farrah Fawcett." She laughed and rolled her eyes.

They finished tuning and quieted as the conductor took the stand and tapped his baton to silence the orchestra. Rehearsal began, and continued for an hour before the first break. Scott walked to the chairs that held his coat, violin case, and a brown paper bag with snacks Ava had packed for him. He listened to the chatter around the room. What were people preparing for All New England Festival auditions in a few weeks? What was the best strategy? An easier piece that could be played solidly, or a more risky and impressive one that might be riddled with mistakes?

Scott dreaded the thought of the audition, and was already preparing the only piece on the audition list he felt he could remotely handle, Beethoven's *Romance No. 1*. The double stops were very difficult. He knew he would never deliver them all correctly, but at least the rest of the piece he had a shot at playing well. Unfortunately, so would everyone else. His nervousness grew until the sound of the conductor's tapping baton silenced the chatter and everyone returned to their seats.

On Monday morning, Scott woke up early to try on his costume. Ava had made it for him by splitting a solid white sheet and sewing it together lengthwise to form a makeshift robe. She added a trim. A black piece of fabric was rolled, braided and pinned into a turban. He came down the stairs into the kitchen where Ava was preparing breakfast. She turned and surveyed his look.

"Looks good," she said as he entered. "You think anyone will know what it is?"

"They should. It's 'Current Events'," Scott said. "Maybe I need a sign."

"We have markers and construction paper," Ava said. "Look at the *Time* magazine cover to get the spelling right. There's one in the rack next to the chair in the living room."

Scott went to the playroom to get the paper and markers, then went to the living room and dug in the magazine rack until he found the magazine with Ayatollah Khomeini on the cover as man of the year. He brought everything back to the kitchen table and made a sign by folding the paper horizontally and writing with small capital letters. Ava used two safety pins to affix it to the back of his robe. Satisfied the costume was complete, Scott carefully removed it, went to his bedroom, and folded it into his backpack.

When he got to school, he kept an eye out and saw about half the school had dressed up, but in costumes themed to popular culture, like the Bionic Man, Michael Jackson and the ladies from ABBA. Did he get it wrong? He decided to wait until his first class to see more costumes.

He found his friend Lisa sitting on her desk and dressed with a wig, a plaid jacket, pearls and red lipstick.

"Looking good," he said as he walked up to her. "Who are you?"

"Margaret Thatcher," she said, smiling.

"Maybe you need a sign," Scott said.

"Totally," Lisa said. "You should have dressed up."

"I brought something," he answered.

"Where is it? Put it on!" Lisa said.

Scott pulled it out of his backpack and tried it on for her.

"Amazing! It's definitely current," she said. "Love the sign. I need to make one, now."

She got a piece of paper, wrote out the label, and dug in her purse to find two pins. They sat through class, and when the bell rang, both walked out together to the crowded hallway toward their next class.

Immediately, a large guy Scott didn't know rushed over toward him.

"Who you supposed to be?" he demanded.

Scott turned and showed him the sign.

"He's an asshole. You like him?"

"Of course I don't like him," Scott said. "But it's happening now. It's current. Read the news."

"Who cares," the guy said and pushed him.

Scott and Lisa continued down the hall and he continued to attract attention.

"Hey sheik! What the hell?" yelled a new guy.

"Go home, traitor!" shouted another.

They hurried along, down a flight of stairs, and into a new hallway toward their next class.

After a few more shouts, Lisa said, "They don't get your costume."

"They think I support him," Scott said. "I'm gonna change the sign."

They entered their classroom and Scott turned his robe around and unpinned the sign. He folded it, and on the other side, wrote: Ayatollah Ass-a-hola.

"Ya think they'll get it now?" he asked.

"Definitely funnier," Lisa said. "That fixes it."

Scott pinned on the new sign and pulled the robe over his shoulders. He wanted to try again, because Ava had helped him make the costume he wanted. He felt guilty wasting it.

As they sat though Trigonometry, Scott nervously planned his route to his next class. He only had to walk a U-shape through the hallway to get to Oceanography. If he left the instant the bell rang, there would be less people in the hallways and he could make it half way before anyone even saw him. He watched the clock and waited until the minute hand got close to the session close and slipped his notebook into his back pack. When at last the bell rang, Scott quickly got up and was the first one out the door.

It seemed his plan was working and the halls were nearly silent. But within 30 seconds, the classrooms emptied and students spilled out and suddenly filled the corridors with a cacophony of laughs, chatter and colliding pathways as they weaved their way toward their destinations. Scott imagined he heard voices criticizing him and couldn't tell if they were real or imagined, until someone large darted toward him from across the hall.

"What are you, Casper the Ghost?" he asked.

"No," Scott answered.

"Then, what?"

"The Ayatollah," Scott said. "It's in the news."

"You shouldn't be wearing that," the guy said, and pushed his shoulder.

"Read the sign," Scott said as he swiveled around and turned his back.

"Ass-a-hola, that's for sure," he said.

Scott continued walking quickly and it seemed the guy faded into the crowd as Scott got further down the hallway. He heard more shouts and laughter and watched as people pointed and tugged at his robe. Someone pushed the turban down into his face from behind. He heard aggressive voices but kept walking, until he suddenly was forced up against a row of lockers by someone he had never seen before and asked, "Who the hell are you?"

"Read the sign!" Scott shouted again, and wriggled free to expose his back.

He escaped and quickly pulled the turban off his head. As he continued walking, he reached over his shoulder, removed his robe and started rolling it into a ball. He bunched it with the turban and stuffed them into an open slit in his backpack as he rushed to get to his classroom. When he entered, he found a seat, took out the book and notebook he needed, and finished pushing his costume to the bottom, so no fabric would stick out. He would never dress up or participate in another school "fun" day. He obviously got it wrong and would never make the mistake again.

As his classmates entered and filled out the desks around him, his friend Brian asked, "Where'd your costume go?"

"Took it off," Scott answered. "It was stupid."

"Don't be chicken. Everyone looks stupid," Brian said and pointed to the others seated around them. "That's the point."

Scott felt relieved when class started. He liked Oceanography, and also looked forward to the break for lunch that would immediately follow it. He looked around the halls and wondered if anyone would recognize him as the Ayatollah, but nobody seemed to care.

The rest of the day passed without incident, and after school he went to his regular practice for the cross country team. He had joined his sophomore year, out of a sense he needed to make more friends, because everyone else seemed to have more.

He loved his orchestra friends, but like him, they were mostly quiet and not as extroverted as the people he watched who played sports, or the singers he saw in the chorus. He was in awe of the ease with which they laughed and interacted with others, and in awe of the way people reacted to them. Where did the confidence come from?

He was determined to put on a different personality from his "real" one that got lost within a symphony and didn't like talking to anyone. So the cross country team seemed like his best option. He wasn't good at any team sports, but he was skinny and could run. He would try to put on an outgoing persona and copy the way the confident people acted. He would also join the chorus, because he had a musical ear from the violin and knew he could sing from grade school and church. And unlike the serious orchestra people, the chorus people made plans to do things after school, and even went to parties.

He needed to make changes or nothing was going to change by itself. Today had proved it. He couldn't be himself. His ideas weren't popular. He wasn't popular. He didn't fit in.

As he walked home after practice, he thought about the camaraderie of the team. They had nicknames for each other and supported each other when racing to beat their best times. He liked who he was around them. It wasn't who he really was, but people liked it better.

He acted cool and slowed down his talking and didn't need to say much of anything about himself. He only had to go along with the jokes, and try to better himself as a runner, so he could contribute to the team's success and not be the worst one on the team.

In chorus he was someone different, because people acted silly and social and the girls were charismatic. They seemed to always have something melodramatic going on with their personal lives and boyfriends and didn't hesitate to share the information. He was a good listener, and he played the role in such a way that no one expected him to talk about himself in return.

In a semester's time, after a quiet start, he found himself gaining status, because it turned out he was one of the best tenors and it seemed to make him more popular with people in the chorus. It also made him a target by other tenors who saw him as a threat, and he tried to avoid the aggressive ones, who frightened him.

But it was a new feeling to have guys against him because he was good at something, and not just because he was weak and unlikable. His orchestra persona remained serious and guarded, and he felt great responsibility to carry the first violin section and to play loudly, to make up for their sparse numbers. Meanwhile, it isolated him because the guys around school looked at orchestra as nerdy, and he often felt like a target dragging around his violin case.

It was exhausting to play the different roles people wanted so they would like him.

When he arrived home, Robert and Ava were in the kitchen, sitting at the table, and dinner was in the oven. Pamela was out with friends and the table was set for three.

Scott sensed Ava had *the blues* because of the downcast look on her face he had come to recognize over the years. It still made him very nervous when he sensed she was sad, or annoyed by something, or a combination. He always wondered if he had something to do with it, and would be in trouble. He remained on alert. Robert didn't seem to notice as he read the newspaper.

"How was practice?" Ava asked as Scott approached the table. She smiled.

"Good. But really muddy. I'm gonna hang up my shoes overnight to dry," Scott said.

"You can hang them in the garage if you want," Ava said. "There's room on the line along the back wall."

Scott pulled his shoes out of the bag, and went to the garage. He was relieved Ava seemed to perk up somewhat from what he sensed when he first walked in. Maybe everything was fine. He returned to the kitchen and put his backpack on the counter.

"How did your costume work out?" Ava asked.

"It was awful."

Scott pulled it out of his backpack and put it on the counter.

"Why? What happened?"

"They teased me and made fun. Nobody liked it," Scott said and paused a moment. His eyes teared up. He suddenly felt a wave of shame and frustration from the hallway hostilities.

Ava and Robert stared in disbelief as he erupted.

"I *hate* this place! I *hate* living here. They wore stuff from TV like the Bionic Man. But that's not current events. It's pop culture. They don't even know the difference. It's so obvious! So expected. So backwoods up here. There must be a place where people get things and are smarter. I'm moving as soon as I can to find it. I'm getting out of here. It's the middle of nowhere. Why did you bring us here? I *hate* it!"

There was silence for a moment, then Robert spoke.

"Maybe you will move someday. That's okay. Nobody said you have to stay here. When you're on your own, you can move where you want."

Scott nodded silently. He left the costume on the counter and took his backpack up to his bedroom. After a few minutes, he returned to the kitchen for dinner. They didn't speak about the costume or his outburst again. He gave short answers to questions and nodded from time to time, but was far away from the table. He had already shared too much.

Mid-summer before his junior year, a new family relocated from the other side of town to their street. Scott knew their son, Tom, from school, because he played on the varsity football team and was one of the most popular guys, but they weren't friends. A few weeks after the move, they ran into each other on the sidewalk.

"You're Scott, right?" Tom asked.

Scott wondered how he knew his name. "Yeah. Tom, right?"

"Guess we never met." They shook hands.

"How do you like the neighborhood?" Scott asked.

"It's great. Close to school. Can even walk to practice," Tom said.
"It's already started."

"Yeah, for me, too."

"Cool. What sport?"

"Cross country."

"When's your next practice?"

"Tomorrow at 3."

"Mine too. Want to walk over?"

"Supposed to rain."

"Doesn't matter. My Mom can drive us."

They agreed to meet at Tom's house at 2:30 the next day. As Scott walked away, he was excited, but puzzled, by what had happened. How did Tom even know who he was? Or want to talk to him? He immediately got nervous thinking about the walk to practice. He was going to have to act tough and cool, because Tom was popular and a jock and he couldn't let Tom find out he might be neither.

The next day, Scott showed up in front of Tom's house at exactly 2:30. No one was outside, so he rang the doorbell. After a moment, a women answered the door.

"Hi, I'm Scott, from four houses down the street."

"I'm Tom's Mom. So nice to meet you," she said and opened the door. They entered the kitchen. "He'll be right down."

Scott rested his backpack with his running clothes on the floor.

"He told me you're a brain, and also play in the orchestra," she said, and smiled.

"I'm not a brain. My sister is. She's at M.I.T. now," he said. "But I do play the violin."

"That's great," she said. "It's a difficult instrument."

"I like it. I'm also on the cross country team."

How did she know about the orchestra? Did Tom tell her? He knew already?

"Have you started looking at colleges?" she asked.

"Yeah. But still not sure which one, or what to major in."

"Maybe you can help Tom. He's not sure he wants to go. Needs to get his grades up."

They heard thumps coming down the stairs and Tom entered the room.

"Hey! Looks like the rain held off," Tom said.

They chatted a bit and Tom's mother volunteered to drive them to practice. Later, they could walk home or call her if it was raining.

In the few weeks before school resumed in September, a pattern began to form. The two of them would walk to practice or get a ride most days of the week, and they sometimes met in the evenings at Tom's house to play UNO with his older sister, Katherine. Tom also met Ava and Robert, and sometimes joined them for cook-outs in the backyard.

Scott began to see Tom as a role model. He had never known someone from the football team, and was inspired to push himself in the pre-season training on the cross country team. He beat his personal best times and made team practices his main priority.

Scott had to call to push back the time for a critical audition to establish seating for the fall season of the Vermont Youth Orchestra, because it conflicted with an important 10K practice race. He felt prepared for the audition, and was fully satisfied with his performance of the piece for his violin teacher the day before. They both agreed he had nailed it. But he collapsed under the critical attention and scrutiny of playing alone while being judged and ranked in an audition. It terrified him. He played far below his ability because he imagined what was required was unattainable and exceptionally, exponentially difficult. Everyone else got all the double stops correct. No one else fumbled a passage. And when he did, it made things worse as his ability to deliver his best performance on even the easier sections unraveled. Why did he just mess up a run he always played correctly? Was it as bad as he thought? Or was he imagining and amplifying the mistakes? Why was he fixating on mistakes instead of focusing on the performance? Stop it and concentrate! Mantras buried somewhere deep inside that he was scarcely aware of came to the surface: I Hate My Life. I'm Such an Idiot. I Have to Get Out of Here. Please Help Me.

When he finished playing, the conductor was kind and told him he played well. Then, he asked him, "Why did you need to postpone the audition?"

Chapter 3 / 1978

"We had a big, pre-season cross country meet," Scott answered.

"Is that your priority?"

"No, of course not," Scott said. But he knew he was in trouble. The conductor saw him as a jock, even if no one else did.

When seating was announced Scott dropped a stand from the previous season instead of holding his own or moving up. It was humiliating, but at least he was still mid-way in the first violin section. He wasn't going to major in music, anyway. He wasn't good enough. Maybe he deserved to be punished for pretending to be an athlete so he could be more like Tom.

The fall semester at school was well underway and Scott got a ride every morning with Tom and his dad, who had to drive by the school anyway on his way to work. It was faster than walking, and he liked spending time with Tom. He still couldn't believe they were friends. Tom had made co-captain of the football team and was rugged, muscled, handsome and effortlessly popular. Scott saw himself as the opposite. He had no real idea of how he looked, beyond the skinny part. Was he good-looking? It wasn't something he had a sense of when he looked in the mirror. Sometimes in a photo he would be surprised when he came out looking good.

But now everything was changing. He and Tom would arrive at school together and then meet during lunch period. Scott got to sit at a table with a whole new set of friends who were cooler and more popular than anyone he'd ever known before. The guys were mostly jocks, and Scott was constantly on guard with this new group, who had their own set of rules. He had to act tough and removed. He could never relax with them the way he could with his friends from chorus or orchestra. The cross country friends were laid back and fell somewhere in the middle.

But Tom hung out with an A-list group of jocks, cheerleaders and assorted good looking people who were known for throwing great parties at their parents' houses. Scott couldn't believe he was being accepted by this new crowd because of his friendship with Tom. No one seemed to remember or care that he was just a skinny, quiet violinist.

When practices were finished after school, Scott and Tom talked on the telephone, and often Scott went to Tom's house to study. Tom's parents liked him, and he sometimes felt he talked to them more than he did with Ava and Robert. They projected an interest in him that felt nice. He would talk for a while in the kitchen, and then go upstairs to Tom's bedroom to study. He and Tom spread a pile of books on the bed and completed homework assignments or crammed for tests in the classes they shared.

Compared to Tom, Scott was a much better student and was able to explain things that confused Tom in Trigonometry and Statistics. Katherine had saved her old Chemistry exams, and Tom got them from a box in the back of her closet and they used them as study guides. They also wasted time just laying around and talking. Tom went through lots of girlfriends and Scott did his best to give advice, even with no dating experience of his own. Tom's girlfriends sometimes approached Scott during the day and asked him for insight, or tried to pry information, because now everyone knew they were often together. It was the first time he had such a close friend, maybe even a best friend. And to Scott it still seemed improbable, even impossible, that Tom even liked him — and it could end at any time.

With winter came the end of the cross country season. The practice time after school Scott gained was replaced by pit orchestra rehearsals for the spring musical and chorus rehearsals for upcoming All State and All New England competitions. He was usually home by 5 p.m. and would help Ava set the table in preparation for dinner as they awaited Robert's return from work.

Scott kept a close eye on the TV Guide and studied it every week for any show or movie that was likely to feature fist fights. *Vega$* was required viewing. Also, any movies with Bruce Lee. *The Dukes of Hazzard*, *Starsky & Hutch* and *CHiPs* were on his must-watch list. The timing was often difficult because he would have to stop what he was doing when a show came on.

He would click on the TV at the beginning of a show to see if it would be a good episode. Most repeats he had memorized, so he knew immediately what time the fight would come on, or if it was a dud. New episodes were problematic, because he had to watch the whole thing.

He had no idea why he had such a strong compulsion. It was a pattern that had been established for as long as he could remember, and was simply a given. He sometimes wondered when it would stop or if he would grow out of it. The first time sperm came out was a big surprise and he thought something went horribly wrong or he had somehow peed. But he remembered Robert had given him a talk, and a book to read called *Almost 12* that explained it.

Dinner time was tricky because reruns of *The Six Million Dollar Man* came on and ended at 6 p.m., usually just minutes before Ava would have dinner on the table. He had to disappear unnoticed after quickly setting the table and quietly click on the television upstairs in his parent's bedroom. Sometimes he felt great relief if he knew the episode was a bad one. He could turn it off and go back to the kitchen or his bedroom to study. The worst was if he knew a fist fight was imminent, with Steve Austin pitted against a robot, a martial arts master, the Seven Million Dollar Man, or Sasquatch. Then his heart would start to pound and he knew he was powerless to do anything other than watch.

Sometimes Ava would come upstairs and he would have to jump up and suddenly sit with his pants pulled up like nothing was happening. The instant she left he would hop back down. He wondered if the fear of getting caught was part of the attraction. He felt defiant, as if he was somehow pushing back against a world that would strongly object if it knew what he was doing. Then the fight would end, and he would regain control of himself and quickly clean up and click off the TV as if nothing had happened.

If there was still time before dinner, he would read. He loved horror novels and also big dramas about abuse or depression. *Sybil*, *Lisa Bright and Dark*, *Mommie Dearest* and *Ordinary People* fascinated him, and he liked to read about characters who were struggling. What they faced was horrible. On some level he understood. He had a generalized, vague, bad feeling about his own childhood. It felt like a void he didn't want to think about or ever return to. It was a shadow land that existed on an isolated island somewhere beyond a fog.

When school closed for Christmas vacation, Scott and Tom hung out most days. They each had a snowmobile, and followed the trails traversing the hills and fields of Bundy's farm. A small footbridge now crossed the creek at the bottom, and it was easy to speed across.

One Friday, after racing home just as nightfall started to approach, they made plans to meet later that evening to play cards and watch TV in the finished basement at Tom's house. Kathleen was home from college and could get them a six pack.

After finishing dinner, Scott showed up at Tom's house. They went to the basement and immediately opened the mini-refrigerator and got two beers. For a while they played cards, took breaks talking and sitting back on the sofa, got more beers, then turned on the TV. Tom started flipping through the channels.

"Nothing's on," he said.

A few more flips and he stopped on the *World Wide Wrestling Federation*.

"You like this?" Tom asked.

"Yes," Scott answered. It was a favorite.

They watched for a while and Tom suddenly got up from the sofa. He walked to the chair where Scott sat by the card table. He put his fists up and started to throw air punches at Scott.

"Think you could ever take me?" Tom asked.

"You're a lot bigger."

"You chicken?"

"No." It was an irresistible challenge.

Scott stood up and started to push the card table toward the wall. Tom grabbed the other end and both of the chairs to create open floor space. He entered the middle of the floor and again put up his fists like a boxer.

"Let's see what you can do."

Scott didn't hesitate and immediately rushed him. He jumped up and pushed Tom backward while managing to get a leg wrapped behind to trip him and take Tom to the floor. They rolled several times until Tom extended his legs and used his weight to pin Scott by laying on top of him while he reached down and squeezed the edges of Scott's jaw.

"Give?" Tom asked and continued to squeeze.

"No!"

Tom increased the pressure and Scott quickly yielded. "Okay. Okay!"

Tom released the pressure and got up.

"What was that?" Scott asked, rubbing his jaw.

"The submission move."

Scott stood up. "Let's go again."

Before Tom could respond Scott was on him and took him to the floor again. He clung to Tom's back and immediately reached his arm around his chest and thrust his hand upward to squeeze Tom's jaw as hard as he could. He managed to pin Tom on his side as he continued to apply pressure.

"I give!" Tom said.

Scott released his grip and rolled onto his back.

Tom sat up and rubbed his jaw. "Now, you're dead."

They both jumped to their feet and crouched down with arms extended as they faced each other while trying to catch their breath. They went a few more rounds, Tom dominating most of the rest of the matches due to his size advantage, and anger at having lost a round. Scott's jaw was throbbing and he touched it carefully as they sat back on the floor, leaning against the sofa, both sweating through their shirts and out of breath.

"You really had me a couple of times," Tom said. "Surprised me. You're tough."

The wrestling matches became routine throughout the spring semester. They met to study and hang out after school and, depending on where they were and who was home, they would fight in the basement, living room or sometimes at Scott's house at night on weekends when everyone was asleep. The rules of submission expanded to include digging a knuckle into the opponent's breastbone.

One morning Ava noticed bruises and swelling on Scott's jaw.

"What happened to you?" she asked.

"My jaw?"

"Yes."

"Tom and I wrestle sometimes. For fun."

"That was the noise last night? The thumps?"

"Yes."

"Why your jaw? I've noticed it before."

"It's how you win. Squeeze it until someone gives."

"I don't like it," Ava said. "It needs to stop."

Weeks later, when it was obvious it didn't stop, Ava took matters into her own hands. She went to speak to Tom's mother while their sons were at school. When Scott and Tom got home, they were both informed of the conversation and ordered to stop. If the wrestling continued, they wouldn't be allowed to see each other for a couple of weeks. Maybe longer.

Senior year arrived, and Scott did not prepare for the SAT exams. He scored just above average on math and only slightly better on verbal. He did not take them a second time. It was good enough. He knew he could never approach Pamela's near perfect scores. His only goal was to get away. He didn't even know why, it was only an impulse coming from deep inside.

He convinced Ava and Robert to let him study Journalism as long as he double-majored with something more employable, like Computer Science. The University of Vermont didn't offer Journalism, so he would have to go out of state. He applied to other state universities in New England, because they had a reciprocal tuition agreement. His grades and extra-curricular activities were solid enough to get into any but the elite schools and he managed to make the National Honor Society his senior year. He visited the University of Maine at Orono with Ava and Robert, and they agreed it looked good. Scott liked that it was big, and as far away from home as he could get. He knew Pamela's school was expensive, and his tuition would be a bargain in comparison. He didn't want to feel guilty about being an added expense. It was as reasonable a decision as anyone could expect.

Chapter 3 / 1978

Scott was surprised when he was called to the auditorium to be photographed for the yearbook senior superlatives. He had been voted Class Bubbles, along with his friend Kerry, a pretty girl with long blonde hair. He had no idea what it meant, and asked his friends. Half said it meant he was funny and social and floated around like a bubble. The other half laughed and called him Space Man. They said he was always spaced out when he was spoken to, as if he wasn't listening. He did at times catch himself daydreaming through conversations, though not for lack of interest, but because he felt uncomfortable being the focus of someone's attention. Spacing out gave a quick escape. Floating around like a bubble was meant to deflect attention. If he played funny and carefree no one would bother to ask serious questions, like why he didn't have a girlfriend or how he felt about things.

One late afternoon, when the school was silent and the hallways were empty, he returned to his locker after a rehearsal. As he walked alone, for what he knew would be one of the last times before graduation, he started laughing: the other students would die if they knew there was a gay in their school. It was the first time he used the word to describe himself. In that instant, he admitted the fights he watched and fantasized about were always between men. Involving a woman in the fights didn't work. It changed the whole dynamic into something distasteful, overly-violent and off-putting. He didn't like seeing women hurt. With men, no fight went too far.

But the moment of clarity soon evaporated. He still didn't know about real sex and he tried to convince himself things would change. Fights weren't like sex with a naked person, anyway. He had never even tried.

Graduation came and went. Scott didn't like the attention and felt awkward receiving a gift from his parents. He saw it as an obligation. He didn't feel he deserved it. He didn't know why. Ava seemed especially listless. Was he the only one who saw it? Scott felt like he walked on egg shells, doing anything to keep her mood upbeat. Was she somehow disappointed in him? Was she sad he would be leaving for college? Was she angry his jaw was swollen again?

Near the end of June, Tom went to Scott's house for dinner on a Wednesday night. They finished eating and relaxed on the back porch, playing UNO with Katherine and drinking Riunite Rosé Rosado on ice. Tom's parents came in to join them. They told Scott it was their weekend to use the family cabin on Lake Champlain, and they invited him to join them. They rotated it with other extended family members, and it was set up with a boat, water skis, and a barbecue. It would be the perfect way to celebrate graduation and to kick off the last summer before college was to begin and everyone would go their separate ways. He gratefully accepted the invitation. The timing was perfect. As the card game continued, they excitedly planned activities and what they should bring. They would go, they decided, rain or shine, because there would be plenty to do. They could fish in the rain and they had poles they could use off the sides of the dock.

Scott was elated on his walk home. Any time he could spend with Tom was important, now that the calendar was racing toward August. It was his top priority. He was leaving for Maine, and Tom was going to a college in southern Vermont, and Scott knew things would never be the same. He had never had someone call him a best friend before Tom, and it felt really good. As unlikely a pair he thought they were in the beginning, they had somehow bonded, and it worked. He felt proud someone like Tom thought he was cool. It went against everything he felt about himself.

The next day, Scott got up and made breakfast. Robert had already left for work, Ava was out running errands and Pamela had her own schedule, since she was home from college. Ava had left a note saying she had driven Robert to work, so Scott could use the car to get to his job, and they would see him afterward for dinner.

Scott started at 11 a.m., working for a contractor who fixed up, painted and restored the condition of condominiums for owners before new rental leases began. He cleaned up his breakfast dishes, got dressed, and drove to work.

When he returned that evening at 6:30, Robert, Ava and Pamela were gathered in the kitchen. The table was set, and everyone was quiet. Scott sensed immediately something was wrong and got nervous. Ava looked despondent. He approached the table cautiously.

"I got some bad news from Uncle Frank," Robert said. "Your cousin, Natalie, is very sick with what looks like a rare kind of cancer. We're going to visit them this weekend."

"Everyone?" Scott asked. He barely knew his cousin.

"No, just your mother and I."

"Where are you going?"

"Boston. There's a hospital there with cancer specialists. We're going to drive down in the morning," Robert said.

"When are you coming back?" Scott asked.

"Sunday evening. You'll stay here with Pamela."

Scott felt trapped and paused before he said, "I already made plans for the weekend."

Everyone stared at him.

"I got invited by Tom and his parents to go to their camp on the lake."

No one spoke for a moment.

"You'll have to go another time," Ava said.

"Why?"

"Pamela doesn't want to stay alone in the house," Ava said.

Scott looked at Pamela. Their eyes met and Pamela's expression was familiar to Scott: *Shut up and don't make trouble.*

Ava continued, "She's afraid to be by herself. It's better if you stay home."

Scott gave up and listened as they explained more about his cousin's condition and where they would be staying. They would leave a phone number where they could be reached. Dinner arrived at the table. Scott didn't talk. It didn't seem fair he couldn't go. What difference would it make? Pamela wasn't a baby who couldn't stay alone. She was going to be a junior in college. And his cousin wouldn't care. Was he supposed to sit home and pray?

When they finished eating, Scott helped clear the table and did the dishes. He excused himself and told them he was going to Tom's to explain about the weekend. As he walked over, he was determined to find a solution. He knocked on the door and entered the kitchen. Tom, his parents and Katherine were cleaning up their dishes. He greeted them and waited until they finished. Then he told them what happened to his cousin and about his parents' trip. They offered condolences and hoped he could come another time.

Katherine was quiet for a moment. "Why not come out Saturday and head back Sunday morning? Just one night. I'm sure Pamela would be fine."

It was a perfect idea, and certainly different from spending the whole weekend. Scott agreed, and said he would try. Obviously, he really wanted to. He, Tom and Katherine went to the porch to play cards. On his walk home, Scott wondered if he should ask again, or just go without permission.

The next morning, everyone got up earlier than usual. Robert took the day off from work and bags were already packed and waiting by the front door. The vibe in the house was tense. They ate breakfast quickly, and Ava packed lunches for them to take on the road. Robert brought the bags to the car, and within thirty minutes they were ready to leave.

Ava left a list of phone numbers on the kitchen table in case of emergency. She specifically told Scott to behave for Pamela. And he was to keep her company and not go to the lake. Ava and Robert kissed them goodbye and then waved as they drove away.

Pamela and Scott went back inside to finish their breakfast. She offered to drive him to his job, and pick him up when he was finished so she could use the car. They decided they would make dinner together later. Scott suggested they could watch TV or go to the movies afterward. He was going to spend as much time with her as possible before Saturday morning when he would leave with Tom for the lake. His mind was made up. He wasn't so sure it would be easy to just switch to another weekend, because he sometimes had to work, and Tom had many other friends he could choose to invite, instead of Scott. He was lucky to be chosen.

He called Tom and told him his plan. He would even wash the car Saturday morning, just to butter up Pamela. He would be gone for 24 hours, max. She needed to grow up. His parents didn't even need to know.

The next morning Pamela came out into the driveway as Scott was finishing up the car.

"Looks good," Pamela said.

"Thanks."

"You're up early."

"Yeah. It needed a wash," Scott said and paused. "Do you think it would be okay if I went to Tom's camp just for the night?"

Pamela looked annoyed. "Mom and Dad said you couldn't go."

"I know. But are you really scared to be alone?"

"No."

"I'm not going for the whole weekend like they thought. It's just one night. I'll be back tomorrow by this time."

"It's up to you," Pamela responded.

"The weather's perfect. I might not get another chance," Scott said, and went back to the whitewalls. He wanted to go bad enough to risk getting caught. She might not tell.

Pamela turned and walked into the garage. Scott gave the car a final rinse, put things away and headed into the house to take a shower. He cleaned the grit and grease from his hands and arms, and walked with his hair still wet with a towel wrapped around himself back to his room. He had already laid his clothes out on the bed, and carefully folded them into his backpack. He didn't need a lot. Just a sweatshirt, a bathing suit, shorts, a tee shirt, underwear and socks. Plus suntan lotion and Ray-Bans.

He headed to the kitchen and found Pamela reading the newspaper.

"Here's the number at Tom's parents' camp, in case you need me" he said, and handed her a slip of paper. "I'll come right back. It's only an hour away."

"Okay, thanks," Pamela said, and put it next to the list of numbers Ava had left on the table. "See you tomorrow. Be careful."

Scott grabbed his backpack and headed outside. He felt a sense of freedom and excitement as he walked toward Tom's house. It was stupid to just sit home on such a beautiful day. Everyone wanted to control him, and he was no longer cooperating. Spending time with Tom was more important than blindly obeying. He was aware Tom had a pull over him that overrode all other concerns. Scott couldn't resist. Anything he wanted, Scott would do.

Tom was shooting basketball hoops in the driveway when Scott arrived.

"Sorry I'm late," Scott said.

"No problem. You're right on time." Tom shot one last basket. He tossed the ball into the garage and closed the door. His bag and keys were already in the car. "Let's blow this clambake."

They got in the car and backed out of the driveway. Tom revved the engine while the car was in neutral, and then locked into gear with all the force the Toyota Corolla could muster. The wheels spun a bit as they sped forward and Scott started laughing.

"I'm glad we're going," Scott said.

"Me too," Tom said. "That was close."

"I know. Probably get in trouble, but I don't care."

"Who cares? It'll be worth it."

"Weather's amazing."

"Have to take advantage," Tom said.

"Not much time before August."

"Wonder what college will be like?"

"Think we'll keep in touch?" Scott asked.

"Of course!"

"Kinda scary and depressing, the way everything changes."

"I know."

"Changes are forever," Scott said. "Maybe that's the way life is."

"Nothing's gonna be the same. That's for sure," Tom said. "Some people already left."

They continued driving in silence for a moment.

"Gonna miss hanging out," Scott said.

Chapter 3 / 1978

"I know. Me too," Tom said.

They turned the radio up and rolled down the windows. Tom drove fast, and they made it to the lake in less than an hour. Tom's parents and Katherine greeted them after they made their way down the winding, dirt road and pulled up in front of the cabin.

"Fantastic you made it!" Katherine said to Scott, and led him from the car to the open lawn overlooking the lake. Tom followed with his bag and they stopped at the picnic table to enjoy the view of the lake, with seagulls above and sailboats in the distance.

Tom, Katherine and Scott went inside the cottage, changed into bathing suits and went to the dock. They drove the boat out and took turns water skiing, alternating drivers. When they returned, lunch was on the grill and everyone ate outside. The rest of the afternoon they played badminton, walked to the public beach to go swimming, and took the boat out again to go fishing. Tom's parents grilled steaks for dinner, and afterward they played cards, drank beer and talked until it was time for bed.

The next morning after breakfast they had time for another boat ride before Scott and Tom decided to leave at 11 a.m. Scott needed to be home with Pamela. Maybe she would even forget he left by the time his parents got home later in the day.

The drive home went quickly, and Scott made it back to his house by 12:30 p.m. He thanked Tom for the ride and they made plans to talk when Scott had scoped out what was going on. The car wasn't in the driveway, so Pamela was already out someplace. Scott got the spare key from behind the thermometer hanging in the garage and let himself in. He went upstairs and unpacked his backpack. He relaxed for a while and then decided to call Tom since Pamela still wasn't home.

"We just got invited to a pool party," Tom told him. "Lisa's house."

"Perfect. What time?" Scott asked. "No one's home here, anyway."

"Like, starting now. Until whenever."

"Be right over," Scott said and hung up the phone.

He wrote Pamela a note and brought it down to the kitchen table. He was home and heading to Lisa's house with Tom. She lived near the neighborhood. He would be back soon. He looked up her number and added it to the bottom in case she needed to call him. To cover his tracks, he threw away the other note he had left with the phone number at Tom's camp on it.

Scott walked to Tom's house, and together they headed to Lisa's. They didn't drive because it wasn't far, and they would probably be drinking. As they approached, they heard music coming from the backyard. When they walked around the back of the house and turned the corner, the lawn was packed and most of their friends were already there. It was an impromptu, post-graduation party, Lisa informed them. Her parents were away.

They headed to a plastic tub filled with ice and beer and joined the crowd. As the afternoon unfolded, volunteers left to bring back more beer and supplies to make hamburgers. The party was full tilt when Scott checked his watch and saw it was already 5:30. He told Tom he had to leave because his parents would be home soon and he would call later.

As he approached his house, he saw a car in the driveway, and it wasn't the one Pamela was using. His parents were home earlier than expected. The party was over. His heart pounded.

He entered the garage and quietly opened the door to the kitchen. No one was there so he paused. He heard Ava and Robert talking softly in the living room. He breathed deeply and accepted he had to face them. Maybe they didn't know anything. He slowly walked through the kitchen and turned the corner to the living room.

"Welcome back," he said as he entered.

"Yeah. Welcome back, you son of a bitch," Robert replied.

Scott's heart started racing, and he knew it was going to be bad. Robert had never sworn at him before. Ava just sat and glared.

"Where were you?" Robert asked.

"A party at Lisa's house."

"Are you drunk?" Ava asked.

"No."

"You look drunk," she said.

"He's lying," Robert said. "Smell his breath."

They walked over to him and he closed his mouth and held his breath.

"You stink like beer," Robert said.

"We told you not to go to Tom's camp," Ava said. "You blatantly disobeyed."

"It was only one night," Scott said. "Not the whole weekend." How did they find out? Why couldn't Pamela just lie for once?

"We told you to stay with Pamela. We depended on you," Ava said.

"Not such a big deal," Scott said. He was thankful he was drunk. He dared to talk back.

"We're trying to help my brother who's dealing with your cousin's cancer and you carry on like this?" Robert said. "You are grounded for a month."

"What about work?"

"Grounded as soon as you get home," Robert said.

"Forget about seeing Tom," Ava added.

Scott gave up. He said he was sorry and went to his bedroom. At least they didn't hit him. He was too old.

The next day, Scott was glad to get out of the house and go to work. Breakfast was tense, and he didn't speak to Pamela. The whole thing made him angry. They blew it into a catastrophe, and it really wasn't. Just like always.

When he got home, he realized he would have to suffer through dinner with them. No one spoke much, and Ava moped around the kitchen. He acted dutifully timid even though he could not care less. They all sat at the table and Scott daydreamed halfway through dinner until Ava suddenly spoke.

"I saw Katherine working the counter at the drug store today. Was going to keep quiet, but couldn't stop myself. Walked over to her and gave her a piece of my mind. Told her they were wrong to invite you when you had already explained the situation with your cousin and you weren't allowed to go. Told her off good. We simply asked you to stay home. It wasn't a lot."

"Not her fault," Scott said.

He was mortified and silent for the rest of the meal. Scott was aloof as he dried the dishes after Pamela washed them, neither of them speaking. He went to his room.

Later, he sneaked into his parent's room to use the telephone to call Tom.

"Won't believe what your mother did," Tom said immediately.

"Tell me."

"Screamed at Katherine while she was at work. In front of customers. In front of her boss."

"Oh, my God."

"Made her cry. At her job."

Scott was silent.

"Your mother's crazy."

"I know."

CHAPTER FOUR
1981

What should have been an exciting, celebratory summer before embarking on a new journey with the start of college was, instead, joyless and disappointing. Within two weeks Scott asked if he could be released from the captivity of being homebound except for work and church. Ava and Robert allowed it, but a chill continued in the house and Scott felt he was continuously under scrutiny.

His relationship with Pamela suffered. She felt entitled to have reported the facts when confronted with a question. Scott felt betrayed by a sister who could have covered for him if she wanted to. It seemed college was changing her into someone he didn't know anymore — someone who acted like a superior, rather than a sibling.

His first stop on reprieve from being grounded was Tom's house. He didn't tell anyone where he was going, because he felt it would be taboo to mention Tom or Katherine's name. He knocked on the screen door to the kitchen and saw Tom and his parents sitting at the table. They motioned for him to come in.

"Nice to see you," Tom's mother said.

"Been a while," Scott said, entering and closing the door behind him. "Sorry about all the trouble."

"Big drama."

"Katherine still talks about it," Tom said.

They told Scott how upset she was for days, especially since her boss was present and he almost fired Katherine until he learned Ava's screed had nothing to do with work. They felt Katherine was owed an apology.

Tom and Scott headed downstairs and talked like before. But in the days that followed, the incident cast a pall over Scott's relationship with Tom's family. He knew they didn't blame him, but needed to create distance from Ava, because she had crossed a line. Sometimes Tom wasn't available to hang out, and Scott was never invited for dinner or to the lake again. He blamed Ava for complicating — or even ruining — his friendship and relationship with Tom and his family.

In the evenings when Tom wasn't around and Scott was alone in his room, he laid on his bed with the lights off and the music turned up loudly in the earphones of his Walkman. He had discovered an incredible, new kind of music. Lisa had blasted it at her backyard party, and everyone stopped what they were doing to listen. What exactly it was, no one could say for sure. Punk, maybe. It was a song called "Planet Claire" by *The B-52s*. For Scott it blew away anything played on top-40 radio, which was awash with songs by Barbara Streisand, *The Bee Gees*, *Peaches and Herb*, *The Doobie Brothers* and Olivia Newton-John. The whole *B-52s* album had an excitement and originality to it that sounded like a middle finger pointed at the music that was shoved down everyone's throat. Slam dancing at a *Sex Pistols* concert in London had made the front page of *The Burlington Free Press* and Ava had pointed it out to Scott with the admonishment he was not to ever consider listening to them. His earphones now defiantly blasted "God Save the Queen" inside her house, and he loved it.

The reality of leaving for the University of Maine hit home in August, when Ava and Robert took him shopping for things he'd never needed before, like a trunk to transport clothing that could double as a shelf or end table in a dormitory room. He used two yellow milk crates to store and transport his record albums.

He felt the goodbyes to his friends — especially Tom — were awkward and unsatisfying, because everyone was nervous but trying to pretend things were fine. Thoughts and emotions were already focused on new lives that, for many, had already started.

Before he knew it, the station wagon was packed and Ava and Robert drove him to Orono. There were no interstates, only winding, truck-clogged routes that passed through the White mountains of New Hampshire and continued deep into Maine just north of Bangor. A sense of isolation grew as the trip continued and he realized he hadn't mulled over what it would be like to actually live in a very rural location. It was much more remote than his suburban neighborhood close to Burlington. He admitted he didn't consider realities during the college selection process. His only priority was getting away. And now he was going to find out exactly what he had chosen without much forethought or investigation. He was more nervous than he thought he would be.

He had a campus map and needed it to help Robert find his dormitory on the large, sprawling, picturesque campus that was situated on an island between the Stillwater and Penobscot Rivers that flowed southward into the ocean. It was hard to get to, but now that they had arrived, the campus appeared as a beautiful oasis in the middle of nowhere.

They pulled into the parking lot in front of his dormitory and joined the other families who were unpacking their cars and bringing multiple loads up to the rooms. For the first semester, he was in a triple. Ava and Robert met his roommates, who seemed nice, and already knew each other from high school. Scott didn't like that he was already the outsider. And why had he agreed to let Ava assign him to a quiet section of the dormitory? People he saw in the hallway seemed studious and nerdy and a bit like misfits. Even he was cooler than them, and that was not a good sign.

They finished unpacking, and stood outside the empty station wagon in the parking lot. Ava and Robert would spend the night in a local inn before making the return trip in the morning. Scott surprised himself when he teared up as he hugged them and said goodbye. He felt very alone and the reality of being dropped off and left on his own affected him in a way he was unprepared for. They wouldn't meet for dinner because it was best for him to make friends with his roommates. He watched and waved as the station wagon he knew for so many years pulled out of the parking lot, drove down the road and disappeared behind a hill.

A few days later Scott found himself in a large lecture hall awaiting the test results of the math placement exam that all freshman majors in Computer Science were required to take to determine their course selections. When his name was called, he went to the front and took a seat next to one of the professors calling out names.

"You scored in the top percentile," the professor told him.

"I did?" Scott didn't believe his ears.

"Yes. Look here," the professor said, and pointed to the score on the top page of the exam. "We want you to enroll in the advanced session of Analytic Geometry and Calculus."

Scott didn't speak for a moment. He figured he had only gotten lucky on the exam because it featured a lot of Trigonometry that he had studied in the last semester of high school and was still fresh in his head. He remembered the tricks and secrets. He would never be able to handle an advanced level college math class with new material. It would lead to failure.

"I'm can't. I'm not good in math," Scott said.

"Your test result speaks otherwise."

"What if I can't do it?"

"There's a withdrawal period with no penalty. Give it a try."

Scott agreed and left the lecture hall. He was surprised. Like orchestra auditions, he had imagined college to be exceptionally, exponentially difficult — something almost impossible, that only the smartest people could pass. He was terrified to get in over his head.

The same week, he was contacted by the conductor of the University orchestra and asked to audition, because the admissions committee had notified him of Scott's musical experience based on his application. Scott was wary about getting involved in extracurricular activities until he got a handle on his course load, but agreed to the audition. He performed well, perhaps because he felt the stakes were low and didn't care if he got in or not, and scored an outside seat in the middle of the first violin section.

Scott was mystified how everyone around him was making friends, except for him. It seemed to happen overnight. Within days, multiple groups had formed in his dormitory. Everyone had already split off into cliques.

He liked his roommates, but because they knew each other they often went off with their buddies from high school and didn't think to include him, or Scott would decline an invitation because he felt intimated to meet their group. Meals in the dining hall became a torturous ordeal he would ordinarily do anything to avoid, except he needed to eat. He would walk with his tray, looking for a place to sit, astonished that everyone was grouped up or paired off, except for him. How could he be the only one by himself? What was wrong with him? What was he missing? He imagined they talked about him as he walked by. A loser. A loner. He heard the whispers and saw the looks.

His first classes were equally distressing. He hated standing and introducing himself. It was an excruciating process he had to endure every day for the first week of classes. He was never sure if his imagination got the better of him. Did the other students dislike him? Their indifference to him and obvious ease with themselves contrasted starkly with his obvious shyness and awkwardness.

As the spotlight inexorably approached him and got closer to his seat, the mantras from his childhood would silently infiltrate his thoughts, unnoticed at first, but becoming a focal point and buffer against whatever was happening around him. I Hate My Life. I'm Such an Idiot. I Have to Get Out of Here. Please Help Me. He shocked himself when once he stood and spoke in a thick Vermont accent, using "crick" instead of "creek" and "ruff" instead of "roof." If they were going to hate him, he might as well create someone else entirely, and then it wouldn't matter, because it wasn't him, anyway.

As the semester wore on, Scott made friends in his dormitory and classes, but came to realize he had a warm-up time when meeting others that was significantly longer than people around him. He kept a distance around himself. He didn't know why. It was just the way he was.

The isolation allowed him to get things done on his own time, and he started to collect every new wave and punk album he could find in the college bookstore's record department: *The Go-Go's, The Clash, Bow Wow Wow, Bananarama, Joy Division, Adam Ant, Devo, The B-52s, The Smiths, The Cure, The Waitresses, X, Talking Heads, The Psychedelic Furs, Romeo Void*, and many others.

Most of the other students living on his floor in the dorm were purists who only listened to bands like *The Doors, The Rolling Stones, The Beatles*, and *Pink Floyd*. When Scott left his door open they would stop by to listen to what was new and debate the merits of old music versus new music, or just trash his taste. But for him there was no contest. The old music stood for *obvious* and *mainstream*. The new music pushed boundaries and valued excitement, anger and abandon over technical mastery of a guitar or drum set. The whole point was to reject the brainwashing apparatus of the entertainment machine that followed a formula to "market" their music "product" to the masses.

He noticed other students around campus who dressed in a definite punk or new wave style, and he tried to get ideas from them. He got his hair cut spikey on top, but longer in the back. He used gel. He wanted to show he was a part of this movement and couldn't stand to be seen as "normal" or a suburban-looking, generic, pseudo-prep. He faithfully read the *Trouser Press* to learn everything he could about the new bands that emerged every month.

Sometimes weeks would pass with no word from Ava and Robert. He didn't understand why other parents contacted their kids weekly — some even daily — and yet he could go weeks with no phone call.

He often found himself depressed. He thought about going to the counseling center, but rejected the idea because it was normal to feel lonely the first semester at college. When Ava did send letters or care packages, it surprised him that he cherished everything she sent. He used a coffee mug she had given him over and over even after it cracked on an outside edge. But he grew angry when it came time to talk. He felt like a phone call was too little, too late, and there was nothing to say, anyway. They only wanted good news. He told them the first round of Prelims went well, including Analytic Geometry & Calculus, which was a shock. Yes, he told them, he had made some friends. And yes, he would be home for Thanksgiving break.

When a conversation ended, he felt a complicated mix of sadness, anger and regret. Why was it so hard for him to talk about things? Had he sounded annoyed? He could have been nicer. Maybe he should call them back and try again?

The phone booths were in the common lounge area on the dormitory floor, and Scott walked back to his room one Sunday evening after a talk with his parents. His roommates were out with their usual group of friends. He laid on his bed and replayed the conversation in his head.

After a while he flicked on the TV. A few more clicks and he found what he was looking for. His new top show was *Matt Houston*, a private eye who used only his fists to take out rivals. He watched for clues the episode would lead to a final fight, and he sized up the adversaries. Until the villain was defeated, nothing else mattered. The masturbation routine that had started more than a decade ago never abated. When would it stop? Why was it still happening? What was wrong with him?

The night before the last day of classes before Thanksgiving break, a party erupted on the dormitory floor and Scott and one of his roommates, John, broke out what beer remained in their mini-fridge and joined it. Their third roommate lived only a few hours' drive away and had already left for the week. Most dorm room doors were open and stereo wars ensued in the hallway. Quiet Section rules were abandoned; perhaps the RA had already left, too. Scott liked to drink, and joined the mix of people colliding, laughing, and talking in the hallway.

Students on the floor he had never spoken to were amazed they had never met. Where had he been? Why was he so quiet? He was actually funny? No one had known. He was amazed by the breakthrough and chance to make new friends. Beer, and now the vodka shots that were flowing were definitely the answer to the friendship puzzle he had been trying to solve. He had discovered the key.

He bumped into John halfway down the hallway talking to another guy. He introduced Scott and they both remembered he was the guy who had rented them the mini-fridge in their dorm room back in August. It was his side-business. They invited the mini-fridge man to their room. They all did a shot, opened another beer, and suddenly found it very important to blast "Touch-a, Touch-a, Touch-a, Touch Me" from *The Rocky Horror Picture Show* and to direct the speakers out the door. They reentered the hallway.

The party continued for a long while but started to dissipate as pizza deliveries arrived and students drifted back to their rooms to eat. Scott and John invited the mini-fridge man to join them and they finished two pizzas. They drank until it was no longer possible to continue and still consider making morning classes. Because the mini-fridge man was too drunk to drive, they invited him to crash on their roommate's bed, since he was already gone.

Hours later Scott awoke, aware that a hand was touching him, rubbing his stomach and probing him below. His heart started pounding and he faked he was still asleep. He didn't dare move. It had to be the mini-fridge man. He pretended he was dreaming and rolled over. The hand stopped and moved away. He lay silent for a moment, still unsure of what to do. The hand returned and Scott was mortally afraid. What if he discovered Scott was awake and tried to kill him? Who was this psycho, and where would it end?

Scott coughed, and the hand moved away again. He coughed again, shook his head and sat up. He pretended to obviously awaken. He sensed very clearly it was best to not let on he was aware of anything. The guy might panic and get violent. Scott mumbled aloud he had to go pee, pulled on some shorts, and left the room.

In the hallway he was shaking. Should he run? Call the police? What would he even say? Their room was covered with beer cans. He quickly went into the bathroom, but felt he had no choice but to return to the room. John was in there alone with the guy, and it wasn't safe.

He quietly opened the door and they both seemed to be sleeping. He checked the clock. It was 4:30 a.m. He would wait until 6 a.m. and then get up, pretending he had to be up early to meet his ride home, or go to a morning class. He would tell the guy he had to leave.

Scott got back into bed with his shorts still on and rested quietly, trembling, hoping the mini-fridge man would stay down. He knew he would never be able to sleep and decided he needed a better plan. At 5 a.m. he got up and turned on his desk light. The guy opened his eyes.

"You still asleep?" Scott said.

"Just woke up."

"Cool. Gotta get an early start. Gotta clean this mess up and get packed."

The mini-fridge man just stared at him.

"You're gonna have to get up. We gotta clean our roommate's bed," Scott said.

At this point John woke up and asked what was happening.

"Yeah, I gotta get going," the guy said. "Thanks a lot."

"Take it easy," Scott said. He nonchalantly walked to the door and let the guy out. He closed it and quietly bolted it.

"What are you doing up so early?" John asked. "What's going on?"

"I'll tell you later," Scott said. "Go back to sleep." Scott turned out his desk lamp and got back into bed.

In a few hours, Scott awoke. He felt relieved light was coming in from behind the blinds. It was morning. He abruptly shook John awake.

"What? Stop it!" John said.

"Something bad happened. Gotta tell you," Scott said.

John sat up and listened.

"That guy. The Refrigerator Man. He was rubbing me. Touching me."

"What? Are you joking?"

"Under the covers. Last night. I woke up. His hand was all over me."

"My God."

"You can't tell anyone," Scott said. "Swear it."

"I swear," John said. "Are you okay? What are we gonna do?"

"Don't know. Gotta think about it. Steer clear of that guy."

Scott had one morning class, then time for a quick, early lunch before his ride home was picking him up at noon. He went to the dining hall, put a few things on his tray and found John sitting at a table.

"I'm really freaked out," John said.

"I know. Me too," Scott answered. "You can't say anything."

"I know. I won't. But you were molested."

"I guess so. I don't even know. It's weird to have someone touching you," Scott said. "The scariest part was thinking he could kill me or both of us if I woke up. I pretended I didn't know. He might be crazy. Never go near him again."

"Can you tell me more about what happened?"

Scott got up from the table and gave John a hug. He had to get away.

"Have a great Thanksgiving. See you next Sunday."

Scott left the dining hall, and returned to his room to get his bag. He headed outside and waited for his ride in front of the dormitory. He had contacted a sophomore who'd said on the Student Union's Ride Board that he was looking for a passenger to share expenses for the drive to Burlington.

The ride home was fun and felt like an adventure. The sophomore was friendly, and they were both content to listen to the radio as the drive wore on. Scott had time to think.

The mini-fridge man was obviously gay, and kept himself hidden. He probably targeted other guys throughout the dormitory system. It was his base of operation. A means of access. Should Scott tell someone? Probably, yes. But easier said than done. It would be a messy, scary, sordid kind of report he would have to file, complete with under-age drinking. Who had bought them the beer? And the mini-fridge man was actually nice. Good looking, too. But it was terrifying to wake up in the middle of the night with an uninvited hand probing around. Did the mini-fridge man target him because he thought Scott was gay? That was a horrifying thought. Did Scott seem gay? What a disaster that would be. And whatever happened in the bed held zero attraction for Scott. He hated being touched. He felt violated and dirty. Maybe Scott wasn't gay, after all. Shouldn't he have theoretically enjoyed it? He didn't. It was just frightening.

When the car approached his parent's driveway, Scott put what happened with the mini-fridge man the night before into a compartment, closed it, and never spoke about it again. It wouldn't be the first time something bad had happened to him he never told his parents about. He had always hidden things from them, things parents should have been told about: Bucky the Bus Bully, The Newspaper-Carrier Killer Car, and now, The Refrigerator Man.

When he walked in, Ava, Robert and Pamela were gathered in the kitchen like old times. Scott assessed Ava's mood. He greeted everyone with hugs and they chatted for a few minutes.

"Your hair's different," Robert said.

"Yeah. It's punk," Scott answered.

"No one here wears their hair like that."

"Well, it's big at school," Scott said. "It's a movement."

"About what?" Ava asked.

"Against dumb suburban concerns," Scott answered. "Don't complain. Next time it might be blue."

With that the topic changed and they sat down to dinner.

At the start of the second semester, Scott found himself isolated again. He had made friends in the dorm, but people were moving to different floors or different dormitories or apartments off-campus, and it wasn't enough. His one extracurricular activity — University Orchestra — was unfolding exactly as it had in high school: no one was particularly social. He felt he was repeating the same pattern and finding himself alone much of the time.

Scott felt lonely and depressed and needed to take steps to meet more people. He watched groups of friends interact all over campus and was bewildered. How did they do it? Why was he alone? What was wrong with him?

He decided to audition for the University Singers. It was a select group that had scored a spot at a music competition for the East Coast the year before. The conductor, a professor in the music department, liked Scott's voice and his attuned ear from playing the violin. He was accepted as second tenor and quit the orchestra. He felt bad to leave, but it was a matter of survival.

His first rehearsal with the University Singers was overwhelming. People were all over him. Where was he from? Where did he live? What was he studying? It certainly seemed his tactic to switch from orchestra to chorus was the right move in terms of making friends. They were open and welcoming and he suddenly felt his friendship network jump in one afternoon. There would be multiple concerts through the semester, cumulating with a Spring Tour at venues between Bangor and Washington, D.C. in April. He would need to buy a tuxedo but his new friends knew of a store downtown, and said they would take him.

Rehearsals were every afternoon from 3 – 4. A month later, there was a weekend retreat an hour or two north of campus, on a potato farm belonging to the parents of one of the members. It was designed as a bonding experience for the group, complete with a boozy night of team-building games that ended with an intense late-night discussion where members sat in a circle in the middle of a barn-room floor and shared personal stories.

Scott watched and listened with fascination. Some people were crying. How did they dare to talk about such things? When it was his turn to speak, Scott silently passed the ball to the person sitting next to him. He had nothing to share.

When sophomore year began, Scott felt smarter, as if a fog had lifted. His grades from the first year were all As and Bs, even in Analytic Geometry and Calculus. Why had he felt so stupid in high school? He was discovering he wasn't. His college professors and his classmates stimulated him, especially the newswriting classes that started in the second year. He could tell when a professor liked his work, and the positive attention fueled him.

Scott loved the way newswriting was different from his other classes. An assignment was given and immediately the starting gun was fired and the clock was ticking toward the deadline. The world became the game board where anything and anyone relevant to the story could be called upon as needed to complete it. The challenge unfolded in real time, with few parameters, except getting the story correct with enough real life sources to support it. There wasn't a text book. His other classes relied on memorization of facts, formulas or text from an expert, material that would later be tested in a controlled environment designed to measure comprehension. In newswriting classes, he would fail if he regurgitated a fact from a source without question or examination.

The concept of "critical thinking" was drilled into his head from his professors, and Scott saw it as nothing less than mind-altering. He applied the concept to the world at large, especially TV news, where commentators mindlessly repeated quotes from sound bites by Ronald Reagan without question or verification of facts. *USA Today* was a sickening new concoction that offered short, "happy-news" snippets with no depth and was suddenly the largest circulation newspaper in the nation.

It tied into and fueled his devotion to the punk and new wave scene. The musicians and everyone involved shared a distaste for and rejection of mass-marketed brainwashing from both politicians and corporations. And the biggest offenders were the white suburbanites who believed corporations were kings in a Disneyfied nation where it was of the utmost importance to discuss the virtues of vinyl siding so the paint wouldn't peel on the houses they built with enough space around them to fully isolate the occupants against contact with others outside their like-minded circle, safely ensconced in sprawling, cookie-cutter housing developments. And yes, nuclear war was an acceptable option to protect the freedom to consume as much as possible without regulation, taste, or limits. Communists would stop all that. They had to be crushed, or they would spread, and free markets would shrink.

Scott began to exhibit a new-found confidence. He still sometimes ate alone in the dining hall because there were no familiar faces. But it bothered him less now, because he belonged to a group that liked him. His friends in the University Singers became a bedrock that supported him. He was often hugged at the start of a rehearsal and it felt good. He joined the excited conversations and laughter. Life was better feeling liked, and without trying so hard for it to happen. In the world outside he still dreaded meeting new people and was sure their first reaction would be to dislike him. But at least the sense of overbearing loneliness and depression that came with the dread had lifted.

He followed a local punk band, *Zero Mentality*, and eagerly sought out the black and white concert announcements that sprung up around campus on Xeroxed poster collages taped to Student Union windows and pinned on telephone poles. He went to concerts by himself, and began to recognize the other fans. He felt good when they acknowledged him the next day walking around campus.

Scott got a job the summer before his junior year with a lake resort in the small mountains just north of Portland. College students from all over the county worked there, most of them music or theater majors at conservatories looking to make theater-related money over the summer. Many of the guests returned yearly from Boston and New York, and contacts could be made.

The first day, Scott was nervous not knowing anyone. But he soon met a Lebanese vocal student at Boston Conservatory named Rachel who would work in the dining room, a grounds crew staff member from the University of Wisconsin named Paul, two pals from Potsdam University named Beth and Laura who would work in housekeeping, and an openly gay acting student from Webster College outside of St. Louis named Carl who would also be stationed in the dining room.

Because he could sing competently, Scott auditioned and got cast as Prince Dauntless in *Once upon a Mattress*, and cast in the chorus of the large production numbers that would rotate different nights of the week. He wasn't a music student, and felt lucky to be included with the performing staff, because it would make the summer more fun. Scott found it interesting that the Prince he would play was shy, nervous, withdrawn and innocent.

The employees stayed in a cluster of cabins situated behind a parking lot that connected to manicured grounds. There, a main lodge and guest cottages were scattered about on the banks of a crystal lake that reflected the surrounding mountains. Scott worked with the grounds crew, and in the weeks that followed, the entire staff juggled their assigned duties — grounds crew, housekeeping, or dining room — with rehearsals and nightly performances. They rotated free time.

Everyone from the various departments liked him, and it seemed to happen overnight. With this job, Scott felt he was living a dream. Beth, Laura, and Paul turned out to be his party buddies.

Rachel and Carl were melodramatic and complicated. On free afternoons, they would take car trips to thrift shops in Bridgton, or to outlets and a restaurant in nearby North Conway, New Hampshire. They were both neurotic about performing and prone to pronouncements and mood swings. Scott loved watching their interactions with the world. They called the shots and made the plans, and Scott was happy to go along and to be included with the two biggest divas on staff. Maybe they liked him because he was quiet and nonthreatening. But whenever they wanted to do something, he was happy to tag along. He would wait and hope they would invite him. Spending time with them became his priority.

Scott was particularly infatuated with Carl. He was the first openly gay guy Scott had met who had no problem with it and, in fact, embraced it. He was handsome and athletic and defied the stereotype Scott had always heard about: weak, effeminate, simpering, lisping, pining for affection. There was one openly gay student on the second floor of his dormitory, and he was taunted mercilessly. Carl embodied the opposite experience. Everyone at the resort liked him — including guests — and he carried himself with a charismatic confidence that fascinated Scott. How could he not even care what anyone thought?

Sometimes Scott and Rachel would discuss Carl when they were alone, dissecting his moods, bouts of mania, or, conversely, depression when he wouldn't talk to either of them for several days. He had a pull over them and his silent bouts made them feel left out. They wondered when the silent treatment would end. Scott liked it when Rachel felt the same way; it meant he wasn't imagining things. A day later, Carl would suddenly return to normal as if nothing had happened, ask them where they'd been, and the three of them would pick up exactly where they had left off, making plans to play tennis or meet on the staff beach in the free hours before dinnertime.

Scott felt the world was like magic, as the summer played out with daily work duties mixed with a few hours of free time, then performances in the evenings after dinner. He was nervous playing Prince Dauntless one night a week, but the character allowed for imperfection and audiences seemed enthusiastic. He got some loud laughs and applause.

After the shows, everyone was free and would often sit by a bonfire near the Staff Quarters. Scott began to visit Carl's cabin on a nightly basis. They talked about Carl's life in St. Louis, fears of life after college, and Scott's dream to work as a newspaper reporter. Carl told him he had to force his way toward what he wanted, no one would do it for him.

Scott felt special he was considered important enough to get one-on-one time with Carl, the star of many of the evening performances and popular. Sometimes Rachel would join them in the late night talks, and Scott could only imagine how wonderful it would be to live in a big city as he listened to the details of their daily lives in Boston and St. Louis. Someday, he would move to one. After all, finding work as a reporter would require it.

On a very hot night in early August, Laura, Beth, Paul, Carl, Rachel and Scott all sat around the bonfire and joined the rest of the staff, each contributing their drink of choice to a cooler on the sidelines. Someone added a boom box, and a full-blown party erupted. Everyone was aware that the end of the summer was approaching, and in a few weeks they would all scatter about the country and resume their studies.

When the music quieted and the group began to dissipate, Scott followed Carl to his cabin. He watched as Carl turned on a lamp and lit two candles, one on the nightstand by his bed, the other on the bureau. Carl took off his shirt and laid back on the bed with his feet resting on the floor.

"Come here," Carl said.

Scott froze where he stood.

"Come here," Carl said again.

Scott walked to the bed, grabbed one of Carl's arms, and tried to pull him to a sitting position.

"Get up. You're crashing."

Scott continued to pull on his arm until Carl was upright.

"Sit here," Carl said.

Scott's heart was pounding as he sat down next to him. Carl reached his arm around and pulled Scott toward his chest. Scott felt the odd sensation of whiskers on the side of his face as Carl continued to pull him closer. Scott stood up and quickly moved to a chair next to the bureau.

"When are you going to stop playing games with me?" Carl asked.

Scott could scarcely breathe.

"I'm not playing games with you," Scott said. "I already told you, I'm not gay."

"I don't care what you are," Carl said. He lay back again.

Scott was puzzled by the response and just sat for a moment.

Then he walked toward Carl and again tried to pull him to a sitting position.

"You're drunk," Scott said.

"If you pull on my arm one more time I'm going to punch you," Carl said.

Scott stopped and went back to the chair. No one spoke for a moment.

"You never really wanted to be friends all along," Scott said.

"That's not true."

Scott waited and then walked back to the bed to see if Carl's eyes were open.

"You know what you're thinking," Carl said. "Stop playing games with yourself."

"What are you talking about?"

"You know."

"What?"

Carl said nothing and stood up. He walked to the lamp and switched it off. He blew out the candle by his bed. Scott walked to the bureau and blew out the other candle.

"Party's over," Scott said and left.

The next day at lunch, Scott sat next to Paul and grew nervous when he saw Carl enter the dining hall and walk toward him. Carl approached slowly and sat across from him.

"What time did I go to bed last night?" Carl asked. "I don't remember anything."

"Twenty to twelve," Scott said.

"I was out of control. That's why I don't get drunk very often. Not a pretty sight. No one likes to be around me."

Scott didn't respond and finished his lunch. Two days passed without more than an exchange of "hellos" between them in passing. Scott quietly continued his duties and began to hope Carl would make another effort to talk to him. Scott would not approach him first.

That evening, Scott waited alone off stage while awaiting his cue. Carl spotted him and walked over.

"Why have you ignored me the last two days?" Carl asked. "Was I rude or something the other night? I really don't remember. I was trashed."

"We'll talk about it later," Scott said. "You were rude." It was time to enter the scene and Scott walked to the stage.

Later that evening when the show was over, Scott exited the music hall and saw Carl outside talking to Rachel on the pathway.

"Wait! Aren't we going to talk on the way back?" Carl asked as Scott walked by.

Scott stopped and waited. Carl caught up to him and again told Scott he couldn't remember anything.

"I don't buy it," Scott said.

"I'm sorry you don't, but it's true," Carl said. "Now, let's hear the dirt so I can apologize."

Scott told him what happened in his cabin after the bonfire party. Carl told him he was sorry and they hugged. It was a warm, moonlight night so they decided to head to the beach to take a swim. They left their clothes on a wooden chair on the side of the lake and entered the invigorating water. Scott wanted to show Carl the damage had been repaired. They were nude and swimming and talking and didn't touch. They treaded water while watching the moonlight reflect on the waves. Carl was Scott's friend again, and it meant everything to Scott. They didn't have to be gay. This was plenty close. All Scott could absorb.

The few remaining weeks of summer passed quickly. Scott savored any time he could spend with Carl, and they played tennis, went running on country roads, swam, and made quick shopping trips. Scott considered it the best time of his life. He loved his friends and dreaded the day they would have to part.

Paul lived the furthest away, and was the first to go. They held a keg and corn roast in his honor the night before he left. Beth and Laura were next, and they cried when they hugged Scott to say goodbye and promised they would write.

The night before Carl left, Scott gave him a card and met him in his cabin. The card read:

I know you hate sentimental goodbyes, so I'll make this short.
Thanks for being my friend this summer. I really do love you.
See you in Boston? St. Louis? Who knows?

They hugged for a long time, and to Scott it was the warmest feeling he had ever experienced.

Scott and Rachel were the last of their group to remain. They talked about Carl and how much they already missed him. They promised to keep in touch, and hugged when they finished packing the car for her drive back to Boston. When her car disappeared down the road, Scott felt completely alone.

The fall semester back at school was excruciating. Scott desperately missed his friends from the summer. He got two short notes from Carl. Scott called him, but the conversation went nowhere and he hung up the phone despondent. He called Rachel and she told him Carl asked what his problem was and why he hadn't written. So Scott sent him a card for Halloween, then one for his Birthday. At the end of the note, he wrote:

Write soon, but don't bother if you're just patronizing me.
I'd rather you didn't.

He waited for phone calls that never came.

Meanwhile, pressures from his studies were mounting. He was heavily involved with the daily student newspaper and was producing front page stories. But he hated conducting interviews, and was terrified each new story assignment would be the one he couldn't do. He assumed sources wouldn't want to talk to him and felt awkward calling them, like an unwanted guest.

He grew suspicious of his friendships in the University Singers. The chatter before rehearsals he once found open and welcoming he now saw as cheesy and fake. He became aloof, and barely joined into conversations or activities. The music, rehearsals, and performances he liked, and was excited about the spring tour to New York City, but he no longer trusted anyone.

He had put his heart into friendships over the summer, and what had they amounted to? He would never make the mistake again. It wasn't worth the pain in the long run. He couldn't understand how Carl, Rachel, Laura, Beth and Paul could just disappear. What happened? Why would people do that?

A depression descended on him. He declared himself in a state of 'personal emergency' and would protect himself by turning inward, because he thought a lot about suicide and it worried him.

He focused on the newspaper and became a Managing Editor. Twice a week he was in charge of the headlines, subheads, layout and production of the next morning's edition and getting it out on time. If they missed the pick-up, they would have to drive the mechanicals to the printer themselves, which meant not getting home until 4 a.m.

Chapter 4 / 1981

He continued to immerse himself in the punk and new wave music scenes. One Thursday night, he went to a *Zero Mentality* concert in the basement of a local nightspot called Barstan's. The crowd was particularly enthusiastic and gathered in front of the band to dance. Scott joined in.

Slam dancing was tough and physical, but it fit the music and he liked it. When the sound switched from a surf rock beat to a sudden, thrashing explosion, the crowd would react with a violent burst that briefly turned brutal. Scott accidentally clipped the side of his eyebrow against another dancer's head and got a black eye.

As he walked back to his seat, a group of four fraternity guys were sitting against the wall. He could tell by their shirts they weren't fans of the music and were there only out of curiosity. No one into punk would wear Greek letters to a concert. Greeks were the ultimate conformists on campus.

"Oh, you're real tough," one of them said to Scott as he passed, and pushed a chair with his leg to block Scott's path. Scott grabbed the back of the chair and forcefully threw it to the floor. He stepped over it and continued walking, his heart pounding in preparation for a fight.

He was shocked he had dared to defy them, and had not simply walked around the chair. They were invading *his* space, not the other way around. He looked over and they still seemed to be sitting. The chair rested where he pushed it over, lying on its back. His days of cowering before white guys were over. They always traveled in packs, like cowards. It was easy to bully people when traveling in packs. And it was always white guys who bullied. The campus was diverse, and he had never had one incident with anyone other than whites. He despised them, the Straight White Suburban Males, who dictated the rules and made sure everyone obeyed or were bullied into compliance. They were the ones responsible for the spectacle of burning jeans in barrels on the front lawn of several fraternity houses to protest Gay Jeans Day: a one-day event when students were asked to wear jeans in a show of support for gay rights. Jeans were selected as a symbol because everyone had them, and gays were everywhere, even though there were none in sight. Scott had watched the flames from afar with disgust and fear. Their hatred of students in a far weaker position than themselves was sickening, and he hated them back.

Weeks passed, and Scott was unaware that the depression and anger he felt was exacerbated by the cold distance he maintained between himself and his friends and family.

He was encouraged to keep a journal for one of his writing classes. He liked the idea because there was no one to talk to. In a journal entry the last day of classes of the fall semester, Scott wrote:

Sometimes I get very bitter and think I'll never again put so much into friendships. It's not worth it in the long run. I contemplated suicide all through September over my loneliness, and pressure from newswriting. It's not worth it. Carl wasn't (isn't) worth any more of my thoughts after the summer. It's so hard to understand why Carl, Rachel, Laura, Beth and Paul have blown me off. I don't believe they've changed. That's what's so puzzling. What has happened? Oh, fuck them all.

Who I thought were my greatest friends turned out to be nothing. But I really did grow out of this whole thing. I know I did. I'm a much stronger person because of this. I have a stronger crack threshold now. You can only suffer so long without growing out of it all. So with this I end thinking about the summer and its aftermath. I don't ever want to hear from or think about those people again. I've wasted enough time being miserable about it all, and it's time to stop. I don't care about it anymore. Next time I write here, it will have nothing to do with the summer ever again. Bye.

With that, the semester ended and Scott returned home for winter break. He took solace that while he scored one 'C' in newswriting, it was largely due to spelling a name incorrectly or small mistakes that were outweighed by the support he got from his professor about his writing in general. He convinced Ava and Robert to let him drop the Computer Science part of his curriculum, and to declare a single major in Journalism. They agreed, but with the caveat that he had to get his grades in newswriting higher.

Chapter 4 / 1981

During the spring semester, Scott met and became friends with a member of University Singers named Josh. He was from a suburb west of Boston and was sophisticated and popular. Josh told Scott he found it interesting Scott kept himself away from the main shenanigans of the group, but at the same time Josh had been afraid to approach Scott because Scott was so aloof. Josh was also a tenor, and Scott liked when he saved a seat for him at rehearsals if he arrived slightly late. They began to sit together every day.

Scott shared his plan was to move to a big city, and they both eagerly awaited the spring tour. They looked at maps together and plotted out things to see in New York City. Though he resisted at first, Scott felt happier as a friendship with Josh began to grow.

They made plans to meet for dinner, and sometimes met in the Language Lab. Scott studied Spanish all through college, and hoped to use it in a city after graduation, and Josh had a work-study assignment in the lab. They met for pitchers of beer many nights at the Bear's Den or Pat's Pizza. Scott found himself questioning what Josh saw in him. But nonetheless, he liked having a companion after the loneliness of the previous semester.

As Spring Tour approached, Scott and Josh signed up to be roommates. The route would take the group to concert locations at churches and school auditoriums scattered between Orono and Southern Maine, with further stops in Massachusetts, Connecticut and Long Island. The final concert would be in New York City, with the next day free for sightseeing.

The tour committee organized host families to house the singers along the route, and the trip took place over spring break. Scott and Josh sat together on the bus and became inseparable. They listened to mix tapes they made on Scott's Walkman, which had two headphone jacks.

"You've got the best music," Josh said.

"You're the only one who thinks so," Scott said. "Not mainstream enough."

"Maybe not around here. But huge in Boston."

"That's why you get it."

"I miss the city. The music. The style. Modern people."

"I need to get away from group hugs."

"Before rehearsals?"

Scott nodded. "Too much and too fake."

"You're a cynic," Josh said. "I like that. Like Zooey. Handsome and cynical."

Scott was intrigued that Josh called him handsome, and also that Josh liked Scott's favorite book, J.D. Salinger's *Franny and Zooey*. Scott wasn't sure how he appeared to people. He didn't see "handsome" when he looked in the mirror. But it felt nice to hear.

When they got to New York City, Scott was enthralled. As he crossed each avenue, he would pause momentarily in the midpoint of the crosswalk to absorb the view of buildings spread in all directions for as far as the eye could see. It was unimaginable to him contrasted with the hills of Bundy's farm, or the seclusion of the University of Maine campus. He knew in that moment he would move. It was a simple realization. A fact. There was nothing to question. Life was short and difficult, and if he didn't take control and put himself here, something would rise up to stop him and he would waste his life pining for a dream that would never happen.

Scott and Josh shared a room in the Roosevelt Hotel. It was small, dark and depressing with a view into a brick wall, but the hotel lobby was fantastical, buzzing, and ornate, perfectly preserved in reds and golds from its opening in 1924. They marveled as they passed through the revolving doors to walk the streets for hours, talk, people-watch, dream of the future.

On the bus ride home, they were energized. The trip was an inspiration. Maybe Josh would move to New York someday, too. They made plans to be roommates for senior year. Josh lived in a house off-campus with two other roommates, and they had an opening for Scott.

In the weeks before the end of classes in May, Scott and Josh spent as much time together as possible. Josh hung out at Scott's apartment on campus between classes when they had free time before rehearsal at 4 p.m. Every evening, Scott walked to Josh's place off campus. They studied, listened to records, and Scott met his future roommates.

Scott and Josh were aware time was growing short, because summer break was soon to start. Scott was offered a job back at the lake resort. He wrote to Rachel to see if she was returning. She was but didn't know about anybody else, including Carl. She hadn't heard from anyone, either. Scott decided to accept the job, partly to get answers. He secretly hoped Carl would be there.

One afternoon, Josh closed the book he was reading in Scott's room. They sat on the floor with their backs up against the lower part of a bunk bed. Scott's roommate was at class. A record played on the turntable.

"You ever wonder what it would be like to kiss another guy?" Josh asked. He paused. "Ever thought about it?"

"Yes," Scott said.

"With who?"

Scott hesitated. "You."

"Me, too."

There was silence for a moment. Then Josh leaned forward and kissed Scott's cheek. Scott rubbed the side of his face slowly up and down against the wetness of his lips, and turned his head. They kissed. It continued for a long while. Then it was time for rehearsal.

Scott felt elated and dazed as they walked to the center of campus. The kiss was exciting. He had made out with girls at parties, especially when he was drunk. This felt the same. Except for the whiskers. Kissing a guy wasn't something shocking, like everyone imagined.

"That was cool," Josh said.

"Really interesting."

"Thought it would be strange."

"I know."

"Glad about it."

"Me, too."

They went to rehearsal and sat together. At the end, they made plans to meet later at Josh's apartment. It was more private and he had his own room upstairs. Scott returned to his apartment to get what he needed to study, and notes for a story that was due the next day. He rang the bell at Josh's apartment, and a roommate let him in. Scott went upstairs to Josh's room, knocked on the door and went in. Josh was waiting for him, and as the door was closing went over to Scott and grabbed him without speaking. They held each other, standing, and kissed. An hour later, Scott had his first sexual experience. He didn't know what to do. He closed his eyes and thought about a fight he had watched on TV during the week.

In the weeks that followed, they met every night. They talked about what was happening between them. They agreed they had never felt it before. One night they walked to Josh's apartment and lay together on his bed, listening to music. Josh pulled out a notebook and took Scott through his journal entries of the last three months. He shared how he felt about Scott. He described a sexual episode when there was no Kleenex to be found, and he had to use a dirty sock next to him on the floor to release himself. The latest entry said he was falling in love.

"Not just falling," Josh said. "I am in love with you."

"I feel the same," Scott said.

They held each other and Scott spent the night in Josh's room.

When summer break arrived, and Scott prepared to leave for the lake resort, Scott assured Josh time would pass quickly. Josh helped Scott move his winter clothes and what he wouldn't need over the summer into his new room on the first floor of their house off campus. Scott gave Josh the phone number and address at the resort. Josh would remain in Orono, to take a summer session course and continue to work in the Language Lab.

They spent their last night together in Josh's room, and it felt strange for Scott to simply walk downstairs to find his own clothes in what would now be his new bedroom. Josh told Scott he was happy to see his things in the downstairs bedroom because a part of him would remain in the house. Then it was time to leave, and Scott drove away.

Three hours later, when he pulled into the parking lot behind the staff quarters at the lake resort, everything changed. All the memories of the previous summer came back with a rush of adrenaline and Scott was suddenly alarmed. Could he do this again? Why had he thought this would be okay?

Chapter 4 / 1981

Scott parked the car and brought his bags to the cabin he had been assigned for the summer. He unpacked and tried to relax until the staff meeting at 3 p.m. He missed Josh, but now he had bigger problems. Was Carl here? Would he and Rachel still talk to him? He nervously checked his watch until it was finally time for the meeting to start.

When Scott entered the dining room, the people he knew smiled and waved to him. He saw Carl and Rachel sitting together. They both stood, waved, and held out their arms for him to come hug them. Scott greeted them.

"Great to see you," Carl said.

"You, too," Scott said. "What happened to you?"

"He's in a relationship," Rachel said.

"With who?" Scott asked.

"Someone from school. A year older. Already graduated but lives in town. It's serious. There's drama," Carl said. "What's your excuse?"

"Excuse for what?" Scott asked.

"Your silence. You disappeared," Carl said.

"Just got very busy," Scott said.

"Seeing anyone?" Rachel asked.

"No," Scott said.

"Same here," Rachel said. "We'll have to listen to Carl all summer."

The staff meeting started, and things immediately felt familiar. Duties were assigned, and training sessions would start the next day. When the meeting broke up, Rachel challenged Scott and Carl to tennis matches. They played for a while, then walked to the beach. It was too cold to swim, but the lake felt good on their toes.

Scott felt himself switch. Now, he was someone else. There was nothing he could do. It would be impossible to integrate Josh into this new situation. He would store Josh away until August, when it was time to return to school. It was as if Josh were a dream that suddenly didn't exist. Gone. The new bedroom. The kisses. The feelings he had felt. Everything was distant and foggy and out of sight and lost.

On Wednesday, Scott ate lunch with Rachel and Carl. The office manager brought mail that had arrived and distributed it. She called out Scott's name. He was the only one to receive something. She brought the letter over to him at the table.

"Who's that from?" Carl asked, laughing and snatching the letter away from Scott. "Josh Henderson? Who is Josh Henderson?"

Scott was mortified and grabbed the letter back.

"A new housemate," Scott said.

He put the letter face down on the table as if it were meaningless and started a new conversation. Why had Josh already written? Was he crazy?

On Friday another letter arrived, and Scott felt like a baby receiving mail the first week of the summer when no one else did. Scott put the letter on the table and Carl turned it over.

"Again from Josh?" Carl asked.

"Yes. Our new apartment house. Financial stuff. Mind your business."

That evening Scott called Josh from a pay phone booth in the back of the main lodge. He told him to stop sending so many letters. Scott didn't say so, but he found it annoying and weak.

"How was I supposed to know?" Josh asked.

"Not your fault," Scott said. "But it makes me nervous."

"Why? I miss you. Thought you would like it."

There was silence on the line.

"Miss you, too," Scott said.

"You sound weird," Josh said. "I'm hanging up."

In the weeks that followed, the letters slowed in frequency, and Scott wrote a few in return. He explained it was busy and difficult to find time to write, but he looked forward to seeing Josh at the end of August.

In early July, news spread of a killing near the University of Maine campus. Three white teenagers chased a gay man named Charlie Howard, yelling anti-gay slurs while Howard ran for his life. They caught him, kicked him, and threw him over a bridge in downtown Bangor, where he drowned in the water below. He had pleaded with them not to drop him over the rail because he knew he couldn't swim. The news sent a chill through Scott. Being gay was dangerous business. You could be chased and killed for it.

Scott spent most of his free time with only Rachel and Carl. It became clear as the summer unfolded that it would not be a repeat of the one before it. Carl was moody and apparently having arguments with his boyfriend. Some days Carl would go off by himself and Scott would hang out with Rachel. They sat in her room and talked, played tennis, or took out a small sunfish sailboat. Sometimes they kissed. It was more of an experiment than anything else, but they both enjoyed it. Rachel was innocent and Scott liked her sweetness. Carl thought their attempt at a fling was ridiculous, and said so.

In August, Scott wrote Josh a letter saying he decided he was straight and needed to continue with Josh as just friends, as they were before. He no longer wanted a sexual relationship. Two days later, he was called by the office manager to the main lodge to take a phone call.

"Got your letter," Josh said. "Can't believe it."

Josh was crying.

"I'm sorry. I can't help it."

"What do you mean?"

"I've changed."

"Can we at least talk about this in a few weeks when you come back?"

"Not much to talk about," Scott said. "We can be friends just like before."

"Can't be just like before," Josh said. "It won't be."

"Then, that's your problem," Scott said. "Not mine."

"But, I love you. You told me you loved me."

"I know. But, I've changed. I met a girl," Scott said. "Look, I can't talk right now. I'll explain more when I get back."

The phone call ended.

Why was Josh being so weak? It wasn't the end of the world. He should be fine with it. They were friends for months before they did anything sexual.

Scott went through the motions of the rest of the summer. He and

Rachel mutually decided it would be foolish to continue any kind of relationship. They agreed with Carl to meet at Rachel's apartment in Boston for October break. Scott felt more level-headed and in control than the previous summer. He would see them again in October, and that was good enough.

Scott was already hardened when he pulled into the driveway at Josh's apartment house. They went up to Josh's bedroom to talk. Scott couldn't focus on what was being said. His thoughts drifted wildly away and he felt removed from the room as if observing the conversation from a perch somewhere above. Listening to it, watching it, but not a part of it. Josh was crying, and Scott wanted to calm him, but he couldn't. Scott had gone too far in the first place, and got too close. Now he had to protect himself.

Scott asked Josh if he wanted him to move out. They agreed it would be difficult to find a replacement now that the semester was about to start. They would try to be friends, or at least cordial housemates.

What was supposed to be a great senior year became an endurance test. Scott tried his best to be kind to Josh, seeing his obvious pain as the weeks unfolded. But a point came when he felt Josh should have recovered and was now weak, needy, and pathetic.

Scott withdrew and spent more time away from their apartment. He became a DJ at the campus radio station. With friends, he put on a party persona that masked any inner turmoil.

He continued work with the campus newspaper, but switched to a more private, quiet role as Copy Editor. He won a Maine Press Association Scholarship for his last semester. He was a finalist for a job opening at the *Bangor Daily News*, but failed the typing test on an IBM Selectric typewriter, after working on a computer keyboard for years. He imagined the speed they expected on the test to be exceptionally, exponentially fast. He sat in the confines of the testing room. I Hate My Life. I'm Such an Idiot. I Have to Get Out of Here. Please Help Me.

The highlight of the year was a European tour with the University Singers in the spring. In London, Scott could scarcely sleep due to his excitement. On the last night, Scott sneaked out of the hotel and made his way to a huge nightclub, the Camden Palace. It was like being transported to another world. He reveled in the exciting mix of people all around him. He had never been in so impressive a space, and the lights, the new wave music, the whole experience overwhelmed him. He watched clubgoers in wild outfits on the dance floor below from an elevated balcony, and tried to absorb the frenetic scene as it unfolded. When he got the courage, he went down the stairs and danced by himself, lost in the crowd.

He returned to the hotel in time to make the morning bus that would take the group to the ferry crossing, but when he told them about his adventure, some in the group found his behavior reckless. Something could have happened to him alone in the middle of the night in a big city he knew nothing about. They whispered about it. He sneaked out to a nightclub and barely made it back in time.

Josh was worried and sat with him on the bus. Scott convinced Josh he was fine. Would it have been better to sit in his room and miss one of the best, most memorable experiences of his life?

In Venice, he again sneaked out of the hotel and spent the night drinking beer on the floor of the train station with travelers from all over Europe. They discussed politics and life with the young American. The Cold War was unending, fear of nuclear war was palpable, and *99 Red Balloons* was a huge, worldwide hit. Everyone wanted to talk to him. He felt fully alive and invigorated.

When the tour ended and only a few weeks of classes remained, Scott kept to himself and made plans to escape to a place where he could disappear. He got accepted to a program for the summer at New York University. Ava and Robert agreed to pay for it, especially since he had won a scholarship his last semester.

The night before graduation, he said goodbye to Josh. In his heart, Scott knew the only mistake Josh had made was showing him true love. Scott sabotaged it. He didn't know why. He only knew he had to get away.

CHAPTER FIVE
1985

It was early June, and Scott was back in Vermont. He and Pamela were together at home, because their cousin Natalie had died of cancer after four years of treatment. Ava and Robert traveled to Boston to stay with Robert's brother for a few days and to attend the funeral. After graduation from M.I.T., Pamela had landed a good engineering job in Burlington and couldn't take off from work to attend the funeral. Scott was leaving for New York in a few days, so was also excused. They both knew they didn't want to go. They barely knew their cousin, or their aunt and uncle for that matter.

The last time Scott and Pamela were home alone together, Scott had disobeyed orders to stay with her, and left to spend the night at Tom's camp on the lake. This time things were different. Pamela had her own house 10 miles away. She returned to check on Scott because he had a stomach virus. She carefully prepared a chicken broth for him to calm his system. She made sure there was other food in the house for later, and checked to ensure Scott had a ride to New York University since Ava and Robert would be unable to take him.

Scott had lined up a friend from high school to drive him who was curious about seeing the city. He didn't mind dropping off Scott, then spending a free day on his own. Pamela was satisfied and hugged him goodbye. She couldn't understand why he would want to move to such a dangerous place, but wished him well. They would see each other at Christmas.

Scott didn't believe in laboring decisions. His whole life had been rural. Now, he wanted urban. The center of a big city. He knew on his first visit to New York he wanted to live there. Others weren't sure, or thought everything was too crowded and dirty. He was sick of the prissy tidiness of white suburbia, and the attitudes that went along with it.

His friend found a place to park a few buildings down from Brittany Hall on East 10th Street in Manhattan. They took turns unloading the car. Scott registered at the desk, then moved his things close to the elevator. He pushed the down button. Nothing happened. There was no basement. He looked back at the attendant who rolled his eyes. Scott pressed the up button. The door opened. He had only been in a few elevators, and wasn't used to them. He thanked his friend and said goodbye. He owed him a lot. Then the elevator doors closed and took Scott seven floors up to the start of a new life.

Scott found his room and met a few of his suitemates. There would be five or six of them total. They were all in different programs, either law, business or publishing. They would all have different schedules and agendas. Scott unpacked his things.

He got out to the street as soon as he could. He loaded his Walkman with the best mix tape he had put together as a DJ at school and played it loudly. "We Live as We Dream, Alone," by *Gang of Four* started the list. The music served as a connection and anchor as he walked. He was unafraid of getting lost because the address of his dormitory was simple to locate. He wandered without destination. He discovered single, 16 oz. cans of beer placed in brown paper bags could be purchased at Bodegas and Korean delis and could be consumed in the street while walking. It was an ideal combination: Loud music and a can of beer in a bag while exploring Manhattan. It was all he needed.

The publishing program began on Monday. Scott nervously entered the auditorium the first day for orientation. He nodded and smiled to those around him and found a seat. He braced himself for the inevitable introductions as they started around the room. Students came from Berkeley, Bennington, Louisville, and Los Angeles. The professor told him Orono was a frequent New York Times crossword puzzle answer and Scott felt better, almost exotic. He was from the most rural background. During the break, five students came up to him and introduced themselves. They were outgoing and enthusiastic and treated him as an equal. It didn't occur to him to question why he sensed he was somehow lesser.

Over the next three months, the students made contacts and learned about opportunities in book and magazine publishing. Scott was still interested in newspapers, but wanted to learn about related industries. He had no idea how to navigate this new world, so he concentrated on what connections he could garner from the program.

He explored New York with the new friends he made. As the end of August approached, those who wished to remain in the city felt a sense of panic. Jobs needed to be found, or they might be forced to return home, and the whole summer would be a waste.

Scott landed a job as an Editorial Assistant at a book publishing house. It was the first job he applied for. He didn't have the luxury of an extended job search. It wasn't a newspaper, but stakes were high and the job guaranteed he could stay in New York. That was his primary objective. Other jobs could be found later.

But first he had to find out who he was.

He needed to find a place to live he could afford on his starting salary of $12,000 a year. He scoured the ads in the *Village Voice* and quickly found what he was looking for. A bedroom was available in a two-bedroom apartment in Long Island City. It was close to Manhattan and a quick commute to his job in Midtown. Scott got on the 7 train and met the man who placed the ad. His name was Jorge. He was handsome, in his thirties and from Bogatá, Colombia. Scott liked he would be able to practice Spanish with him.

Jorge told Scott he was gay. He said it with shame and regret, as if it were a liability, and for that reason he offered the spare bedroom inexpensively. Scott instantly liked him for it. It was honest and heartwarming. Scott smiled and said he didn't care, but shared nothing about himself.

Scott took the room in Jorge's apartment. He hired a Man-With-A-Van, also found in the Voice, to help him move his belongings from NYU on September 1st. Jorge welcomed him and showed him a few things in the kitchen he could use if he wanted to cook. They would share the bathroom. Jorge was surprised and delighted when Scott spoke to him in Spanish.

At least four of Scott's friends from the program stayed in the city. They met for drinks on weekends and formed a bit of a support network. They introduced him to the Pyramid club on Avenue A, one of the epicenters of the new wave scene in the East Village. Scott found himself there every weekend. The music was exactly what he liked, and the crowd was cool and interesting. It was dark, and a long wooden bar extended from the front door to an archway that led to the dance floor in back. The bathroom was a pit. It was best to take a deep breath before entering, because the smell was putrid. Something inside had passed the point of being fixed or cleaned, so it was left to fester.

A few weeks passed, and Scott discovered Sundays were "gay night". He knew he had to explore it, though it made him very nervous. He was a regular on Fridays and Saturdays, so if he showed up on a Sunday night he could pretend he didn't know, if questioned.

When Sunday came, he put on what had now become his uniform: black t-shirt tucked into gray jeans with suspenders and rolled to be narrow at the bottom, paired with combat boots or shiny black shoes with white socks. He got his left ear pierced and wore a small jack knife earring on weekends. His hair matched a lot of people who went to Astor Place to get their hair cut: short all around and spike-y on top, a "flat-top" hardened with Stiff Stuff.

Jorge questioned where he was going on a Sunday night, especially since he had to work the next day. Scott told him he was meeting friends. But he was alone.

Chapter 5 / 1985

His heart pounded as he approached the bar and the bouncer outside. But the guy smiled and let him in. Inside, he didn't have to pay. Scott was one of the first to arrive because it was only 11 p.m. He had discovered nothing got going in New York until at least midnight. It would make it hard to go to work, but it was a sacrifice he was prepared to make to find out what a "gay night" entailed. There was no other way.

He stood at the end of the bar and watched as people began to enter. The bartender sometimes gave him free beers. Scott had learned to tip one dollar for every drink without fail. He studied the guys around him. They looked normal, just like on Saturdays or Fridays. By midnight the room was packed with men. Some were big, some were handsome, and some he could never imagine could be gay. He watched men dance alone or in pairs and it all seemed perfectly natural. Why did straight people think it was such a big deal? He felt lied to.

Sometimes a guy would catch his eye and Scott would instinctively look away. He couldn't hold eye contact. He was aloof, exactly like his last year at school. An observer.

Scott was terrified of AIDS and overheard people in the bar talking about it. He wondered if he could have caught it from Josh. They never had intercourse, but no one really knew how it spread. He heard kissing might even pass it. Any exchange of fluids.

At 2 a.m., Pyramid was full tilt, but Scott had to leave. There was a train ride ahead and work at 10 a.m. He could still get six hours of sleep. He knew he would be back next Sunday.

Weeks later, Scott stood at his perch at the end of the bar near the dance floor. A guy came up to him. He introduced himself as Tim and shook Scott's hand. Scott had noticed him before, but never dared to look too closely. Tim had a handsome face and a body one would expect on a high school or college football jock. He was hard to resist.

"Seen you here a couple of times," Tim said.

"You look familiar," Scott said.

"Where're you from?"

"New England," Scott said. "What about you?"

"Houston. When did you move here?"

"In June. Went to a summer program at NYU."

"Where do you live?"

"Long Island City."

"You look local. Didn't think bridge and tunnel."

"I want to move. Would love to live in the East Village," Scott said. "What about you?"

"Just across the park," Tim said. "Want to dance?"

Scott nodded and Tim led him to the dance floor, directly in front of a small performance stage that formed the back edge of the room. A DJ sat in an elevated booth to the left of the entrance to the room. They danced for an entire set, sometimes touching each other. After a while, the music stopped, lights came up on the stage, and a drag queen named Lady Bunny appeared. She did a comedy act, lip-synced, and introduced guest performers. When the show ended, the lights dimmed and the DJ took over again.

Tim leaned toward Scott and asked, "Want to come over?"

Scott agreed and they left the dance floor. They walked through the front bar area and went outside. To avoid Thompkins Square Park, they used the North side of the street above it as a safer route to the other side.

Scott was nervous, but excited. He couldn't believe a guy as attractive as Tim was interested in him. He might not ever get another opportunity with a guy so hot. He had to see how this would unfold. Tim led him to his apartment building, unlocked the front door, and continued up the stairs. Tim had a roommate, so they had to be quiet when they entered his apartment. They crept into the entrance hallway, crossed the kitchen into his bedroom and closed the door.

"Nice place," Scott said. He was amazed by the art work and spacious rooms. How could Tim afford this? Were his parents paying for his apartment, like Scott's friends from NYU?

They went to Tim's bed and kissed. Scott was ecstatic. He hadn't kissed anyone since Rachel the summer before. And not a guy since Josh. They had sex the only way Scott knew how. He rubbed on top of Tim.

"That's good," Tim said. "Safe sex."

For Scott it was nothing more than a pattern repeated since childhood. In his mind, Tim was losing a fist fight.

When they finished, they lay together for a while, until Scott sat up because it was time to head home. He had to work in the morning. They exchanged phone numbers.

The next day Scott was exhausted at work but it was worth it. He couldn't wait for the day to end. Did Jorge have an answering machine?

That evening, Scott called Tim from his room and they talked for more than an hour. Tim had graduated from Rice University in Houston the previous year. He had studied architecture. His roommate was an up-and-coming painter who knew everyone, and, yes, Tim's parents helped Tim with the rent since he was still starting out. They made plans to meet on Friday night. Scott hung up the phone excited. It was his first date with someone he barely knew.

When the weekend arrived, Scott met Tim at the Yaffa Cafe on St. Mark's Place. From there they went to King Tut's Wah Wah Hut on Avenue A. As they drank beer, Tim asked Scott if he wanted to take ecstasy. He explained it was an amazing, mind-expanding drug he got from his friends in Houston, the epicenter of ecstasy laboratory science. It was gentle and euphoric and made dancing really fun until later when it made closeness, cuddling and sex irresistible.

Scott was intrigued. Did he dare? Everyone knew drugs were bad news.

Tim continued to outline the evening: they would go to The World, the best nightclub in the East Village where only the coolest people could get in.

Scott asked if ecstasy had side effects.

"Just really tired the next day," Tim told him.

Tim took out the pills and showed him one.

"You'll need to stay hydrated. Drink a lot of water, not beer. You'll just waste the alcohol, anyway. You won't feel it."

Scott continued to think. "If I freak out, you've gotta help me."

Tim laughed. "You won't freak out. You actually become smarter. Your mind opens."

He put the pills back in his pocket.

"It takes at least an hour before you even feel anything. Sometimes longer. It's very subtle. Suddenly, you just kinda realize you're completely high."

"We should do it," Scott said.

"Great. We will," Tim said. "It's still too early."

They finished their beers, then headed across the street to the Pyramid. There was a line in front, but the bouncer saw them approach and waved them in. They stood at the bar to order beers, and Tim held Scott's hand even though it was Friday, and not Sunday. Nobody cared. It felt good. They stayed until midnight, then they each took an ecstasy pill.

The walk to East 2nd Street was dangerous. They crossed North of Thompkins Square Park to Avenue B, and headed south. Side streets were to be strictly avoided, but from Avenue B to the entrance of The World, foot traffic made it feel safer. There was a line to get in. Tim walked up to the bouncer, who opened the red rope for them. Scott was impressed with Tim's influence. He obviously knew people.

The scene inside was pure decadence, in the best possible way. Ornate gold framed mirrors hung on chipped, red walls extending up to a black ceiling in the small rooms closest to the main entrance. The sparseness inside was accented by 1940s furniture on wooden legs, upholstered with patterned fabric. A huge mahogany bar extended along the near wall in the main room, facing a cavernous dance floor with wood plank floors and crystal chandeliers overhead. A disco ball spun and the twinkling lights cloaked the room with a dream-like gauze. The music thundered a mix of post-punk, new wave and rap that literally shook the walls. The crowd was beautiful and dressed in extravagant outfits they had put together themselves with a creative wit that prized originality over any kind of department store fashion or functionality.

Scott and Tim made their way to the bar and ordered waters. They weaved through the crowd on the dance floor and found a spot. They danced with no one in particular; everyone seemed to be on their own, anyway.

Scott hadn't felt so free and excited since his one night in the Camden Palace in London. But that had felt lavish, friendly and spectacular. This felt edgy, raw, and somewhat dangerous. Like anything could happen. A cool, detached vigilance was required.

He noticed a very good-looking dark-haired guy dancing with another guy. They kissed. But the dark-haired guy soon drifted to his female friend who danced with her breasts exposed like it was nothing. And in here it *was* nothing. Her outfit required it. He watched them dance together and felt a subtle, yet perceptible tweak. Something was happening. He concentrated, and it faded. But in a moment when he relaxed and scanned the room, it happened again, this time with more strength.

"I'm feeling something," Scott said to Tim.

"Yes. It's starting," Tim answered and smiled. He grabbed Scott's hand.

A small series of waves began. They pushed in, then receded. It was fun to catch himself drifting away with each pulse.

"I love it," Scott said.

"Just wait."

Scott concentrated to keep a hold on reality, to play a game against the waves, and delighted when it became impossible. A wave came in strong and this time did not recede. Scott felt his senses become enhanced, more sensitive. He felt euphoric, like it was the best thing he had ever discovered. Even the music was different, with certain sounds rushing forward and popping out from nowhere. Drum beats and twanging guitars became an important, overpowering force that needed to be reckoned with on the dance floor. Scott and Tim danced enthusiastically with everyone surrounding them. Sometimes they would touch and rub against each other and sometimes against strangers. Everyone was okay.

Hours passed, and the rush of excitement receded to a constant, steady, pleasurable pulse. Scott talked effortlessly to Tim, and didn't fear touching him in public. They kissed and rubbed each other, fixating on stomach, arms, chest. Tim knew of a place nearby. An after-hours club. Scott was amazed such a thing even existed. New York was even better than he thought.

They weaved their way off the dance floor, maneuvered through the crowd, and found their way outside. They walked back to Avenue B and Tim led Scott into Save the Robots. They descended the stairs and found seats, content to sit together, touch, and listen to music. After about an hour, Tim suggested they head back to his apartment.

They arrived about 6 a.m. and quietly went to Tim's bedroom. They undressed and got under the covers. They couldn't sleep and spent hours kissing, talking, and touching each other with an intensity that varied from gentle to passionate. They slept in spurts and didn't get up until late Saturday afternoon. They were famished, and went to a diner. As they waited for the food to arrive, Tim invited Scott to join him at a big, annual reunion ball at his alma mater in Houston the next weekend. They would need to take Friday off from work. Scott immediately agreed. He was thrilled Tim wanted to spend more time with him. He would do anything Tim wanted. He felt like he was falling in love with him. When they finished eating, Scott got up to leave, and they agreed to talk later.

On the train ride home, Scott felt dazed. The night had been an overwhelming blur. He couldn't stop thinking about Tim. Maybe they could meet again tomorrow.

When Scott walked into the apartment at 7 p.m., Jorge was annoyed.

"Where you been?" he asked.

"Decided to stay at my friend's apartment," Scott said.

"You gotta let me know. I almost call the police."

Scott apologized. He had never considered Jorge would wonder where he was. Next time he would call and leave a message.

Scott went to his room and rested. He didn't sleep well and woke up Sunday in a depression. A dark heaviness weighed on him and got worse when he called Tim, who sounded distant and didn't want to meet at Pyramid that night. Scott would drop everything to see him, but Tim apparently didn't feel the same. They talked about the Houston trip, and Tim said he would call with flight information when he knew more.

The depression continued the next day. It was worse than his usual ones. He figured the ecstasy caused it. He got permission from his editors to take Friday off, and that evening he waited for Tim to call. The phone rang at 8:30 p.m. and Jorge knocked on his door and told Scott the call was for him. Scott always let Jorge answer first, since it was his apartment. Tim told Scott he had booked flights leaving Friday afternoon and returning Sunday night. They got a good price, and Scott could write him a check. They talked a bit more, and Scott felt better. He was excited to spend a whole weekend with Tim.

On Friday the depression still lingered, but the thrill of traveling with Tim overpowered it. In Houston, they took a cab from the airport to stay with Tim's parents. Scott felt special, and was surprised to see they were fine with their gay son and his friend. He wondered if he were Tim's boyfriend.

The next day, Tim took Scott on a car tour of Houston. They played *Propaganda*'s album "A Secret Wish" loudly and on a constant loop. They went to the Galleria and Tim showed Scott around Rice University.

That night they put on suits and went to the gala event of the architecture school. When Tim introduced Scott to his friends, Scott felt under scrutiny. Were they attacking him or just trying to get information? Scott found a lot of them pretentious and dismissive of him. He suddenly realized he was very nervous, especially given that Tim was comfortable being seen publicly as gay, but he was not. Scott was a curiosity. A gay Tim had found. A show-and-tell artifact. Scott felt tolerated, but not welcomed in the tight-knit group, and did not enjoy the evening. Tim was in high demand, and sometimes disappeared. Scott felt stranded.

The next day there was a brunch event, and Scott again felt like an outsider. They knew Tim as a three-dimensional former classmate, but Scott was the gay invader. He felt it immediately. He had to defend himself, and contributed little to conversations.

On the plane ride home, Tim asked Scott why he was so quiet. Scott denied it. But Tim had stopped touching him and was acting cold. Tim made a joke, securing the seat belt very low and tight against his crotch, but it didn't feel genuine. It felt like Tim was playing with him.

During the week, they spoke on the phone and Scott hoped they could meet. But Tim already had plans. Scott tried again the next week, but it was the same thing. Obviously Tim didn't like him or he would make time for him. Scott didn't want to beg. He had been dumped. Probably all Tim had wanted was a date for the ball at his school reunion.

Scott went into a depression and vowed not to fall for someone again so easily. People were unpredictable and untrustworthy. They liked you, then they dropped you. He should have learned his lesson after his summers at the lake resort.

He avoided Pyramid and decided to explore a place he had heard about called Boy Bar on St. Marks Place. He had walked by several times, but had never dared to enter. It was an obvious gay bar and it scared him to be seen approaching the door by people on the street. He waited until the sidewalk was clear.

The atmosphere inside was simple and inviting. On the first floor, near the front door was a large bar that opened onto the dance floor. A DJ spun post-punk, new wave and sometimes generic dance music. Upstairs was another, smaller dance floor with a jukebox that played 45-rpm records, another bar, and a coat check above the stairs. Scott liked that he could sit at the bar by the door and watch people, and the bartenders talked to him. He decided he would come back.

Over the next several weeks, Scott became a regular. The bar had a reputation for having the best looking guys in the East Village. The crowd was trendy, different from the West Village (clones) and the Upper West Side (preppies). The doormen came to know him and he always got in for free. Bartenders recognized him sitting in the same spot at the bar and offered two-for-one beers, just for him and other patrons they liked. He gradually made friends and a small clique formed. A young photographer from Virginia Beach named Ed was one of them. They met Friday nights, and would repeat weekly at Pyramid on Sunday nights.

Chapter 5 / 1985

One Saturday afternoon in the spring, Scott left his apartment in Long Island City and started his daily walk to the 7-train. He passed a group of guys on the street, and one of them spit on him.

Scott continued to walk, but turned to watch the spit dripping down his calf on the back of his leg. It felt degrading. He felt empathy for other people who throughout history had been spit on. No one knows how it feels to be spit on by a complete stranger until it happens.

He turned the corner, and wiped off the spit with a Kleenex. He surmised they thought he was gay because he dressed trendy and they dressed "regular." Or maybe he no longer fit into the neighborhood with his Astor Place haircut. He wanted to move to the East Village, but it was hard to find an apartment. Especially with an Editorial Assistant's salary.

That night, he met Ed at Boy Bar. He told him about the incident on the way to the subway. Ed said he had a friend from work named Lourdes who lived in the neighborhood and was looking for a roommate. She was an actress, and wanted to become a director. She had attended Emerson College in Boston. He would introduce them, if the room was still available. Ed called Scott the next day and quickly arranged a meeting with Lourdes, because someone else was also interested in the room. He gave Scott the time and address.

Scott was excited by the possibility of living in the East Village, where his entire social life had become focused. The apartment was on 14th Street between Avenues A and B. It was loud, and the streets were dangerous, especially after dark. But you could walk anywhere if you took precautions, looked like you belonged, and knew the blocks to avoid.

He found the building and pressed the buzzer for apartment No. 8. A female voice told him to go to the second floor. The door buzzed, and Scott pushed it open. A stench hit his nose as he stepped inside and realized dirty mop water had been used on the stair case and the bucket was still sitting in the hallway. It was a five-story walk-up and each stair creaked as he ascended. On the second floor he turned and saw a pretty, petite brunette peeking out the cracked door.

"Scott?" Lourdes asked.

"Yes. Lourdes?"

She smiled, pulled the door open, and extended her hand. "So nice to meet you."

They shook hands and Scott went in. The door closed behind him and he surveyed the room. To the right of the door was a small, white combination gas stove/oven. It butted against a kitchen sink that butted against a porcelain bathtub that stood on four legs situated against a wall with a window facing 14th Street. A shower curtain encircled the tub. A water closet butted the back of the bathtub. A small kitchen table stood in the middle of the room against a wall that opened to a bedroom on the left, and a short hallway on the right.

"This is the living room, kitchen and bathroom," Lourdes said and started laughing. "Take a seat," she said, and motioned to the chairs by the kitchen table. A gold lamé table cloth covered the table. A topless female mannequin stood in the corner by the entrance to the hallway.

Scott sat down. "Cute place."

"It's a dump, but I make it work."

"Great location," Scott said.

"If you love the neighborhood."

"I do," Scott said. "The only place I go. Except for midtown to work."

"Where do you live now?" Lourdes asked.

"Long Island City."

"We've *got* to get you out of there," she said.

Scott relaxed and they continued to talk. He told her he moved to the city in June, went to college in Maine, though he was from Vermont. He wanted to work a newspaper but was now working for a book publisher.

She was from the Upper West Side, her mom from Puerto Rico, and her dad from Venezuela. She spoke Spanish, though secondarily to English. Scott told her he studied Spanish through college and wanted to keep it going.

"*Hay, que lindo,*" Lourdes said. She stood and pulled aside a curtain covering the doorway to the bedroom behind him. "This is my room. You can take a peek," she said.

Chapter 5 / 1985

Scott stood and looked inside. A loft bed rose above a desk below and a large rack of clothes. A window looked out onto 14th Street.

She let the curtain go, and led Scott to the hallway behind the mannequin.

"Let me show you your room."

They walked five or six steps down the hallway and the bedroom opened to the right. An upright piano was set against the wall closest to the kitchen, and the foot of the bed extended from below the keyboard. Sitting Indian-style on the bed was the only way to play it. A window looked into the alley in the center of the building.

"Comes with a piano," Lourdes said. "The previous tenant couldn't deal with moving it, so just left it. We can move it if you want. But I don't know how we'd get it out of here. Can you play?"

Scott leaned over the bed and touched a few keys.

"It needs a tune up," he said and started laughing. "I play the violin."

"That's adorable," Lourdes said. "Do you have a lot of things?"

"No. Just a small bureau. A record player. My records. Plus clothes."

"Perfect. That should all fit. There's a bar hanging in the hallway you can use as a closet," Lourdes said and pointed to a steel rod suspended by 2x4s in the hallway opposite the doorway. "Do you like it?"

"I love it," Scott said.

His share of the rent would be $400 a month. It would be tight, but he could do it.

"I have a good feeling about this," Lourdes said, and led him to the kitchen. "When can you move in?"

"Gotta talk to my roommate, but probably Saturday."

"Oh. Full disclosure," Lourdes said. "There's a junkie who lives on the first floor. She sometimes gets locked out of the apartment and yells for her boyfriend, Walter, to unlock the door. But you can ignore her screams. She's harmless."

They exchanged numbers, hugged, and Scott left. He was ecstatic for the chance to move to the East Village where he felt like he belonged. There was nowhere else he wanted to be.

When he got back to Long Island City, he spoke to Jorge and told him about the apartment, and the chance to live in the city. Scott had paid his share for the whole month so Jorge would have time to find someone else. Jorge said he had enjoyed having a roommate, but now had saved some money and wanted to live alone again. Jorge wished him well.

Scott hired the same Man-With-A-Van he had used eight months before. On Saturday afternoon, they unloaded the van and created a pile with his things on the street in front of the building's door.

Lourdes buzzed them up. They propped the door open and took turns going up the stairs. Lourdes came down to stand guard outside. Scott arranged things in his room, and when he finished unpacking, Lourdes called him to join her at the kitchen table.

"Only carry the money you need in your front pocket with your keys. At night, keep a $20 bill in your shoe, just in case. Leave your wallet here. You won't need I.D., anyway. Never dress fancy. Walk fast, like you know exactly where you are going. Never walk 13th Street. Ever. They rob you, even if you are neighborhood. Be careful on Avenue B. Don't go lower than the Chicken place around the corner. Use Avenue A, instead. Forget about Avenue C. You look like a white boy."

They met Ed at Pyramid later that night to celebrate. Scott thanked him for introducing him and Lourdes. They joked about meeting guys.

"He doesn't dare look at people," Ed said, and pointed at Scott.

"Gotta teach him how to cruise," Lourdes said.

"I don't get it," Scott said.

"You catch someone's eye," Ed said. "Then look again, this time holding the gaze a little longer. Gotta be more aggressive."

"I'm not good at that," Scott said. "Can't do it."

Weeks passed, and Scott loved living steps away from anywhere he wanted to go. It was a different life from taking a train back to Long Island City. He met Ed every weekend, and their circle of friends grew. They were recognized by doormen and bartenders, and rarely paid. They went out Fridays, Sundays, and usually Tuesdays. Saturdays were secondary because locals got displaced by hordes coming from the outer boroughs and suburbs.

Lots of guys looked at Scott, but he never dared to hold their gaze, then went home feeling stupid and angry for having blown his chances. Why was he so afraid? It was a pattern that repeated over and over. One night a stranger walked up to him and informed him he was beautiful, that he couldn't be cuter, it just didn't happen. Scott thanked him and then disappeared into the crowd, unsure of how to handle such a complement, except to run. Another night, he overheard two guys whispering as they passed each other in an inside stairwell. "Yes, he's hot," one said. "But he doesn't fuck. He's a Yankee." It bothered Scott they had information about him and talked about him. People were dangerous.

Something held him back from daring to approach and pursue and push a conversation with guys he was interested in. Scott felt inferior, and didn't question why. It was simply a given. A loneliness overpowered him. The AIDS panic exacerbated matters. Everyone was terrified of contracting it. He replayed sexual encounters in his head, examining any possibility of fluid exchange. He thought about Tim on the ecstasy night. Had it been safe?

If kissing were dangerous, then everyone was doomed. He even thought about Josh in Maine. Before he met Scott, Josh had a gay friend who ran around Boston. Josh had hooked up with him. Could Josh have infected Scott? Some encounters had been messy and uncontrolled. Now, everyone around him was a potential risk. Everyone around him was *at* risk. Everything was suspect. Scott wondered how and when he could possibly meet someone, given his fear of initiating contact with people and fear of catching AIDS. The situation was hopeless.

In the apartment, Scott shared his worries with Lourdes. They talked after work, or late Saturday mornings. Sometimes she came in and sat on his bed and propped a pillow against the piano. Sometimes they sat at the kitchen table and drank a pot of coffee. He told her he got depressed and had started taking St. John's Wort. It was an herb he had read about and could be purchased in Korean delis. She said she was already taking it and it definitely helped.

As fall approached, Scott asked Lourdes for advice. She was a year older and he trusted her judgment. He had spent a year in book publishing and regretted he did not pursue work with a newspaper. He feared life could pass him by. It would be a mistake if he stayed in book publishing simply because it was the first job he took, and allowed himself to get trapped. He was copy-editing manuscripts and proofreading, but doing little original work of his own. Even letters to authors had to be approved by his editor before sending. He found an ad for a job at a weekly newspaper similar to the *Village Voice* that was published in Brooklyn. The job was for layout of the paper, not newswriting. But least it was a step into the newspaper world. The position was freelance with no benefits. Lourdes thought he should make the move. This was the time to take chances.

Weeks later, Scott got the job at the *Brooklyn Phoenix*. He was good at newspaper layout because it had fallen under his duties as Managing Editor of the newspaper in college. The editor was intense and smart and sometimes had a temper. Everyone was equally intimidated by him, and respectful. There was much to learn from him. Scott enjoyed the newsroom environment with its independence, camaraderie, interesting personalities, and pressure to perform under deadline. The offices were on Atlantic Avenue in downtown Brooklyn, and Scott liked discovering a new borough he knew nothing about.

One Saturday afternoon, Lourdes asked Scott if he wanted to go in on some blow. She and her boyfriend were getting some, and there would be a snowstorm that evening in the living room. Afterwards, they would go out dancing. Scott had never tried cocaine, and wanted to. He said yes.

Lourdes stood by the kitchen table and looked in the full-length mirror hanging on the door to the water closet. She wrapped her long hair high on top of her head into an improvised beehive, sprayed it heavily, and added a scarf.

"I like to look good for a drug deal," she said.

Her connection was on Avenue A and she would be back in 20 minutes.

Chapter 5 / 1985

That night Lourdes, her boyfriend, and Scott sat at the kitchen table, listened to *Kraftwerk*, and passed around a small glass vial with a black plastic top with a tiny spoon inside. They talked for hours about politics, life and the problems of the United States. They went to a bar with a dance floor and stayed for hours. Scott noticed how, every half hour, the compulsion to refresh the high with another bump became overpowering. He didn't like that part. But the bad feeling went away instantly with the vial and a trip to the bathroom stall. When the supply started to run out, they decided to head home.

By mid-afternoon the next day Scott felt an overwhelming depression. He asked Lourdes if she also felt it, and she said she wanted to kill herself. It was meant as a joke, but at least she shared the feeling. It was the price of doing drugs. Whatever high was attained, a depression would follow the next day, sometimes for a week, she told him. Maybe it wasn't worth it and they shouldn't do it again.

Over the next several months, Scott continued to go out at least two, and as many as five nights a week. His job at the newspaper didn't start until the afternoon, and the hours extended into the evening, usually 9 p.m. Staying out late didn't interfere. The only problem was sometimes his paychecks would bounce. He always got the money, but it was a hardship because he lived from check to check. Lourdes lent him money if he needed to get through a weekend until the business manager at the newspaper adjusted the accounts on Monday.

Scott watched as people he met in the club scene began to spin out of control. He didn't want to do the same. He met Michael Alig soon after he moved to New York from Indiana. They spoke one night upstairs at Boy Bar, and Scott enjoyed the conversation. Michael was handsome, clean-cut and came across as polite, genuine and friendly. Two weeks later he was transformed, almost unrecognizable, with a new haircut and extravagant Club Kid outfit. Scott thought he went too far too fast. It unsettled him.

Another night, Scott ran into Tim. They hadn't seen each other for a year after the trip to Houston. He was now boyfriends with Dean Johnson, nightlife royalty and lead singer of *Dean and the Weenies*. Scott worried Tim was getting in too deep.

Meanwhile, Scott never turned down cocaine if it was offered it to him. One night in Pyramid he had spent all his money and was desperately thirsty. He cupped his hand to get a handful of water from inside the holding tank of the toilet and drank it. Another night he took an ecstasy pill with three friends at the Limelight. Something didn't feel right and he went upstairs to try to gather himself in a bathroom stall. An intense, horrible, flashing sensation was happening inside his brain, and he needed help. Was he overdosing? He ran downstairs and left the club, intent to find a hospital or police station. He walked a half block, and suddenly the feeling passed, as quickly as it came. He returned to the club and found his friends, as if nothing happened.

The next morning he vowed to stop taking drugs, primarily because of the week-long depression hangovers that always followed. He felt depressed anyway, and the drugs only exacerbated the problem.

Two-and-a-half years had passed in New York, and Ava and Robert still hadn't visited him. Scott resented it. Pamela had become a Yuppie. That it didn't even occur to them to offer him support angered him. He refused to call. In a journal entry, he wrote:

> *What have I been missing? I guess I really am separate from them all. They really don't know me, nor I them. The sick thing is, I don't give a shit. I've wanted them to want me — always have — but it's always had to be on their terms. I didn't share their views/ interests/mindset and so I was deemed uncooperative and not interested in being a part of them. There is a lot of furor involved here and I'd better sign off. It's far too frustrating.*

After six months with the Brooklyn newspaper, Scott started looking for a new job because he could no longer tolerate his paychecks bouncing. He found a job with a magazine focused on the real estate industry. The topic didn't interest him, but the publication was part of a larger group with many other titles. There might be room for growth or advancement. Plus, they offered full benefits. It was risky, not having health insurance.

Chapter 5 / 1985

Around the East Village, Scott admired a strikingly handsome guy named Frank. He was masculine with short, spikey hair and, for Scott, he epitomized perfection. He shattered every stereotype of what it meant to be gay. Scott's friend Ed actually knew him, but even so, Scott didn't dare talk to him. Scott didn't think he was good enough. Frank was hot, and he knew it, and always had guys after him. He was intimidating and confident.

Then, Frank disappeared from the club scene. After a few weeks, Ed told Scott he'd heard Frank had AIDS. Scott was horrified that it had struck the guy he had built up in his mind as the dream boyfriend. It felt somehow symbolic and very scary.

One night in October, 1987, Scott navigated his way down Avenue A. He had a preferred route to The World on East 2nd Street. It got scary below 6th Street, and he tried to look tough and unafraid as he quickly walked south, where he would hope for the best as he entered the dark side street and continued beyond Avenue B to find the club entrance.

Scott made it safely to the door and entered. He had been a few times since his ecstasy night with Tim. He surveyed the crowd congregated in front of the bar. He didn't seem to know anyone, so he found a spot at the bar and ordered a beer. After a few more, he went to the dance floor and stayed for almost an hour. He walked back to the bar area and noticed Frank standing by himself, watching the lights and the crowd. Scott was determined to talk to him. He had to muster the courage. The image of Frank alone was unsettling, because Scott had always seen him surrounded by friends. Where were they now? Scott decided it was the best chance to meet Frank he was going to get, and forced himself to walk up to him.

"How's it going?" Scott asked as he got close and stood beside him.

"Good," Frank said, and smiled.

"Frank, right?" Scott asked. "I'm Scott."

"I know you," Frank said. "Seen you around. You're friends with Ed."

"Yes! Glad to finally meet you in person," Scott said.

Scott was amazed that Frank knew who he was. They spoke for a while, and Scott asked Frank if he wanted to hang out sometime. Frank enthusiastically nodded. He liked to do things. Go to movies. He was feeling good now. They didn't mention AIDS.

The band came on, and the crowd surged toward the stage. Scott moved with the crowd and told Frank he'd find him after the show. Frank waved and smiled. Scott wiggled his way forward to find a better spot to watch. He loved the band, *Dean and the Weenies*. After a few songs, the vamp beat and guitars began for their signature song, "Fuck You." The crowd cheered.

Dean Johnson, the lead singer, started quietly:
"*Why are you staring at me?*
When I look back at you, I don't like what I see.
Your lack of character shows.
I hate your clothes.
And you've got something disgusting hanging out of your nose.
Why are you talking to me?
Please leave, immediately.
Where is your dignity?
Please get away from me.
Why don't you choke on a fashion accessory?"
The music got louder, and the energy in the room crackled. Dean continued:
"*I cannot remember your name.*
And I could not care less.
I could have more fun talking to the I.R.S.
Why don't you take your problems to analysis?
Take your foot out of your mouth, and suck on this."
Then, a shout: "Fuck you." And the crowd roared.
Dean called out: "Everybody now!"
"Fuck!" The crowd and backup singers shouted.
"*The telephone company,*" Dean sang back.
"Fuck!" the crowd echoed again.

"*National security.*"
"Fuck!"
"*The prime interest rate.*"
"Fuck!"
"*The Secretary of State.*"
"Fuck!"
"*Union Carbide.*"
"Fuck!"
"*Third World genocide.*"
"Fuck!"
"*Thermo-nuclear war.*"
"Fuck!"
"*Mary Tyler Moore.*"
Dean then sang a last refrain:
"*So, go tell it to the judge.*
Because I don't care.
You'd look cooler if you wore a Frigidaire.
Get lost. Eat shit. Drop dead. Go screw.
We're in big trouble, baby.
And the trouble is you."

The crowd cheered. Scott joined in the frenzy. The performance encapsulated the rage and cynicism of the mostly-gay audience. After the final song of the set, Scott made his way back to the bar area. He looked around for Frank, but couldn't find him. He checked his watch. It was late and he had to leave. Work at the real estate magazine would begin at 10 a.m.

The next day, Scott called Ed and told him he met Frank who was by himself at The World. Scott asked Ed if he had Frank's number. He shared it. They both found it strange that Frank had been alone. It didn't fit. Were people avoiding him?

On Friday night, Scott called Frank. They talked for twenty minutes. Frank invited Scott to see a movie.

When the phone rang at noon the next day, Scott was excited. They would meet in an hour in front of Paterson's Silks on 14th Street and Union Square West. Frank was already waiting when Scott arrived. They walked to Washington Square Park and looked at movie listings in the *Village Voice* Scott had brought with him. They chose "My Life as a Dog." There was time to kill before the show, so they went to a cafe and ordered cannolis and cappuccinos and talked for an hour.

When the movie started, Scott wondered if it was a mistake, because it was in subtitles. Frank had told him his medication made it very hard for him to read. Scott asked him if he could focus, and, yes, the type was large enough. Scott relaxed. Later in the movie, an alarm went off on Frank's pill box. It was loud and pierced the silence. Frank took it out and popped an AZT tablet.

When the movie ended, they walked to Sixth Avenue, then south to Christopher Street. They continued to the Hudson River to the pier to watch the sunset over New Jersey. They sat on the river's edge and talked. Frank's sister had been killed a few months earlier by a drunk driver. Scott wondered how much pain one family was required to endure. What about his parents? Every moment they sat there felt precious. Frank was happy and alert and interested in Scott's opinion. Frank lived with his boyfriend on Columbus Avenue, but got lonely when his boyfriend had to work. Frank told Scott about his good times in the film industry. He told Scott he'd had a happy, fun, full life. He was 25. He had no regrets.

They walked to Frank's bus stop on Hudson Street. Frank put his arm around Scott's shoulder, and Scott did the same, and they waited. Frank told Scott he had a really nice day. When the bus arrived, Scott patted him on the back.

"Call me," Scott said. "Anytime."

"Anytime?" Frank asked.

"Yes."

"How about 4:15 tomorrow morning?" Frank laughed and climbed the stairs to the bus.

Scott wanted to help Frank. He didn't understand why he felt so strongly about it. Perhaps because Frank had symbolized perfection to

Scott, just a year ago. Scott was willing to open himself to Frank, because it wouldn't last. His time and closeness with Frank was guaranteed to end. There could be intimacy, with no ramifications or aftermath. Scott could love, then be alone again. That evening, he wrote in his journal:

I feel a strange bond with Frank and I really just met him. I'm very depressed by all of this, but at the same time am very thankful to have the opportunity to become friends with him and give all of myself to him while he's still around and in need of support. I'm so glad he wants to be my friend. I really can't believe it. We never knew each other before his illness. Now we seem to be on track to being close. It's strange. How I will miss him. How sad I am. How determined I am to give all of myself while he's still here. Life is so very sad.

Halloween fell on a Saturday, and Frank and Scott spent the day together. They headed to Union Square where a rally was being held demanding government attention and focus on the AIDS crisis.

Scott wrote in his journal when he returned home that evening:

It was very moving. A runner gave a speech in which he mentioned each of his friends who had died of AIDS. Frank started crying very hard and grabbed me. I held him and caressed his face. It broke my heart, but at least I was given the chance to show him that I care about him. When he recovered himself and stood next to me, he brushed my shoulder with his hand. I thought it was to wipe away a tear that had fallen on my jacket — but it was to wipe away the flakes from his skin that stuck to the fabric when he put his face on my shoulder. AZT eats away at him.

The next Saturday, the phone rang at noon. It was Frank calling, and Scott asked him if he was coming downtown.

"Is that an invitation?" Frank asked.

"Yes," Scott said.

Frank appeared an hour later. With him he brought a box of 45-rpm singles his boyfriend had collected from the 1960s and 1970s. They sat on the bed in front of the stereo in Scott's room and made mix tapes.

Later they went to the kitchen table and smoked a joint with Lourdes. They decided to head to the Quad Cinema to see "Matewan."

On Sunday, the phone again rang at noon. Frank invited Scott to his apartment to hang out and watch TV. They ate a chicken pasta Frank's mother had prepared. The freezer was full of dinners she made for Frank, ready to be heated.

Scott sensed Frank needed company. They talked about it. Frank told him he hated to be alone, especially on the good days. It was a waste of precious life. Frank's boyfriend owned a store and had to work long hours to carry the bills of the household. Scott realized he had a role to play, being available to Frank when he was lonely. They spent the rest of the day talking about nothing and everything. When Scott got home, he wrote:

I guess I am accomplishing my objective of making Frank know he can depend on me when his boyfriend is working. I must remember to be unselfish about spending time with him. It is in his best interest to see as many people as possible. I want to be selective about the time I spend with him — offering myself when needed most, when his other friends are unable to be there. I love him.

For the rest of the year, he spent as much time as possible with Frank. Scott helped Frank's mother organize food in the freezer when she brought supplies to Frank's apartment. Scott made a mix tape for Frank's boyfriend to listen to at his store, because he, also, needed support.

During the week when Scott left work he met Frank at Act Up meetings in the Village. The group was instrumental in forcing attention and resources on the AIDS crisis in the face of silence and blatant homophobia from the Reagan administration. "Silence = Death" was the group's motto and coldly, painfully true. A time bomb was ticking and drugs needed to be tested, red-tape had to be cut, and modes of transmission of the virus — if HIV were even the cause — had to be immediately understood and publicized.

Frank and Scott spent a day taking photos and walking around the lower East Side and East River Park. Scott was thrilled to capture him on film. Frank suggested they take a trip together to Europe in the spring.

They could spend the winter planning it out. Frank said he would go himself if no one was able to take the time off to travel with him.

But by spring, Frank's health had deteriorated. Doctors switched his medications, and tried different combinations. He increasingly spent days in the hospital or resting at home. Frank often didn't have the energy to leave his apartment. The treatment strategy was to do anything to hold on — month by month, week by week, day by day — until a drug in test protocols might be released and effective against the virus. The only hope was to see another day. It could be the day that would change everything.

Scott and Frank's time together the previous autumn with walks and talks and movies was the reprieve. The good time. A last spin of life. And then, it was over. Opportunistic infections ravaged him over the next several months. One would be stopped, only to be replaced by another. Shingles followed by pneumonia. In the end came anguished outbursts, signaling the onset of dementia. Frank died in early September.

At the service, Scott watched Frank's mother kneel in front of his body. Scott broke down crying, and had to sit and cover his face with his hand. Not because Frank's mother looked upset. But because she didn't. She was stone-faced. There was nothing left inside her to take. She had lost two children in two years' time. Scott felt arms around him and looked between his fingers and saw it was her. Somehow Frank's mother was able to comfort others.

"He loved you," she whispered in Scott's ear, and hugged him.

CHAPTER SIX
1988

Scott relied on Lourdes in the months that followed. He confided in her about feeling depressed, and she empathized. She had lost friends to AIDS, and was also terrified. She had grown up in New York and wasn't an angel. Frank's sin was that he was handsome, adventurous, unashamed of being gay, and grew up close to the city. He had easy access to bars and guys during a moment in time when no one had an inkling that sex would turn deadly.

Scott now considered himself fortunate that he grew up in Nowheresville. He would keep to himself more than ever. It was a matter of survival. If it weren't too late already.

Scott spent more time with Lourdes. They ate dinners together and became like siblings. They decided to stop going out so much and to divert more energy into their careers. They would stop doing coke because they both battled depression. Lourdes understood Scott had complicated feelings toward his parents. Also anger.

She patiently listened to Scott's nervousness as he made preparations for Ava and Robert's first visit to New York. Scott made reservations for them to stay at the Marriott Marquis in Times Square. He arranged an itinerary of tourist attractions in the city, with a quick stop by their apartment.

He and Lourdes cleaned as best they could, but there was no hiding it was a tenement with a lousy superintendent. When his parents arrived and entered the living room/bathroom/kitchen he could see the shock on their faces. What did they expect? The Waldorf-Astoria? At least the junkie on the first floor stayed in her apartment during the visit.

Scott wondered if they thought Lourdes was his girlfriend. He completed the weekend tour and enjoyed showing them around, but struggled with the same feelings he got during phone calls: Did he sound angry? Why was he annoyed? Why couldn't he just be nice? Why did he feel such pressure inside when he was around them? They were visiting their son for the first time, three years after he'd left home. Did they think that was normal? Maybe he was just feeling sorry for himself. Selfish. Maybe he had actually been the problem his whole life. Ava was the one who needed the attention. She was the one who grew up without a father.

After their visit, Scott planned a vacation. He had never been to California and decided this would be a good time to go. His cousin Deirdre lived in San Diego with her husband. He had always liked her, even though they didn't see each other often. She was ten years older. She sent a Christmas card every year, and always invited him to visit. She was the only one who had ever told what had happened to his grandfather. At least as much as she knew.

Scott called Deirdre, and she was excited. He would fly into San Diego, stay a few days, then continue up to Los Angeles and fly back to New York from there.

A few weeks later, Deirdre picked Scott up at the airport. She always made him feel comfortable, and she chatted effusively with him on the drive home. He would need to visit the Zoo, the beaches, La Jolla. They stopped at a supermarket on the way to her house. It was big, bright and modern, completely different from the dirty, cramped, old supermarkets near his apartment in New York. There was an entire refrigerated section devoted to salsas and guacamole. He had never heard of guacamole, and considered it a major discovery later when they paired it with chips, salsa and beer in Deirdre's kitchen, when her husband came home from work.

They asked him about his life in New York, and were intrigued. He told them about the chaotic fun of the nightlife. He explained how everything was going electronic at work. They were training him in cutting-edge design software on Macintosh computers and he was learning a lot. He was surprised and excited to find he was good at it. His focus was now officially publication design, not writing, and he liked it. He learned from older art directors on staff as an entirely new electronic version of the field emerged. He read books about color harmony and cropping photography.

They opened a bottle of wine as Deirdre prepared chicken fajitas for dinner. Her husband showed Scott the stone flooring he was installing around the swimming pool. Deirdre came out and they watched the sun as it settled behind the mountains in the distance. She refilled their wine glasses.

"We have a lot of friends who are gay," she said.

Scott tried to act nonchalant, but froze.

"Oh, that's cool," he said. "But, I'm not gay."

He changed the topic to the sunset and how different the topography was compared to the Northeast.

The next day, he rented a car and visited the San Diego Zoo. When he returned to Deirdre's house late in the afternoon, she was sitting in the sun on the front lawn. Scott joined her. They were alone while her husband was still at work. Scott told her about the zoo and his drive around the city. He felt relaxed.

"Remember a long time ago you told me about our grandfather?" Scott asked.

"Yes," Deirdre said. "His suicide."

"Did you ever find out anything else?"

"No," she said, and paused. "I'm guessing there could have been gambling debts. Maybe Mafia? My father told David something, but he wasn't allowed to share. The story isn't clear."

"Everyone's so quiet about it," Scott said. "It's taboo."

"I know. It's crazy," Deirdre said.

She adjusted her chair and moved closer to him.

"I moved west to get away from my father."

Scott was silent.

"He used to beat me. He beat all of us. With a paddle, a belt, a rubber hose. Anything he could get his hands on. I just had to move. Get as far away from him as possible."

They sat quietly for a moment.

"Same thing happened to me," Scott whispered. "My mother."

Deirdre looked at him.

"She beat me, too." Scott's heart was pounding. He had never told anybody.

"That's really why I moved to New York," he said. "I couldn't move back home. Too many scary memories and bad feelings. I had to get away."

Deirdre reached over and hugged him.

"I know. Same for me," she said. "That suicide did a number on them."

"Must have been awful," Scott said. "My mother never even met her father."

"I know," Deirdre said. "I think it was grandma who did it to them. Beat the hell out of them. Maybe she blamed them for grandpa's problems? Or couldn't channel her anger."

"Wonder if my mom got hit, too?" Scott asked. "Or, just the brothers."

"I bet everyone got it."

"My mom had moods. *The blues*. Sometimes she would just sit with a sad look. Cried a lot. Especially after hitting me. I think she always thought about what happened with her Dad and the beatings from her mom even though she never talked about it. She said people who needed outside help with problems were weak. Couldn't stand on their own. So she held it all inside. Like grandpa haunted them even after he was gone. No one could see it or stop it. I wish they'd had help. It also got *us*."

They continued to sit awhile, then Scott went to his rental car and took out a map. He and Deirdre planned out his route to Los Angeles, and he left the next morning.

On a Saturday night soon after the trip, Scott met a guy named Kiko at a large nightclub called the Roxy. He was a recent immigrant from Brazil. They talked and joked and Scott met two of his friends from his hometown. They exchanged numbers.

The next day, Kiko invited Scott to his apartment in Queens for a Sunday Brazilian Feijoada his friends were preparing. When Scott arrived, Kiko greeted him and showed him around. He had a small bedroom with a mattress on the floor. He was educated and smart, but had no green card, and his English was only intermediate. He worked as a busboy at a restaurant in Midtown, and found the work humiliating, given that his father owned a construction company in Brazil and he could have a good life there, if he so chose. But he wanted to experience the United States.

Scott and Kiko dated and became boyfriends for two years. They traveled to Brazil, and Scott met his parents, though officially as only a friend. Kiko applied for a green card, but the lawyer he selected in Queens was a crook and Kiko's money, and the application, disappeared.

In the coming months, it became clear Kiko would not be happy remaining in the country as a busboy with no green card. If Scott were straight and Kiko were a woman, they could get married, and the problem would be solved. Scott wondered if his comfort with Kiko were based on the tenuous circumstances. He sometimes admitted to himself he knew the relationship couldn't last, and was therefore acceptable. It was exactly what he wanted. He preferred a relationship with a fatal flaw to one that might have a future. A degree of closeness and intimacy was acceptable if the union was destined to end anyway.

Kiko returned to Brazil. There was no other choice. He and Scott would remain friends, and planned a vacation to Rio for Carnival in February.

Lourdes also had plans to move on. She and her boyfriend were going to try a stint in Los Angeles, and Scott could take over her boyfriend's rent-controlled apartment for a few years. He graciously accepted the offer. They worked out the details. He would visit LA as soon as everyone got settled and could get vacation time.

Scott was now 27, and felt very much alone. In a few years he would be 30, and had little to show for it. People his age outside of New York already owned homes and had children.

Scott could never imagine having kids. The thought of a child looking up to him and thinking he was something special appalled him. He wasn't special. He was barely getting by. He was not worthy of having his own child love him. It was a repellent thought that his mind immediately rejected as soon as it surfaced. He was destined to be alone. He wanted it that way.

He had now spent five years in New York, and Scott decided it was time to talk to his parent about being gay. A side-effect of the AIDS crisis was that gays nationwide were demanding the right to have their existence acknowledged — and even tolerated — by society at large.

A huge gay pride march in New York in 1990 stunned Scott and others, not only with the vastness of the crowd from all over the country, but the very ordinariness of it all. They weren't freaks, as they had always been told they were. They weren't misfits, few in number, pathetic and scattered about. They were everywhere and in far greater numbers than the government or anyone else had yet to acknowledge. The proof was in front of everyone, including editors at newspapers. It could no longer be hidden or suppressed. Scott found a chant at the march particularly apt: "We're Here. We're Queer. Get Used To It. Get Over It."

Gays were encouraged to come out to straights, because exposure reduced the fear of the unknown. It was the best medicine. Old stereotypes were deeply entrenched and could only be erased by contact with gay friends and family members who no longer agreed to hide and remain silent.

Scott rented a car and drove back to Vermont. As he pulled into the familiar driveway, he was desperately nervous. He was not accustomed to discussing serious, difficult topics with his parents. In fact, he had never done so. He had only reacted or kept silent or talked about work or the weather. He never put himself forward.

It was late afternoon, and Robert was still at work. Scott kissed Ava and brought his bag to his room. He thought about postponing his

Chapter 6 / 1988

announcement for a day, but felt his fear would only grow worse. Ava was in the kitchen. Scott thought about entering and asking her to promise she wouldn't get mad like he had the morning after he wet the bed so many years ago.

"I have to talk to you about something, Mom," Scott said.

He sat down next to her on a bar stool at the counter top.

"Okay," Ava said and looked at him warily.

He knew he wouldn't dare if he didn't blurt it out: "I need you to know that I'm gay. I've known about it for a long time."

Ava was silent.

"You have to know. It's best for our relationship. If I don't tell you, then every time I see you or talk on the phone, I'm always hiding something. I can never join in, because I need to keep the secret. That's why I'm always quiet. I can never share anything. I want you to know me better."

Ava looked at him for a moment before she spoke.

"Are you sure you're not just following one of your movements?" Ava asked. "You've always been attracted to the trend of the moment."

"I'm sure. It's not just a movement. It's me. I need you to know."

"Okay. I'm glad you told me." She hugged him. "We'll have to tell your father."

Scott nodded. A wave of relief washed over him. He still wasn't finished, but he had cleared the first hurdle — Ava — without shouts or tears. She didn't reject him and seemed contemplative as she digested the news. Maybe she was caught off-guard.

Scott didn't want to push his luck, so he left the kitchen and went to his room and closed the door. Ava prepared dinner.

When Robert got home, he greeted Ava in the kitchen and found Scott. They hugged and spoke for a few minutes. Robert went to his desk, to work on bills. Scott headed down to the kitchen.

"Are you ready?" Ava asked, and smiled.

Scott nodded. Ava walked in front and led Scott up the stairs to the room where Robert was working. Scott's heart pounded.

Ava entered the room and Scott stood behind her.

"Scott has something to tell you," Ava said.

Robert turned in his chair and looked at him.

"I told Mom, there's something I gotta share because it's best for our long-term relationship. I need you to know I'm gay."

Robert's face grew angry. His eyebrows pulled closer.

"Are you sure?"

No one spoke.

"You will need to be a priest," Robert said.

Scott froze. He puzzled over his father's response. *That* certainly wouldn't solve anything, and what, exactly, was Robert inferring? The priesthood was where gays were supposed to go hide? The old-fashioned view that gays had no other place in society?

"That's not a good solution," Scott said. "I had to tell you or you'd never know. It would always be a secret. I'm not waiting for this country's approval. It wasn't that long ago women couldn't even vote. There are still a lot of people who don't like blacks. I'm not waiting for everyone to like me. They never will. But I only get one life."

Robert didn't speak for a moment as he processed what Scott said.

"What about AIDS?" Robert asked. "Isn't that a worry?"

"Yes. It's scary. I have to be careful. Everyone does."

"You won't have children?"

"No. But lots of people don't."

"What if you end up alone?"

"There's no guarantee for anyone. Some straight people have kids, but end up alone."

Robert slowly stood and walked to Scott and hugged him.

"I agree you had to tell us. You're still our son. We'll always love you."

Scott's eyes filled with tears.

Robert sat back down and swiveled his back to the desk. Ava and Scott left the room.

Thirty minutes later they sat down to dinner and Scott told them about the Macintosh computer, design software, and his new responsibilities at work.

The next morning, Robert seemed completely back to normal. He was upbeat and Scott felt comfortable around him. But Ava was withdrawn and quiet. She was downcast throughout the day, and Scott felt the power she still held over him because he felt guilty and he knew he had caused her pain. Just like old times when Ava had *the blues* and Scott tiptoed around, hoping she would snap out of it, terrified he might set her off. No one mentioned Scott's announcement.

On Sunday, Ava prepared Scott a lunch to eat in the car on his drive back to New York.

Just before he left, she told him: "I'm glad *you* feel better. You got that news off your chest. But now *we're* the ones who have to carry it. You've passed the burden to us."

Scott cried for the first hour of his drive home. Then, he was numb.

Ava's depression continued for months — Scott sensed it on telephone calls and saw it in her disposition when he returned home for Christmas. He felt the return of a cloud of shame and guilt that had smothered him as a child whenever he heard her cry.

In autumn, Scott applied for an Art Director job opening at his company on a sportswear trade magazine. He had hoped working for a publisher with more than 10 magazines would lead to other opportunities, and now he had a chance to move to a fashion-oriented publication. He had never done fashion shoots, but the eccentric fashion director, Lulu, liked that she would control the photography without a power struggle, because Scott would be new at it. The previous art director had left because of too many confrontations with her. Scott had a good reputation at his company, and to his delight, he landed the job.

New York began to change rapidly, and flip flops overcame black boots as the footwear of choice on the masses around town on weekends. Working out in a gym became *de rigueur*. Many gay guys got gym bodies. Scott trained and gained 15 pounds of muscle in two years.

Technology also improved. It made watching fights much more

efficient. Scott set the VCR to record any show he wouldn't be home to watch. He would later fast-forward straight to the brawl. He also created mix tapes filled entirely with fight clips. It was the mainstay of his sex life.

Eventually, Scott met a lawyer named Peter at a fund-raising event. Peter was preppy, unlike any of Scott's friends from the East Village. They decided to become boyfriends after dating for several months. They were both a few years shy of 30. Scott saw Peter's work ethic and stable profession as positive attributes, in contrast to Kiko's difficult journey.

Scott struggled to adjust to Peter's friendship network. They met for cocktails and dinner parties at people's apartments. To Scott, they were uptight businessmen who were obsessed with appearing "straight acting." Scott felt like an outsider and wasn't comfortable around them. He put up his guard, and tempered his behavior to appear as restrained and masculine as possible. Sometimes, at the end of a party, Scott would leave without saying goodbye to the host because didn't feel anyone cared if he was there in the first place.

Sometimes the group liked to meet for "white collar" happy hours after work, at a bar in the West Village called Uncle Charlie's. Scott and Peter joined them and watched videos. One particular segment featured a montage of scenes from the film *Mommie Dearest* that elicited shrieks of laughter from the crowd who found camp humor in Faye Dunaway's portrayal of Joan Crawford, who abused her daughter. Whenever it came on, Scott silently cringed and immediately felt like an outsider. An *Other*. There was nothing funny about it.

After a year, Scott moved into Peter's apartment. It would be the first time Scott lived with a boyfriend, and he liked the idea of sharing a home. Peter had a dog and Scott loved the daily rituals of walks, playtime and treats.

When Scott turned 30, Peter threw him a party in their apartment. Scott's creative friends from the East Village mixed with Peter's business friends. Scott felt it was one of the best nights of his life. He was surprised by how many people had come to celebrate, and that Peter had planned it for him.

Chapter 6 / 1988

Meanwhile, Scott's career advanced and he was producing several photo shoots per issue. Part of the job was casting, and he worked with modeling agencies and the fashion editor to book the right "types" for each shoot. He met Matthew Fox, who he booked for a shoot, but the agency at the last minute canceled, because the actor had won a spot on a new TV show, *Party of Five*, and had to leave for Los Angeles immediately.

Two years later, Scott sent out work samples and got called for an interview with the Creative Director at a young woman's fashion magazine. He updated his portfolio and bought a new suit. He found himself in her office explaining his work. She quizzed him: What were his references for creative concepts? What photographers did he like?

Thirty-five minutes later she walked him down the hall to meet the art director, David. Scott was amazed when he entered the office and immediately recognized the guy from the nights he had spent in the East Village club scene, years before. They had a mutual friend and knew each other.

Scott took David through his portfolio, and each told the other what he had been doing for the past few years. When the interview was finished, David thanked him and said they would be in touch.

Scott left elated, and couldn't believe his luck. Knowing someone made all the difference. Perhaps his crazy nights in the East Village had actually led to something after all.

A month passed with no news. Scott became despondent and thought he was foolish for getting his hopes up. It had been too good to be true. Perhaps they had concluded that his background wasn't good enough. If he couldn't land the job even with the luck of knowing the Art Director, it would never happen.

Then, on a dull Tuesday morning two weeks later, his phone rang at work. It was David. He offered Scott a job as Assistant Art Director. Scott accepted. When was the earliest he could start? Scott told him he needed to give two weeks' notice. They set a start date.

Scott floated through the next two weeks with the biggest sense of optimism for the future he had ever felt.

On his first day on the new job, Scott was terrified. David's assistant took him around and introduced him to the team. The first question from all of them was, where was he coming from, as in what magazine. Scott knew his answer was a dud. It wasn't a publication any of them had heard of. He was already lowered in the pecking order. He felt it.

Camille, the new associate art director above him, didn't seem to care. She was from Paris and also had to contend with meeting everyone. But others in his department treated him with a cool indifference he sensed immediately.

As the week unfolded, his suspicion that they didn't like him was confirmed when he overheard the photo editor complain that a photographer Scott had suggested kept calling her. She said the photographer's work was cheesy and he would never be hired. She said it loud enough for Scott to hear, and he was mortified. He would never suggest another one. He was officially in hostile territory and had to be on guard. David distributed work to the department, and Camille was assigned photo shoots and fashion pages, while Scott designed features and front-of-book layouts. They worked well together and Scott was relieved that at least she could be trusted and was friendly.

Scott began to work closely with editors, and they liked that he had an editorial background, enabling him to quickly grasp what they envisioned.

Weeks passed, and Scott discovered the photo editor, photographer, designer, and art assistant frequently went to lunch together. They were a clique. At least he had pinpointed a common thread linking the hostile co-workers. They questioned him and resisted when he asked to get something photographed or needed scans made. Now he was sure he wasn't imagining it.

In all his previous jobs, everyone had worked together and supported each other. But this was different. People would actively challenge requests and refuse cooperation. Anything one person gained was seen as taking away from the power or standing of someone else. Work didn't used to be that way. Was it because he was in a different league now? Egos were involved? Politics? People were privileged and just didn't care?

Chapter 6 / 1988

The new dynamic had a profound effect on him. That any interaction could lead to a confrontation bothered him to his core, and he felt powerless to control his unease.

He resolved to act more like Camille. She was tough, and spent a lot on clothes. He would do the same. Hide himself. Toughen up. Dress up. Armor himself against antagonistic attitudes. He would offer no information that could be used against him. He would act controlled, confident and unruffled — or least try to, until he fell apart at home.

Scott went shopping and bought fitted, flat-front trousers and black loafers. He studied *GQ* for what shirts and jackets to match. He forced himself into quick, funny conversations with the photo editor and the designer.

A few weeks later, the designer confided in him that she had applied for his job, but had been passed over because she was hired by the previous Editor-in-Chief, and was seen as part of the old regime. Scott showed empathy. They started to talk more, and he asked for her opinion on layouts. Others in the clique were apparently signaled of the shift, because hostilities soon stopped. Scott never knew if unfriendliness in the office or in social situations was real or imagined, and in this case, was greatly relieved it had a cause and had come to a conclusion.

Camille and Scott were given more responsibility. Scott felt a surge of pride whenever he sat on the Editor's couch for planning meetings, and surveyed the view of New York from inside her office. He was so far away from Bundy's farm.

Over the course of the year, David left for another job, and Camille and Scott were promoted. Camille was a difficult and demanding boss, who required the full commitment and loyalty from Scott, her number two. In exchange, she confided in him and taught him how to edit fashion photography, select covers and ensure that photo shoots came back with plenty of variations. She would yell at him if they didn't. She gave him a lot of responsibility and opportunity to learn.

Camille noticed Scott always questioned himself after sending an assertive email, asking her if it sounded too harsh.

"You have to be strong," she said. "You sent it. It was your opinion. So what? It's done."

Two years later, Camille invited Scott to her wedding in Paris. He was honored to be asked, and used his vacation time to attend. Head count was limited, so he would have to attend by himself.

The night before the wedding, Scott met Camille's parents at a reception in their elegant townhouse in the center of Paris. Her friends were polished and sophisticated, some of them in prominent positions in the magazine industry. Scott was awe-struck, and quietly did his best to not embarrass himself. He felt he could easily be exposed as not good enough to be included if he opened his mouth.

It was the most exclusive affair he had ever attended. When asked, he memorized the line he could say on auto-pilot: "I work with Camille."

It was all anyone needed to know and they were satisfied with the response. It kept questions minimal.

The next day, at the wedding, he wondered if his suit was good enough. It looked like a joke compared to the fashion on display by the men and women in attendance. They shopped at Agnés B.

As was the custom, the bride and groom strolled from the church through the streets of Paris toward their reception. The wedding party and invited guests stopped on the way for a toast in one of the most sophisticated spots for a drink in Saint Germain Des Prés.

Scott sat by himself and watched the scene. The confidence and poise of everyone astounded him. They laughed effortlessly, and no one except him seemed nervous. Even other guests on their own somehow managed to make conversation with strangers. How did they do it? Where did the confidence come from? Money? He didn't even deserve to be here. From nowhere, a voice from inside came forward and he desperately wanted to leave. I Hate My Life. I'm Such an Idiot. I Have to Get out of Here. Please Help Me.

When the glasses of champagne at the cafe were finished, people made their way to the reception. Scott relaxed because the structured environment — numbered tables, dinner courses, speeches, a jazz band performance — removed the need for active participation on his part.

Chapter 6 / 1988

A few months passed, and the day after Valentine's Day in 1997, Scott told Peter he thought they should break up.

They had been together for five years, and had evolved into best friends, not lovers. Valentine's Day had made it clear. They hadn't had sex for years. Scott blamed the problem on himself. He knew he only liked sex in the beginning of a relationship. Afterward, he would tolerate it as necessary. He much preferred watching fight clips. Sex didn't stand a chance. It was awkward and strange and what was the point after the initial attraction phase had passed? Peter hadn't pushed for more, so the arrangement had worked for them both.

They agreed it would be best to part ways, so that they would both have a chance to one day find something more. Scott would look for a new apartment, and they would split custody of the dog they loved.

Rents in the city were soaring and finding a new rental apartment was nearly impossible. They would both aim to buy a place, so that they could at least stabilize their living arrangements. It was possible to envision being forced from the city altogether if they didn't. They both studied the real estate ads in *The New York Times*.

In a few weeks, Scott found a large studio that he could afford, near Union Square Park. He remembered when the park had been abandoned when he first arrived in New York, dangerous, infested, fenced off and left for dead. Now the whole neighborhood was coming back to life.

The apartment was in horrible condition with track lighting, a broken window, broken parquet flooring, and an original kitchen and bathroom from 1964. But the raw space and location were perfect. It was a corner unit, with lots of light and a terrace. The broker told him not to hesitate, that it would be the best investment decision of his life. He shared with Scott what he thought would be the owner's lowest possible price.

The same day Scott made an offer and the owner accepted it, contingent on coop-board approval. Extra money he had made from freelance work and saving pay increases from promotions would serve as a 25-percent down payment.

He wouldn't be able to move in until October, so he and Peter agreed to live together until then. A few months later, Peter found an apartment walking distance from Scott's place.

When October arrived, Peter helped Scott pack his things. A moving truck arrived and was loaded. Peter and Scott hugged and agreed to meet that night for dinner. Peter would keep the dog until Scott got settled.

When the movers left, and Scott stood alone in his new apartment surrounded by boxes, he was struck by the silence. There would be no talking because there was no one to talk to. He'd had no idea such a simple reality would feel so lonely.

He surveyed the room and the chaotic mess of his things scattered about. The apartment was a dump. Had he made a mistake? Did the broker trick him? His eyes teared up. He vowed he would never move in with someone again. When it didn't work out, the disruption was too much. He was starting from scratch.

In the weeks to come, Scott descended into a depression, his worst ever. He was 34 and alone. His first live-in relationship had ended in failure.

The only way to meet someone was to go to a bar and stay out late and get drunk and he rarely dared to approach to anyone, anyway. No one seemed to hook up until after 2 a.m. and he wasn't willing to play the game.

He didn't even like sex the same way as everyone else. It was a hopeless situation. He felt increasingly desperate. It worried him, because he didn't see himself sustaining the status quo indefinitely. He thought about suicide in general terms — as something he wasn't ready to do, but one day would be inevitable.

He wondered if his situation was something to talk to a therapist about. He had seen it in movies like *Ordinary People*. But therapists were expensive, and he didn't have any extra money. His salary was fair — the highest in his life — but between his mortgage and maintenance payments, he could barely save anything at the end of the month. He had insurance, but it didn't cover mental health. Even if it did, he would never dare to file claims. Someone in Human Resources would find out.

After toying with the idea for a few weeks, he found a classified ad for a therapy organization with a sliding fee scale. He wondered if he would qualify. He felt desperate enough to call them. It was worth a try. He was told to come in for a free consultation, and he made an appointment. The office was in midtown, and he could walk there after work.

When he arrived, he sat in a waiting area with a noise machine turned on so the voices behind the office door couldn't be heard, or at least were somewhat masked. He was extremely nervous and had no idea what to expect.

In a few minutes, the door opened and someone — presumably a patient — left. Scott was mortified that people who waited could see who was in the room before them. What if they heard something?

He sat a while longer and the door opened again. A woman who seemed to be in her early seventies greeted him and asked him to enter. She closed the door behind them and motioned for Scott to take the chair in front of her desk.

She introduced herself as Dr. Paulson and gave Scott an application with a few sections to fill out. When he finished, she looked at it. She would ask him a few questions to help determine who in her office would be best for him to see.

"Have you ever seen a therapist before?"

"No."

"What brings you here?"

"I'm feeling depressed," Scott said. "Depression."

"How long have you felt that way?"

"A couple of months."

There was a pause as she took notes.

"Was your childhood happy?" Dr. Paulson asked.

Scott was silent. Why would she even ask that? What did she mean? What could that possibly have to do with anything?

He needed help with the here and now. He didn't like to think about childhood. He blocked it because memories came out of the depths cloaked with shame, fear and helplessness. Something wasn't right.

"No," Scott said.

"Why not?"

Scott's mind raced. Was she tricking him? What did she want to know?

"I don't know," Scott said. "Bad memories."

Dr. Paulson changed the subject and asked him a few more questions. They talked about billing and Scott explained his salary sounded high but with housing expenses he didn't have as much money as it seemed.

They agreed on a weekly fee, and she said she would like to continue seeing him if he felt comfortable with that. He would not be referred to someone else in the practice. They could meet at 6 p.m. on Thursdays.

Scott thanked her and left. He averted his gaze from the person sitting in the waiting area as he crossed it to open the door to the main hallway.

Scott returned the next week, and gave Dr. Paulson a check at the start of his session. She guided him to the other side of her office and motioned for him to lie on his back on a black leather couch. Her chair was positioned behind his head so he couldn't see her. She held a clipboard and took notes while he spoke.

Scott told her about Peter and their break-up and the loneliness he felt. She asked if Scott felt comfortable being gay, and he said yes. She asked Scott to tell her about his childhood. Scott said it was complicated and he didn't know what to say.

Over the next several weeks, Dr. Paulson continued to direct the conversation back to his childhood and Scott one day shared that his bad memories came from his mother. She beat him and he had never told anyone except for his cousin Deirdre, who was hit by her father.

Dr. Paulson thanked him for sharing with her and said it would be important to continue to talk about it. Scott found it interesting that she wanted to know so much about it. Maybe it *did* matter.

At a later session, Scott remembered a beating that ended with his mother screaming that she hated him. He abruptly sat up on the couch and shook his head quickly a few times to redirect his focus on the room he was sitting in and away from the memory. He started crying. Dr. Paulson stood and brought him a box of Kleenex.

The next week, Scott returned and told her it would be his last session, because he could no longer afford to come.

He felt much better and said she had really helped him. She asked him to reconsider, and said the fee could be adjusted. Scott apologized. It wouldn't be necessary. He had already learned a lot.

Dr. Paulson told him he made great progress and could return whenever he wanted. Scott thanked her and left.

His depression continued and Scott decided he would try anti-depressant medication. Everyone talked about it. The therapy had been interesting, and made him aware his memories of childhood were powerful and probably more significant than he thought. But they were deeply buried and talking about them was too difficult. It would take too long and what would be the outcome? It was ancient history and he wanted relief *now*.

He found a doctor in the network of his health plan and made an appointment. He was prescribed Celexa. Over the next few weeks, he felt he cared less about what other people thought about him, especially in the office. It was a new feeling. He liked it. It was a feeling of not needing approval, and it and came with a freedom to act without first calculating what would be someone's reaction. He felt his depression had lifted.

But there were negative side effects. Sexual ones and weight gain despite lots of exercise. Scott spoke to his doctor about it. The doctor told him the weight gain was a simple matter of aging and was inevitable for everyone. It had nothing to do with the medication.

In March, a friend convinced Scott to join him on a gay cruise departing from Miami and making stops in San Juan and the Virgin Islands. It would be something different to try after more than year on his own after his break up with Peter.

The ship was enormous and packed with a week's worth of parties, unlimited alcohol and opportunities to explore the ports of call.

Scott enjoyed the time with his friend, but found himself facing the same inability to strike up conversations, something that seemed to come naturally to everyone else.

At the last afternoon party of the last full day of the cruise, Scott saw a guy with a large dragon tattoo on his chest standing alone on a balcony overlooking the crowd dancing alongside the swimming pool.

Scott forced himself up the stairs. What did he have to lose? The cruise would end in the morning, anyway. Scott walked up and stood next to him and introduced himself.

The guy's name was Curtis. He owned a hair salon and lived in Dallas. They decided to get a drink at the bar downstairs and to continue talking.

With a square jaw, muscles, smooth skin, and the tattoo, Scott found Curtis hot. A perfect villain in one of his movie fights. They talked for an hour and continued to drink. Why hadn't they met before the last day?

Scott invited Curtis to his room. They kissed, found they shared a powerful chemistry, and had sex. They made plans to have dinner together to mark the final night of vacation.

Curtis left to take a shower and change his clothes. Scott was excited as he readied himself for the evening ahead. It felt irresponsible and foolish to feel excited, but hook-ups for Scott were few and far between. This last-minute fling was unexpected.

Scott dressed up and found his way to Curtis' room. He knocked on the door and waited in the hall. Curtis came out and told Scott they got reservations in the nicest restaurant on the ship.

At dinner they drank wine and remarked it seemed impossible they had just met. They both felt comfortable, as if they already knew each other. Curtis shared he had been abandoned as a child, and was adopted. He was half American Indian. He grew up in the middle of nowhere in west Texas, and his parents moved from place to place. The large tattoo on his chest was meant to cover a scar below his right nipple from a slashing attack one night when someone tried to rob him. Bad things just happened to him.

He was HIV positive, but his medication made the viral load in his blood undetectable. He always had safe sex, and the chance he could infect someone was minimal.

Scott told Curtis he grew up in New England, but moved to New

York as soon as he could, at 21. His focus was now on trying to build a magazine career.

They finished dinner and went to a lounge to have drinks.

Scott was drawn to his honesty. Scott told Curtis he'd had a bad childhood. Curtis hugged him and thanked him for sharing something personal. Curtis said Scott was like a turtle that stuck its head out from its shell for a moment, only to dart back inside. Curtis called himself a hayseed that blew from place to place.

They exchanged home addresses and telephone numbers on a sheet of paper at the bar. They lived in different cities, but would keep in touch. They promised to see each other again.

After the cruise, Scott and Curtis talked on the phone. Scott received a letter from Curtis with a story he illustrated in ink about the Turtle and the Hayseed. Scott made plans for his first visit to Dallas.

Curtis picked him up at the airport and Scott initially felt awkward, as if the whole premise of the trip was crazy. Scott was quiet and didn't have much to say. They drove to Curtis' apartment, and Scott unpacked his bag. They went to the kitchen and ate salsa and chips and drank beer.

In an hour, Scott had relaxed. He touched Curtis' arm. They went to Curtis' bedroom and had sex on the floor. It was the best sex of Scott's life. He was wildly attracted to the handsome, bad-guy, muscled persona of Curtis. It fit perfectly with the fights in his mind as they wrestled and had sex. It was the first time a partner in real time completely matched what was going on his head. Scott could imagine a fight was really happening.

Curtis became an actual character — a villain — who was losing. Curtis liked that Scott rubbed on top of him. It seemed intentional, given the need for safe sex, and Scott offered no explanation.

At the end of the weekend, they both decided there was no reason they couldn't continue the cruise ship romance.

Curtis sent Scott more letters with drawings and stories about the Turtle and the Hayseed. One story said their union was unlikely, but destined to succeed, because they had somehow found each other. Curtis would help Scott come out his shell. Scott would help Curtis feel grounded. Living in separate cities was a temporary setback that could be overcome.

In May, Curtis came to visit Scott. By now the apartment he had purchased was greatly improved. Floors were sanded, windows replaced, track lighting removed, and everything freshly painted.

Curtis arrived early in the evening on Friday. He took a cab from the airport and found his way to Scott's apartment. When he opened the door and saw Curtis in the hallway, Scott again wondered if the whole thing were a mistake. He felt a distance from Curtis, which was silly, since he was standing in the hallway of Scott's apartment building.

Scott invited him in, showed him around, and made room in the closet for Curtis' things. They opened a bottle of champagne, put on music, and Scott began to feel better. They went to dinner and talked. Curtis said he thought about Scott all the time and was happy to see him again. They went back to Scott's apartment and had a repeat of the kind of sex Scott liked. He felt a control over Curtis that fueled the erotic charge of fighting him in his mind.

The next day Curtis told Scott he thought he was falling in love with him. Scott felt something might be happening, too.

The next month, Curtis invited Scott back to Dallas for a pool party one of his friends was hosting. Again, Scott started the weekend in retreat, but after some drinks was quick to go along with the narrative that a relationship was starting, and the distance between them would eventually be overcome.

On Saturday, they went to the pool party and drank beer and margaritas for hours in the strong Texas sun. Curtis looked every bit the arrogant villain with his black Speedo, sunglasses, dragon tattoo and muscles. They stayed in the swimming pool for much of the afternoon, touching each other. They kissed. Curtis told Scott he loved him. Scott looked in his eyes and said he felt the same.

This was intimacy. He finally felt it. They were going to make things work.

For the next month, Curtis sent more letters and they talked on the phone. In August, he came back to New York for a weekend to visit Scott.

Chapter 6 / 1988

On Saturday, they walked around Chelsea and the East Village. Curtis stopped at salons and told Scott he was looking for a place he might like to work. He could cut hair anywhere. What was stopping him from moving?

Scott said it was too soon. Curtis had an established, affluent client base in Dallas that would be hard to start from scratch in New York.

After walking all day, they mixed some cocktails in Scott's apartment when they got home. They kissed and ended up on the bed. But something was different for Scott. He didn't enjoy the fantasy of a macho Curtis being defeated and dominated. Curtis was now someone real who liked him, and it was no longer exciting. Curtis wasn't a macho villain. He was thinking about moving to New York to cut hair.

Sex would no longer work. Scott held Curtis. He cuddled him. But that would be it. Scott said he was tired.

When Curtis left the next day to return to Dallas, they would never see each other again.

A few days later, Scott called Curtis and said he was uncomfortable continuing a relationship. Maybe he was crazy, but he just couldn't do it. Things wouldn't work out. Curtis tried to convince him to take some time to think, but Scott didn't change his mind. He was very sorry. Curtis was crying when they hung up the phone.

Scott was downcast and sat on the couch with the phone next to him. He thought of his first boyfriend, Josh, who he had coldly dumped in college when it was clear that he loved Scott.

Now, Curtis reminded him of Kiko. Scott had pursued them both because a lasting relationship was highly unlikely to succeed from the outset.

Was it a pattern? What was wrong with him?

At least Peter had been a step in the right direction. They had lived together. But even that failed. After a few months, Scott didn't want sex. Things had morphed into a friendship.

Scott was certain of one thing: he was toxic in a relationship. He hurt everyone.

CHAPTER SEVEN
2000

It was early summer, and Scott was 36. Ten months had passed since Curtis returned to Dallas. Scott wanted to write or call him again, but felt Curtis would take it as an opening and Scott would be unable to resist. It was better to keep the door closed.

Scott wasn't sure if he had dodged a bullet, or if he had mistakenly torpedoed the relationship out of fear. He resigned himself to being alone, and was okay with it. Scott stopped taking Celexa and quickly returned to his normal weight. The doctor had lied, or was ludicrously unaware of the side effects.

Scott went in-line skating on weekends, and met friends at bars or restaurants. On a Saturday night, he went with a friend to the Roxy, the same nightclub where he had met Kiko more than a decade before. It had a small upstairs lounge and dance floor that played 80s music.

Scott and his friend danced and had drinks at the bar. A while later, they noticed an attractive pair looking at them. It became clear after another drink they were interested in meeting. Scott liked one, and it seemed his friend liked the other.

The pair approached the bar and introduced themselves. They were Latino friends from business school who now settled in New York. To Scott's delight, the guy he liked chose to remain to talk to him at the bar while their friends went to the dance floor. The guy was Mexican and named Francisco. Scott surprised him with a response in Spanish. They ordered another drink. Scott explained he had studied Spanish through college and still used it whenever possible. He liked to practice and wanted to be fluent because he felt knowing another language opened a whole other world. He thought all Americans should strive to be bilingual.

When their friends returned, Scott and Francisco were engaged in conversation, so they were left alone. Scott looked much younger than his age, so he shaved off five years when Francisco shared that he was 27. Scott was sure Francisco would reject him if he told the truth.

They had another drink and decided to head to Scott's apartment, because Francisco's parents were visiting. They kissed for a while on Scott's couch, and made plans to go in-line skating the next afternoon along Hudson River Park. They exchanged numbers and Francisco left.

Scott considered it a hook-up, because the start was already shaky. A nine-year age difference *plus* a foreign nationality. It would fit his pattern. An entanglement guaranteed to fail.

The next day, Scott met Francisco at a public sitting area north of the Statue of Liberty on the Hudson River. From there, they in-line skated for two hours along the paved lanes hugging the river's edge, stopping at rest points to enjoy the view and chat.

They returned to their starting point. They talked for an hour. Scott liked his accent. Scott learned Francisco had a difficult time coming out and fought depression because of it. Like Scott, he found the process of meeting people very difficult, and often found himself alone. Consequently, he hated weekends. Scott understood what he felt. Scott also often wished for the structure of the work week away from the loneliness of Saturday and Sunday.

In Mexico, it was unthinkable for Francisco to be gay in his city of Torreón. While living there, he wrote and sent an anguished letter to the Pope asking him to reconsider the church's harsh stance against gays. He shared his own story in the letter. He had done nothing wrong to deserve being ostracized and treated as damned.

Scott was immediately attracted to his honesty and sincerity.

Francisco's heart was pure and had not yet been broken by New York. Scott remembered arriving to the city, and the pain and shock of being dumped the first several times. The gay scene was still difficult to navigate, with a constant pressure to look as close to perfection as possible. Trying to meet people was a fool's game. Scott felt a strong desire to shield Francisco from experiencing the same frustrations he had faced, even if they were only to be friends. He couldn't explain why. Perhaps because he was older.

Francisco said that his company was sponsoring him for a green card, so at least he would not face the immigration problems Kiko had faced. It was one less complication.

Scott still did not share his age. He wanted to continue seeing Francisco and it was too risky to say anything. He was the first person Scott liked since the ill-fated fling with Curtis. They made plans to meet again later in the week after work.

Meanwhile, Scott got a job on another magazine and soon found himself in a pressure-cooker. Each day of the week became an endurance test with endless planning meetings, design of layouts, approval meetings with the Editor, photo shoots, editing of photos, revisions of layouts, and managing of design staff.

Every step of the process presented a confrontation of some kind with someone. Office emails were a new technology, and the endless ringing of incoming messages signaled a sea-change in how offices would function. No one left their desks, except for meetings. Questions that previously would be quickly resolved face-to-face became email rounds that created more confusion and ate valuable time.

Scott steeled himself behind a cool persona. Confrontations bothered him to his core, and they were constant. He didn't understand how others were nonplussed by differences of opinion and outright attacks. Scott was constantly nervous.

Scott offered little personal information to his co-workers. He would show nothing of himself. The Entertainment Editor once got a slight whiff of cologne Francisco had given Scott as a present and announced wearing cologne was "so retro." All other departmental editors were armed and dangerous. One photo or layout the Editor didn't like could easily devolve into a finger-pointing witch hunt. Staff meetings were an exercise in bluster and domination. People spoke loudly to make points, as front-row hand-raisers did in high school.

Scott would look with amazement at an editor who for the fourth time made an obvious declaration. He thought people would see through it, but no one did. Quiet and thoughtful was seen as weak. Leaders, and those who wished to gain promotions, spoke confidently and often. He resented that extroverts were treated as superior to introverts, and rewarded. Scott was cynical and found the daily performances nauseating. He refused to contribute to the spectacle, except when necessary and appropriate.

As the months unfolded, Scott met Francisco often and together they blew off steam. On Thursdays, he went to Francisco's apartment on John Street in the Financial District, and they would go for pitchers of beer and wings at a place in a basement down the street. On Saturdays, they met at Scott's apartment and watched DVDs of music videos, before going out to meet friends. Scott had a green thumb from his upbringing in Vermont, and bought Francisco a vine for his apartment, since he didn't have any plants. He placed it by the only window that got a sliver of light in the concrete canyons of the financial district.

They decided to go on their first weekend trip to the country together. They rented a car and Scott drove on the way north. He needed his sunglasses, and asked Francisco to get them from his duffel bag. Francisco leaned over the front seat and dug around for a minute.

"How old did you say you were?" Francisco asked.

"Don't remember what I said," Scott answered.

"Tell me now," Francisco said, his back still bent over the front seat. Scott figured he was caught. "37."

"That's not what you told me."

"Did you go into my wallet?"

Francisco started laughing and sat down with Scott's license in his hand, and the sunglasses.

"Can't believe you searched my wallet."

"Can't believe you lied about your age."

"I had to," Scott said. "You would have thought I was too old. I look younger."

"You look much younger."

Scott was silent for moment and kept driving. "You don't care?"

"No. We look the same."

Francisco leaned over the seat, and put the wallet back in the duffel bag. He handed the sunglasses to Scott. Over the weekend, they decided they wanted to become boyfriends. Sex was good. Scott imagined a young fighter taking on his coach.

In June 2001, Francisco invited Scott to visit his family in Mexico. He was very close with his parents, and from the beginning shared with them news of the time he spent with Scott. They were worried about their son ever since he told them he was gay. They wanted to meet Scott, and planned an afternoon party in their backyard for Francisco to introduce Scott to his friends.

Scott was nervous, but he and Francisco had been together for a year, and he was pleased Francisco's parents were open to meeting him, and welcomed him to their home. Scott was intrigued by the relationship Francisco had with his parents. They spoke on the phone twice weekly, and Francisco shared everything. Scott watched as Francisco interacted with his family with warmth, openness and affection. It fascinated him.

The day of the party was stressful for Scott, with an onslaught of introductions to Francisco's lifelong friends and extended family members, including cousins who grew up together and were like siblings. Scott thought about his cousin Deirdre, and how little time they actually spent together. Here, it was common for generations to remain in the same city. Francisco was the first in his family, and one of the first of his whole group of friends to move away. It was a revelation to them he had done so because he was gay. But they understood, and now offered support.

Scott tried his best to communicate in Spanish. He was thankful he could extend the effort because they were all bilingual, and it would be embarrassing otherwise.

Scott was relieved when the party ended, because he had felt under a spotlight for the whole event. He was touched everyone tried to make him feel welcome. He was sure he was the first openly gay American they had ever met. He felt vulnerable they had that information, but the reality was inescapable. The party was a learning experience for everyone.

The next month, Scott and Francisco drove to Vermont to spend the Fourth of July weekend with Robert and Ava. He was nervous during the drive northward, but upon their arrival, Ava and Robert exuded a warmth and openness that surprised Scott. They had never spoken about anything gay since he had made his announcement to them years ago. He had no idea what to expect.

Their acceptance of Francisco greatly exceeded his expectations. On Saturday, Pamela and her husband hosted a barbecue at their house, which was within bicycling distance of a lake. Pamela introduced her two sons to Francisco. They told him they were both studying Spanish in school, and they traded questions like *como te llamas?* and *donde está el baño?* Scott felt an uncommon sense of pride and relief his family welcomed Francisco as much as he had felt welcomed in Mexico.

He suddenly felt he would now be able to include talking about Francisco during the phone conversations with his parents that had always felt strained. Perhaps this weekend would signal a new beginning for all of them. His negative assumptions had been wrong. That evening, they all watched fireworks over the lake.

In the fall, Francisco needed to find a new place to live in the wake of 9/11. With Ground Zero just blocks away and smoldering, John Street was dark, desolate and depressing. In time, he found a new apartment about ten blocks north of Scott's place, an easy walking distance. They both liked the idea of having their own spaces, while still living close by.

For the next three years, Scott and Francisco saw each other daily. During the week, they would have dinner together, then one would walk or take the bus home. They spent weekends together at one or the other's apartment. They took vacations to Puerto Vallarta and visited both sets of parents together. They both felt a part of each other's families.

Scott gradually withdrew from sex. After the first two or three years came a reduction in frequency that soon tapered to a halt. As had happened so many times before, sex lost its appeal once someone's body became familiar. He found it odd to have sex with someone whom he now knew so well. The idea was repellent, like having sex with a brother. He didn't understand how people continued to find physical attraction to bodies after the first few months.

Fortunately, Francisco didn't seem to mind that they slept together without sex. At least, he never mentioned it to Scott.

Meanwhile, the frenetic pace at the magazine continued unabated. It was a constant churn of deadlines, meetings, confrontations, crises, and future planning to keep from sinking. He didn't mind when he felt all the effort was leading somewhere. But he increasingly felt trapped, with no forward path.

The field was in active decline, with the advent of the Internet and multiple outlets to get celebrity information and entertainment. Previously, magazine staffers often remained at gigs for stints of only three-to-five years, to remain fresh and not get typecast or locked into a specific subject matter or age group. But now, there was virtually no movement in the industry. People held onto positions for years, because there was nowhere else to go in the face of reducing circulations, and advertising dollars diverted to anything digital. Only privileged standouts in the industry with stellar connections and rarefied resumes had any chance at advancement.

Confrontations at work were endless and constant and bothered him greatly. A debilitating sense of anxiety would set in when a project of his own was rejected by a superior. The belief they doubted his talent and ability to do the job — and were displeased with him — was overpowering.

He would work as quickly as possible on a revision to escape the feeling of being in trouble. He needed to get back into their good graces

— and fast — because the sense of having failed haunted him until he could get the project back in front of the bosses and regain their approval. He assumed it was a normal reaction when work needed a revision. If he wasn't praised, he assumed the opposite: he was under scrutiny and not performing up to expectations and not liked. He imagined they wanted him out.

Scott hated ego-maniac bosses. The editor had a closed door meeting with a half-dozen staffers. At the end, she announced she was looking to buy an apartment and had figured out an ingenious plan to research on-line what the seller had paid for the property. She would then let the seller know she knew what had been paid, and would only offer only slightly more.

Scott thought it was the stupidest thing he had ever heard. The whole point of real estate was to buy low and sell high. But the sycophants in the room praised the clever plan. Scott was confused by their unabashed willingness to enthusiastically support whatever nonsense an authority figure blurted out.

Scott felt the need to keep moving ahead, to walk away and start again. Toward what end was not particularly important. Movement away from stress was. He disliked office politics, and didn't know how others brushed it off.

Scott found a job working with the licensees of a magazine publisher. He imagined the position would be less stressful and he would get the opportunity to travel internationally. In a rapidly-changing media landscape, he felt it might be his last, best option.

Scott moved to the new office and had to make an immediate adjustment. They dressed more formally and politics went far beyond what he had thought was already bad on the magazine. Every email was a potential bomb that could blow up the next day. Why was something phrased a certain way? Why wasn't someone bcc'd? Had a prior email come in that someone else didn't know about? Why wasn't it forwarded?

Scott learned to adjust, but after an overbearing lecture from one of the bosses a month after he started, he knew he had stepped into a trap.

She stood in the doorway to his office with a commanding presence and for nearly twenty minutes loudly explained to him how she wanted things done. He was unable to look away and unable to respond.

The tone in her raised voice and her unflinching gaze triggered him. He felt extremely anxious and trapped, as he had been as a child with his mother. His heart pounded and he felt like a failure.

Meanwhile, Robert and Ava came to New York to visit Scott in 2006. They arrived on a Friday night, and Scott and Francisco took them out for dinner.

Late Saturday morning they walked the perimeter of the Ground Zero construction site, and continued to the Hudson River water front. Ava and Robert meandered along and commented on things Scott took for granted and didn't find particularly unusual or remarkable. The banter was growing annoying.

They stopped by a large shoe warehouse on the way home, and perused the aisles. Scott found himself barely able to control a growing sense of disgust. The time it took them to make a decision — to sit down, to untie a shoe, to test a new one, to discuss it — was excruciating. Robert's toenails needed trimming. Couldn't he see that? Why didn't he groom himself? Ava somehow managed to find the ugliest pair of shoes on the floor. Scott felt they were country bumpkins hopelessly overwhelmed by the scale and pace of things away from their small town. He tried to be patient, but felt he was losing control.

They returned to Scott's apartment, and Francisco would meet them later for dinner. Scott made tea and brought out a cup for Ava, who sat at the table and started to read *The New York Times*. Robert sat on the couch and clicked on the television.

"Have Francisco's parents visited New York?" Ava asked.

"Yes. A lot. They come twice a year and stay with him."

Scott was annoyed. She had a lot of nerve asking. He had lived in the city for 20 years and this was only her second visit.

"That's nice for them," Ava said.

"Why for *them*?"

"To get away from Mexico. The drug wars."

Scott felt his anger rising. "It's not like that. Their city is beautiful."

He paused and decided he wasn't going to stop.

"The whole extended family lives nearby. Siblings, uncles, cousins," Scott said.

"That can be good. Or bad," Ava said.

"Why?"

"Families are complicated," Ava said. "It's hard to do things on your own without worrying about everyone else."

Why did she have to be so opinionated?

"I love it, Scott said. "Francisco's cousin next door is like his brother. We rarely see our cousins. Lots I don't even know. At least he has roots."

Scott felt a sudden rage. Did Ava think their isolation was normal? Did she ever consider what it was like to be floating alone with no grounding or connection to a past that went beyond a house filled with scary memories near Bundy's farm? To be the grandson of a ghost that no one acknowledged, but a ghost that haunted them with shame, isolation, abuse and a cloak of silence?

"We don't have any roots!" Scott said.

He thought about Pamela's sons and the huge amount of time Ava and Robert devoted to their grandsons. Celebrations. Special treats. Little excursions. *That* was normal.

"*I don't even know my grandfather's name.*"

Ava's eyes suddenly teared up and her face flushed.

Robert looked over from the couch. Ava said nothing and looked down at the newspaper.

Scott immediately regretted the outburst and felt a surge of guilt. He had broken the taboo. It was unthinkable and what now?

Scott walked to the window just beyond the table and gazed out.

"The sky's clearing. Won't need umbrellas," Scott said. "I think you're gonna really like the place we're going for dinner. We can walk from here."

Ava smiled.

Chapter 7 / 2000

"I'm sure we will love it," she said. Her face returned to normal.

Scott was surprised how quickly she was able to conceal her emotions.

Scott sat across from Ava and they finished their tea and looked at the newspaper silently.

On Monday morning, Ava and Robert got up early to have breakfast with Scott before he left for work. He felt a sense of regret as he said goodbye. Why had he been so critical of them? Why couldn't he just be nice? He always felt on edge around them, as if he had to be ready to defend himself. It was horrid that his own parents annoyed him.

Scott didn't share his resentment of his parents with Francisco, because it made him sound awful in light of the closeness shared by Francisco with his parents.

A few weeks later, it was midsummer. Scott and Francisco sat together side by side in two folding chairs on the beach. Scott had wanted to say something all day. Now, as the afternoon was drawing to a close, it was time.

"We've been together now for seven years, right?" Scott asked.

"Yes," Francisco answered.

"Are you happy with the relationship?"

"Yes. You?"

"Yes, very," Scott said. He paused. "Do you think it's bad we haven't had sex in like a year?"

"It's more like three years."

"Oh, right," Scott said, and nervously kicked at the sand with his foot. "Ever wonder if we should open our relationship?"

"Open? Like be allowed to have sex with someone else?"

"Yes."

"I've thought about it," Francisco said. "But, I wouldn't want to ruin our relationship."

"Of course. That's most important," Scott said.

"We could try it for a while, and if it doesn't work, we could stop," Francisco said. "We could make rules."

They continued to talk. They reasoned they both had demanding jobs and the only free nights were Friday and Saturday. Fridays were reserved for going out someplace to dinner together. A date night. And Saturday was the only night dedicated to drinking and going out to meet friends.

They decided the only window for any kind of "opening" would be Saturday nights after midnight. It would be the starting point for the new experiment. They would part ways after spending the first portion of the night together and then find adventure.

They both agreed sex with the same partner was boring after a few years passed. It would actually be the best of all possible worlds: they knew they had each other, but would be free to have encounters with guys who didn't need to meet any kind of criteria that would be considered if they were actually looking to date someone. They decided they wouldn't talk about who they met. There would be no repeats. They promised to be honest if they felt bad about the situation.

The time came to test the new system. On Saturday night, they had drinks at Francisco's apartment while watching videos. They met friends at a bar in Chelsea and at about 12:30 said their goodbyes to the group, and to each other. Francisco would head to The Eagle, and Scott to the East Village.

Scott knew of two places practically next door to each other that were known primarily as pick-up bars. He made his way to the first one, and ordered vodka-sodas, alternating with Bud Lights. He knew he would be unable to meet someone unless he was entirely drunk. His fear of making eye contact and initiating small talk remained.

He found himself intrigued by the idea of selecting someone — anyone — out of the crowd. A person based solely on carnal attraction with no strings attached.

Scott felt fortunate to appear 10 years younger than his age. He finally looked like a man, not a boy, and could get guys — if he could muster the courage.

This new, open experiment might be his last chance to make up for all the time he lost in his 20s: paralyzed with fear and unable to meet people, and terrified of AIDS. Then, the lost decade of his 30s with a cycle of serial monogamy that led to nothing.

He decided to target guys he had always fantasized about but never acted on. He got himself drunk enough not to care, and approached a handsome black guy in a corner of the bar, and soon they started kissing. Scott fake-punched him in the stomach and the guy liked it and returned blows. Scott imagined he was with a hot boxer or gangster and the fantasy soon became passionate enough that they decided to leave the bar and go to Scott's apartment. Scott felt exhilarated and free. In two hours the guy left, with no questions asked. He was on the down-low.

The next day, Scott and Francisco briefly traded stories of the previous evening. Scott told him about the black guy. Francisco yelled at him for having sex without a condom. Scott responded he was HIV negative and a top. The possibility of infection was remote for the active partner. That was why heterosexual men were largely spared HIV infection from sex. Francisco didn't want to hear excuses. There were plenty of STDs to worry about. He made Scott promise to always use a condom. Scott agreed, but wasn't sure he would actually do so.

In the months ahead, Scott and Francisco continued their Saturday night solo excursions after midnight. Scott discovered an attraction to Asian guys he had previously not fully explored because of lack of access: immigration patterns to New York had changed dramatically, and bars were much more racially mixed. Asians had been a tiny minority and were now highly visible in comparison.

Scott felt lucky to be old enough to have witnessed the change, and cheated by the limitations of the earlier years. Perhaps he had simply not been attracted to the majority of the all-white crowd in years past. It was another reason he had to make up for lost time now.

But to muster the courage necessary to approach, hold eye contact, and show interest, Scott found himself drinking more heavily on Saturday nights than ever before. It was the only way he would dare to actually do something and not stand on the sidelines.

Everyone around him seemed more naturally confident with the pick-up part of the process. A boom and bust cycle started with an exuberant Saturday night when anything could happen, and ended with a Sunday morning hangover and depression for the remainder of the day.

Scott began to cultivate "bar boyfriends." He told them he had a long-term partner and was in an open relationship. But over time they would find each other late Saturday nights in the East Village and hang out and kiss. Sometimes they would meet during the week, if Francisco was out of town, and one became a sex buddy who encouraged Saturday afternoon rendezvous at his apartment.

Scott liked having several partners lined up, because it was a measure of his worth and attractiveness. In his mind, one was a Japanese fighter pilot in the Imperial Navy, one was a top Korean black belt, and one was a highly skilled Chinese assassin. He later added a Cambodian body guard and a Vietnamese weight lifter to his collection of opponents. When they became friends, the kissing and sex would stop because the fantasies no longer applied, but they would continue to meet up and hang out.

One night, a cocky Latino in his late twenties hit on Scott. They kissed and realized they both liked trading gut punches. They moved to a bathroom stall and kissed while they struggled to pin each other against the walls. They pushed forcefully against each other and with one energetic motion both collided into the door. The latch gave way and they tumbled out into the open area in front of the sinks. Scott split his upper lip with the impact as he landed on top of the Latino, who slammed the back of his head on the floor.

They lay there stunned momentarily, then got up. Scott grabbed a paper towel, wet it, and held it on his lip. The Latino rubbed the back of his head, and they decided to leave. They apologized to each other that it got so rough, and agreed to walk to the Latino's apartment.

When they arrived they got undressed and went to the bedroom. They kissed briefly but Scott stopped because his lip was cut and it would be a dangerous potential means of HIV infection. The reality of the situation killed any remaining excitement, and Scott left after about an hour.

Chapter 7 / 2000

The next morning, Scott's lip was greatly swollen. He treated it with ice before going to Francisco's apartment for lunch. When he entered the apartment, Francisco noticed the lip immediately. Scott told him the story and Fransisco said he was crazy. Scott admitted he was getting out of control.

At work the next day, he told colleagues he fell in-line skating. He was growing increasingly concerned about his career and future prospects. His job had become almost entirely management, and he was rapidly losing the hands-on skills that had been the foundation of his entire career. He wondered if he was living a lie: the trade-off for a window office with a view was a life of soul-killing meetings, politics, manipulation, and games.

He wasn't interested in playing anymore. He had set goals for his position, and, after nearly five years, had already met them.

Perhaps he didn't even deserve the job. He wasn't necessarily better than anyone else. He knew he would never understand or be able to mimic the projection of confidence, privilege and entitlement he saw in the other people around the office. He resented them and didn't aspire to be like them.

He had already traveled far from his rural upbringing and this was where the road would end. The world had changed and there was only a digital future. His journalism degree from the University of Maine had served him well, but the Internet hadn't even existed at the time.

Perhaps if he got a Master's degree he could move in a digital direction and start again. He felt it would be now or never to make a move.

His choice was to hang onto this job for as long as possible — and basically be unemployable when it ended — or to continue his education and hope for the best. He applied to a MFA program in the city that admitted only 20 people. Four months later he was accepted, and decided to enroll. He felt it would be a gift to his future self. An updated education that more adequately reflected who he had become.

When he gave notice at his job in August, people were shocked. No one left a position like Scott had to return to school. He didn't know if he was crazy and making an enormous mistake. He simply felt a familiar call from deep inside himself to keep moving and to get away.

To help pay for school, he rented his apartment and moved in with Francisco. They had been together for nine years and it would be the first time they lived together. It would be a tight squeeze into a one-bedroom, but only temporary. They would still have an open relationship, but sharing an apartment would change the dynamic, and be an interesting experiment. He would need to discard a lot of his possessions and be very selective about what could fit into four storage containers in the basement of Francisco's building.

He threw away many of his photos and scrapbooks including shots of his friend Tom from high school. What had any of it amounted to, anyway? No one kept in touch. He kept his violin, but placed it in a storage bin. It had also amounted to nothing. All that time and energy had been a waste. The violin brought back flashes of childhood that felt extremely unpleasant — a feeling of fear and sadness at his core — and he quickly covered the violin case. Why did he even still have his letter jacket from cross country in high school? He placed it in the trash bag. This would be a time of moving forward, and the past would be erased.

Scott was the oldest in his class at grad school. Somewhat improbably, he became close friends with the youngest in the class, a pretty blonde girl from the Czech Republic named Sasha. She lived nearby and they almost always walked home together at night after the final session that sometimes ran until 9 or 10.

Scott didn't mention anything about Francisco or even the fact he was gay. He kept himself hidden, and hoped his classmates assumed he was in his mid-thirties because he looked young enough.

Scott dreaded a daily part of the art school process: the *crits*. One by one, each student would present their work and face a critique by the other students and the professor. Scott felt exposed and attacked standing in front of the class while listening to the assessment of his work. It was terrifying to him and he often blanked out, missing the gist of the criticism because his mind would flood with the mantras: I Hate My Life. I'm Such an Idiot. I Have to Get Out of Here. Please Help Me.

Often, on the walk home, Scott would discuss the aftermath with Sasha.

"I'm so humiliated," Scott said. "He hated my project."

"What?" Sasha responded. "No, he didn't."

She started laughing.

"He said I didn't even have an idea yet."

"No! He said he liked your design. But your presentation skipped over the nuts and bolts of the idea. Doesn't mean he doesn't like it."

"He said I'm trying too hard to force the project into parameters."

"Yes? And?"

"So, that's bad."

"No! He wants you to be open to what can happen when you stop controlling. To let the project take over. It's a good thing. He believes in you."

"That's not what I heard," Scott said. "Are you sure?"

"Yes! It's always the same thing with you."

Sasha hugged him and continued on her way up Third Avenue as Scott turned onto a side street.

In less than two years, the Master's degree was completed. Scott felt a new-found confidence in his ability to solve problems. He was intrigued with the concept of Design Thinking, and used it to unlock his own projects.

He also found it eye-opening — and worrisome — that his reaction to the critiques was not accurate. Late night walks home with Sasha had provided him with the opportunity to hear an unbiased perspective on the criticism he had faced, and his interpretation did not match hers.

He had felt singled out and attacked. But her perspective was more nuanced and balanced. He wasn't more attacked than anyone else. Anything good in a critique Scott disregarded, if there was also something bad. He didn't know why his interpretation was so different, and it bothered him.

He found a job with a media company working on mobile editions of their magazines. It wasn't a dream assignment, but considering the economy, he felt fortunate.

Scott and Francisco had lived together for two years without a hitch. They had proved very compatible, even in the close confines of the 650 square-foot one-bedroom. They decided to live together permanently, and found an apartment that would be large enough for the two of them.

Scott was able to take his things out of storage and they merged their belongings. Scott stuck his violin on the top shelf of the hallway closet.

While Scott recognized he should be happy — finishing the degree, finding a job, moving in with Francisco — he continued to feel dejected. The compulsion to continue to add to his collection of "bar boyfriends" was a problem because in order to do so he had to be very drunk. He felt intense depressions, especially on Sundays. The hangovers were severe and he felt guilty about the previous evening's hook-ups.

Sometimes he would kiss three different guys in one night, but that wasn't enough, because the week before he had scored four. Was he less attractive now? Other times he would be alone with the Chinese assassin or the Korean black belt and worry that he was crossing the line of agreement with Francisco because he actually *liked* the guys. They weren't just strangers. He felt affection for them. Nothing like the love he felt for Francisco — *that* was in a protected, special class — but feelings nonetheless. How could anyone only like one person? The whole thing was confusing.

By the year's end, Scott felt a growing sense of desperation. He was a full-grown man and repeating self-destructive patterns of behavior, with no relief in sight. It was unsustainable and he knew it. He couldn't talk to Francisco about it, because it was too embarrassing and sounded weak. He told Francisco about the depression, but nothing more. It didn't help matters that Francisco seemed to be enjoying the arrangement, coming home some Saturday nights even later than Scott, without apology.

Scott didn't feel the least bit his age, and not in a *fun* way. It was

Chapter 7 / 2000

more like being stuck in a time warp that left him feeling empty and confused. He didn't *know* who he was. Why did other people have a sense of themselves and of their place in life?

He wanted to age gracefully, but he wasn't. He had become a poster child for dysfunction: anonymous hook-ups, juggling sex with multiple partners, heavy binge drinking on weekends and depression. He had to do something before it was too late.

He thought back to his meetings with Dr. Paulson. She had uncovered that he was bothered by his childhood, and he'd tried to ignore it. Now, he had to see what would happen if he faced it. Maybe there would be a change. There was no other answer he could think of. Something deep inside him felt buried, dark, scary, shameful and off-balance. On Sundays, with a hangover, it was unbearable.

On the Internet, Scott searched around and found a group that offered weekly, free meetings in New York: Adult Survivors of Childhood Abuse. He assumed what had happened with Ava probably counted as abuse, and sent them an email. He quickly received a response with the location and time of the next meeting.

He went on Wednesday after work. At least thirty attendees sat in chairs arranged in a large circle, and he was very nervous as he entered the room. He watched and listened to the main speaker, and then to the stories of individuals who wanted to share as they went around the room. He felt validated by the stories he heard. They suggested that the depression, confusion, and low self-esteem he often felt might be traced back to abuse, and was shared by others. He felt a twinge of excitement there might actually be a reason for his behavioral downward spiral. And if there was a reason, there might be a way to fix it. When it was his turn, he told them it was his first meeting. He was hoping to figure things out by hearing from others.

For the next eight weeks he went every Wednesday. He felt like he had a right to be there. That, in itself, was a big step. He could empathize with the people in the circle. Some of them had been to therapists, and it had helped them, and they were now able to talk about what had happened to them. Scott realized what he wanted most was to talk to someone by himself. He knew he would never dare to share much in a large room. He still couldn't face digging deeply into his childhood memories on his own.

For the next four months, Scott hoped something would change, but nothing did. His behavior was simply not going to correct itself on its own. Something made him wildly excited to enter into a drunken Saturday night adventure — and to feel desired — even though he knew the next day he would wake up shamed and depressed. He liked the attention, and he liked getting drunk. The pattern was going to keep repeating. He was powerless to stop it.

Scott found a website that defined different kinds of psychological issues that could be treated, created a community, and explained the process of therapy. It also offered a search and introduction to therapists, based on parameters such as expertise and location. He liked what he read, and found a listing for a doctor near his apartment who specialized in childhood trauma. Scott guessed it would be as good a starting point as any. He bookmarked the page. Based on his photograph, the doctor was handsome and Asian.

Scott wanted his money's worth if he was going to have the added expense of therapy.

At least the doctor would be hot. A Taekwondo master.

CHAPTER EIGHT
2013

For the rest of the week, Scott thought about sending an email to make contact with the therapist. He continued to read articles on the website. Starting therapy with a real doctor felt like a big decision that once begun would be difficult to retract, at least without humiliation.

On Saturday, Scott and Francisco put on a playlist and started having drinks in the kitchen at 9 p.m. in preparation for the evening ahead. At 9:50, Scott stole away to the bedroom and sat at his computer. He had a buzz on and suddenly felt determined to send the email. Why wait? He knew the next day he would be hung over and wouldn't feel like reaching out.

It was better to do so now, in anticipation of a night out hunting, while he dared to do so. If the doctor didn't write back, or Scott's email somehow sounded stupid, he could shrug it off. Scott was intimidated to write because the doctor looked serious and was employed by a major hospital, Beth Israel Medical Center.

Scott imagined his problems were probably laughable and minor compared to what the doctor had to deal with every day working with patients in a mental health ward that specialized in traumatic stress. What was *trauma*, anyway? It sounded serious and horrible and Scott probably didn't even qualify. He would be looked at as a joke. A frivolous case. A patient to be tolerated and patronized each week for 50 minutes, just for the money.

Scott began to type a message. He thought he had better include something about his childhood or he might not even get a response. Meetings with Dr. Paulson and the peer support group had confirmed the darkness he felt whenever the word *childhood* was even mentioned. An album Ava had given him with photographs of himself as a child was something pernicious he couldn't look at without closing after several pages, and hiding it away in a bottom drawer. Scott remembered some outfits he wore in the photos and could see only sadness in his eyes.

He kept his communication brief:

I am looking for a therapist to help me deal with
residual problems from childhood abuse.
Is this your specialty?
I would need to know what hours of operation you offer,
and also fees involved.
Thank you for your time.
Scott

He reread what he wrote, and yes, he called it abuse. The residual problems he considered were drinking, promiscuity and depression. He hit send. He felt a rush of excitement he had dared to do so, and went back to the kitchen to the music and Francisco and another drink.

The next morning at 10:30 a.m. he had a response:

Hi Scott. Yes, definitely.

The doctor's name was Ken and he briefly explained fees, out-of-network benefit policy, and hours of availability.

Scott was excited by the response and thought about it for two days. Could he afford $250 a session? It would be an extra $1000 a month, at least until insurance kicked in after a $3700 deductible. But at least he had insurance that would cover what they called "behavioral health." It was definitely worth a try. If not now, when?

On Tuesday morning, Scott wrote back, and asked if it was possible to get an evening session, after work.

In 20 minutes, Ken responded: *Tomorrow Wednesday at 7?*

Scott's heart raced. Could he do this?

Five minutes later, he typed: *That's great. Thank you. See you then.*

Scott was excited all day. It would be a new kind of adventure. At dinner he told Francisco he was going to try seeing a therapist, and his first session would be the next evening. He wanted help with the bouts of depression he felt, especially on weekends. Francisco was supportive and thought it was worth exploring.

At 9:30 Tuesday evening, Scott received an email message from Ken: *Sorry, but can we please reschedule for Thursday?*

Scott was discouraged. It was already happening. His case was a joke and would be something to fit around the doctor's busy schedule. Maybe he had picked a doctor who was too important for him and he needed to find one in a regular private practice away from a hospital. He responded Thursday would be fine.

On Thursday, Scott approached the hospital after work, and was extremely nervous. He made his way to the second floor. The hallways were quiet because it was after hours. He saw an open door on the left side of the hall and slowly walked toward it.

He peeked around the corner and saw a man who sat typing at his computer but swiveled his chair around when he noticed Scott in the doorway. They greeted each other and shook hands. Ken motioned for Scott to sit in a chair against the back wall that faced him as he put an "In Session" sign on the outside of the door and closed it.

"So what brings you here?" Ken asked.

Scott hesitated a moment. His eyes met Ken's, but darted away.

"Depression."

"What's going on?"

"On weekends. It gets bad. Plus, I'm drinking a lot on Saturday nights. Binge drinking. The rest of the week is fine. Almost nothing. But Saturdays are bad."

"How so?"

"I have a partner. A guy. We've been together for about 12 years. But we opened our relationship about four years ago and on Saturday nights we can fool around."

Scott paused. "I drink a lot so I can dare to do stuff."

"And what about your partner?"

"He's right there with me. Maybe even drinks more."

Ken laughed. "What about your childhood? You wrote something."

Scott tried to collect his thoughts. It was intense to sit face to face. He had expected to be lying on a couch or something. He looked away from Ken as he spoke.

"I didn't like it. My childhood."

Ken continued to look at Scott, watching his face and movements.

"My mother. She beat me," Scott said.

Scott suddenly felt he was being tested, or measured to see if he was a worthy case. He had to speak up, or he might be dropped.

"This scar on my eyelid. It's something I have to look at every day, in the mirror," Scott said, and pointed above his right eye socket below his eyebrow. "She did it. She shook me by my hair and threw me and my face slammed into the front edge of a wooden toy shelf."

Scott looked beyond Ken and out the window. His foot twitched.

"Have you ever told anyone about this?" Ken asked.

Scott thought about what to say. "One time. One person. Actually, two. My cousin also knows. But I went to a therapist."

"How did that go?" Ken asked.

"It went well. I really liked her," Scott said. "It was about 15 years ago. But I only went for eight or twelve weeks." He paused and reached for memories. "It was different than this. I had to lay down on a couch and she sat behind me and took notes while I talked."

"I take a more active, confrontational approach to therapy," Ken said. "Do you think you can take that?"

"Yes," Scott said. "I think I would like that."

Ken smiled, asked a few more questions, and they went over some paperwork details. He told Scott he had a girlfriend. Scott was relieved because Ken was cuter than his photograph on the web portal. But he seemed to be unaware of his attractiveness. As he sat in his office chair, it was clear he had big, muscled thighs like some of Scott's Asian friends in the bars and gym. He dressed cool. Fortunately, he wasn't gay, or it would be too much of a distraction.

Scott wondered if he mentioned a girlfriend in case Scott wanted a gay therapist. Scott found it very considerate. As the session drew to a close, Scott thought Ken appeared to be a perfect role model: educated, intelligent, poised, accomplished, friendly, thoughtful, energetic, handsome. Scott felt immediately comfortable with him. Scott didn't know why, but he already wanted Ken to help him. It was just a sense he got. An intuition.

"Do you think I would be an okay fit with you?" Scott asked.

"Yes," Ken answered. "Very much so."

They made plans to meet Wednesdays at 7 p.m.

Scott was excited on his walk home. He had somehow lucked into finding his conception of an ideal therapist. It was time to try the experiment. He was eager to see what would unfold. That evening, Scott told Francisco he liked the therapist and that they agreed to continue with sessions on Wednesday nights.

When the next session came, Scott again felt nervous as he approached Ken's office. He wanted Ken to like him, so he dressed his best and quietly, cautiously knocked on his door. Scott wanted to show respect. Ken smiled and waved him in. Scott hung up his coat, closed the door with the sign, and sat in the chair facing Ken.

"How are you?" Ken asked.

"I'm fine. And you?" Scott answered. He hated that question. If he were fine, he wouldn't be here.

Sitting, facing Ken three or four feet away, he felt nervous. There was an intensity to the communication. Ken stared at him. It was nerve-racking. Scott twitched.

"What would you like to talk about?" Ken asked.

"I don't know."

Ken continued to watch him.

"I've been irritable lately," Scott said. "Like, all the time. Nervous, too."

"Elaborate."

Scott gathered his thoughts.

"On the train platform. Or even on the way to the subway. I yelled at a bicyclist who cut right in front of me. He almost hit me and I had the Walk sign."

There was a pause, then, Scott continued.

"I hate arrogant people on the sidewalk who refuse to move or even swivel out of the way for you. It's usually privileged white people. This one woman with a huge Michael Kors bag refused to budge so I kept walking straight and bumped the bag and it fell off her shoulder."

Scott stopped and tapped his foot.

Ken asked Scott to rate the alarm he felt, now, in the office, on a scale of 1 to 10.

"What do you mean, *alarm*?" Scott asked.

"Nervousness. Anxiety," Ken answered.

Scott thought for a moment. "Pretty high. An 8."

"Your alarm is your body's protective mechanism," Ken said. Scott watched him closely. "Sometimes anxiety changes your thoughts and makes you feel something terrible is going to happen, even when there's no way it could happen, or even when the worry is no big deal. The alarm is actually your friend. It's trying to protect you. It's looking for danger."

Scott listened intently.

"But it's your job to figure out whether something is really dangerous or if it's just a pattern of reaction you've been carrying for years with no real reason," Ken said. "It's a habit you can learn to recognize and control."

For the next three weeks, Scott and Ken talked about alarm reactions. Scott's alarm was hyper-vigilant, he learned. Always on and always pro-actively searching for something that might hurt him or for someone who may — or may not — have bad intentions toward him.

They did exercises to dissect the situations that made Scott nervous such as meeting with friends of Francisco or confrontations at work. Ken tried to teach Scott to re-frame his reaction to an anxiety-causing event into a broader, more philosophical action. Did it really matter that people at a party were pushy and rude? He should focus more on simply being grateful for the leisure time to spend with Francisco and feeling confident he was good enough to be there. He could learn to identify when the alarm was kicking in, and to immediately analyze if it were warranted, or just a false alarm making him suspicious and irritable.

Scott left the sessions exhausted, but exhilarated. He made the decision to concentrate on his body's reaction to events, and to recognize the prevalence of the alarm each day.

Scott loved talking to Ken. He thought about him often. It was the first and only time in his life he agreed to share openly with someone. He could never begin to talk to Francisco the same way, because he would look weak or deeply flawed. Ken didn't care. He was being paid for it. But it was satisfying to talk to him, nonetheless. Scott looked forward to the meetings. It was his favorite hour of the week.

On the day of his fourth meeting with Ken, Scott received an email at noon: *I'm so sorry I have a family medical emergency. Can we meet next week?*

Scott was angry. Why would Ken just cancel and not even try to reschedule? Scott's original suspicion he wasn't an important enough case to Ken was probably true and now would being to play out. Scott was foolish to have trusted Ken so quickly.

Scott wrote back: *Ok.*

There was nothing else to say.

One minute later, Ken responded: *Thank you! If u wish or need, I'm free Friday too.*

Why hadn't he said so in the first place? Scott wondered. He responded: *I would appreciate it if we could meet Friday. Is 7 pm possible?*

Another minute, and Ken responded: *Yes!*

Scott felt much better. He was afraid of being dropped.

At the session Friday, he dared to tell Ken how he felt. Ken apologized and said he should have offered an alternate plan from the outset. For Scott, sharing he was disappointed by someone's action was something new and felt very intense and personal. Intimate, even. He liked it.

He decided to push the envelope. Four or five weeks had passed and Scott had never mentioned anything about his childhood beyond the initial intake meeting. He told Ken about the photo album Ava had given him that he never dared to look at. He asked Ken if he could bring it in, and they could go through it together. Ken said he would be honored.

The next week, Scott put the photo album into the bottom of his backpack and took it with him to work. It felt odd removing it from the drawer, let alone transporting it out of the house with the intent of showing it to someone else. Francisco didn't even know about the album.

At his session that evening, Scott handed it to Ken, and together they turned the pages. Ken smiled and laughed, commenting there were happy times evident in the photos. But Scott saw pain behind the smiles, and refused to continue. Ken told him he should go through the album as many times as necessary until it lost its power over him. Scott didn't believe that would work or help.

"And what about your mother?" Ken asked. "Can you tell me what you remember?"

Scott stared at the window beyond Ken. He sat silently, trying to figure out what to say. He wanted to share a memory. He wanted Ken to know. This was the whole point. He had to talk.

"What are you thinking?" Ken asked after a minute.

"The worst memory," Scott said.

He continued to stare beyond Ken. He couldn't look at him. He was awash in shame. He spoke slowly and paused between sentences.

"She told me she hated me. It was after a beating. She always went to her room next door and cried. I laid on the floor and had to listen. Knowing I caused it. Caused her pain. She beat me bad and I was on the floor and at the end of it she screamed she hated me. Right this minute she hated me. I started shaking. She turned and walked out of the room and cried loudly and out of control. I just laid there and waited. I had no idea what to do. Later she came back in, her face red from crying, and she hugged me."

Scott stopped and stared at the wall.

"She told me she loved me because she had to because she was my mother. But she didn't *like me*."

Scott sat silently.

After a minute Ken asked, "Do you ever cry?"

Scott thought about it. He always held it in. "No. Not really."

When Scott walked home from the session, he felt drained but very close to Ken. It felt good to share. He would force himself to do so every time. To get his money's worth.

The next week, Scott told Ken there was a lot more he wanted to share, but it was very difficult to talk about.

Scott said he didn't blame Ava because her childhood had been horrible. Much worse than his. Her father had committed suicide before she was born.

Ken told Scott he could, for now, acknowledge that what happened to him was bad without making excuses for Ava. It was important for him to understand that the abuse mattered. It had an effect on him.

"What effect?" Scott asked. "It was so long ago. How could it still matter?"

"How old were you when the abuse started?" Ken asked. "Your earliest memory."

"I think five. But it might have been earlier. That's just what I remember. I know because I checked the date of TV shows I used to watch."

"For how long a time period?"

Scott thought back. He had a sense it was over when Robert gave him a book to read about puberty, *Almost Twelve*.

"Five or six years. Maybe more."

"How many incidents?"

"Incidents?"

"Beatings."

Scott thought back.

"At one point, almost every day. Sometimes twice a day. If we were on vacation or something and she couldn't do it, she would tell me I would get it later, when we got home. So I would have to wait.

Sometimes I would try my best to act friendly toward her and be really good for the rest of the trip. To make up for the bad thing I did. But she would never forget. And then a week later she would tell me it was time. It almost always happened when no one was around, and my dad was at work."

"How did you feel?"

Scott closed his eyes. "Horrible. Ashamed. Terrified. Never safe. Always gauging her mood. Waiting. The look on her face...."

Scott stopped talking and stared away from Ken.

After watching him for almost a minute, Ken asked, "Where are you?"

Scott paused, then spoke quietly.

"I masturbated to guys fighting on shows like *The Wild Wild West*. Also fist fights in comic books like *Spider-Man*. I did it from as young as I can remember. I think it was an escape mechanism."

"Interesting," Ken said. "Absolutely an escape mechanism. A stress release. A way out. You had nowhere else to go. It saved you. A young child needs nurturing and protection. Abuse from a primary caregiver has a profound, damaging effect."

Scott sat quietly a moment. "I know I had very low self-esteem. I remember incidents from school."

"Of course, Ken said. "Think about the effect of the abuse on your self-perception. Your ability to share. Your ability to trust. You learned love was given, and then taken away."

"Maybe it really did matter," Scott said.

"It definitely mattered." Ken smiled. "And you've been carrying it around alone all this time. You need to share it. Tell Francisco."

A wave of fear shot through Scott.

"I can't. I would never."

"Why?"

"He'd think I'm weird. Damaged goods."

"You don't think people would be caring and supportive?"

"No. It's embarrassing."

"Think of when something bad happens to someone. Like an accident. It's not their fault. People care and show support. Think about how you feel toward someone that's hurt."

Scott sat and stared away from Ken. He removed himself from the room, mentally. He had a lot to absorb and needed to stop.

"What are you thinking?" Ken asked.

"It's okay. I'm just processing."

On his walk home, Scott felt he had made a major realization: the abuse mattered. It wasn't just a dark memory with no ramifications. If he traced it back, he could follow a path. If he started out with shame and low self-esteem, it was reasonable to conclude it would affect how he looked at life, and how he felt in relation to others. It would close him off, hide him away, in an attempt to stay safe. It made sense not to trust people or to open up. Why would he? A horrible precedent had been established by Ava.

The next session, Scott told Ken about his realization that the abuse mattered. Ken smiled broadly. He asked Scott to elaborate.

Scott said it was now clear to see that with no one to talk to, and with no frame of reference — in isolation — he grew up fearful of people and had a low self-image. The low self-esteem as a child made the world a scary place. It was terrifying before and after a beating. He was helpless and lacked any shred of control. Everything was potentially dangerous and threatening, laced with a fear of getting in trouble. Fear of making a mistake. Fear of others discovering he was actually something awful. The secret had to be hidden so that no one would find out. It would interfere with learning, because of the amount of mental energy required to keep the secret. He daydreamed constantly, lost in a fog. It made sense. He was ashamed, because he misbehaved and always made his mother cry. He didn't deserve love, because he was the horrible dark seed somehow planted within the family and disrupting it.

Ken wondered if Scott could talk to Ava about it.

"Absolutely not," Scott said. He refused to look at Ken. He *couldn't* meet his eyes.

"She would deny it, and twist it, and say I was making things up and that this was so typical for me," Scott said. "It would do incredible damage. To me and to her. She would be very upset. Now, she's old. There would be nothing to be gained."

Ken dropped it. They talked more about Scott's reluctance to tell Francisco about the abuse. A goal would be to share more of himself. It would be an important step toward coming out of hiding and establishing *intimacy*.

Scott hated the word, and didn't even understand what it meant. It sounded cheesy and corny. He felt he already had intimacy, even with a one-night-stand when they lay together and held each other in the morning before parting ways. They would probably never see each other again, but shared a nice moment. *That* was intimacy. Scott watched couples picking out groceries together in the supermarket and thought it looked forced, as if they thought what they were doing was so important. If that was intimacy, he didn't want it.

Ken told Scott he could think about planning a time to tell Francisco about the abuse. Maybe over dinner in a nice location.

Scott wasn't convinced sharing news about himself was important or would amount to anything. Why was Ken so relentless about pushing it? He told Scott people liked it when someone confided in them. It made them feel special and, in turn, they would share more of themselves. A pattern would develop. It was how people opened to each other.

Scott agreed to try. He trusted Ken. If he was going to be an active participant in therapy — and take it seriously — he was going to push himself to explore Ken's advice.

Weeks later, Scott and Francisco took a vacation. On the third night, they found a place for dinner with tables outside overlooking the ocean. Lanterns were scattered about, and the only other light came from the flames of a bonfire. Scott thought it was the perfect spot for his talk with Francisco.

He was very nervous. He felt the news he was about to share was like letting a genie out of a bottle. Once out he could never retract it.

"You know the therapist I've been seeing? Do you ever wonder what we talk about?" Scott asked. His heart pounded.

"Yes. Very curious," Francisco said. "You said it was about depression."

"It is. But there's a reason behind it." Scott reached for a glass of wine. "The truth is, I had a bad childhood." He paused. "I was beaten by my mother."

"Well, she's a very strong woman," Francisco said. "I'm sorry."

Scott didn't like the response and sat without speaking.

"So, she hit you a little bit?" Francisco asked.

"I don't think you get it. I was abused. Like, worse than *Mommie Dearest*."

"What's that?"

"Nothing. It's okay," Scott said. "I just wanted to tell you. My therapist said I should share more."

"I'm glad you did," Francisco said.

Scott immediately changed the subject. The conversation had bombed. Francisco didn't get it all. It wasn't about his mother being strong. What did that have to do with anything? Was he taking her side? At least the topic had been breached and now he wouldn't have to mention it ever again. Done. It was out in the open.

After dinner, Scott sat on a bench by the water outside a nightspot while Francisco explored the scene inside. Scott had one priority: to text Ken.

They had agreed not to text or send emails between sessions, but he didn't care. Ken had to know he had tried and failed to communicate with Francisco. He read the text carefully and repeatedly before pushing send.

Scott didn't expect a response because of the time difference with New York. When no response came the next day, Scott stopped checking his phone. He wanted to talk to Ken badly, but forced himself to wait.

What Scott felt for Ken was something new and strong. After 10 weeks of meetings, it was like having someone follow him around, shadowing him. Ken had become a confidant and Scott learned he liked it. He liked sharing. It felt like a real relationship. An important one.

Even on vacation, Scott found himself thinking about Ken and wanted to follow his advice and make Ken proud the next session that he had tried to open up. He wanted to prove to Ken he was worthy of his time. He worried Ken might drop him if he didn't perform, or show signs of improvement. Ken was a professional and didn't seem the type to waste his time on frivolity. Scott had lucked into finding him, and didn't want to blow it.

It bothered Scott the connection he felt with Ken was paid for, like a prostitute. Instead of paying for sex, he was paying for friendship. A relationship preset to expire with the final AMEX payment in a final, bitter twist. Except it wasn't a friendship, because it didn't flow both ways.

Ken kept himself a mystery and only released tidbits of information even though Scott was extremely curious and clung to anything that leaked out, like the neighborhood he lived in, where he liked to get coffee, and that he had a dog. But, Ken somehow had the ability to make Scott want to share.

Ken's eagerness to *know* Scott was intoxicating. Scott wanted him to. Scott looked out on the water and quizzed himself. What was it about Ken that resonated so strongly? Scott felt Ken actually cared about him. To be liked by and close to a person of a different race was profound and interesting. It shattered all assumptions that people carried innate preferences from their birth to favor people who looked like themselves, and would always tend to do so.

At their next session, Scott was eager to talk to Ken about the vacation and the dinner. Surely he must have been curious about the text message.

"Sorry I texted you," Scott said. "Did you get it?"

"Oh, yeah. Right. I think you sent something," Ken answered.

Scott was shocked and hurt. Why was he so dismissive?

"Can we talk about it?" Scott asked.

Ken nodded.

"I listened to your advice. I told Francisco about my mother at a dinner," Scott said. "But, it was a disaster."

"How so?"

"He took my mother's side." Scott answered. "He basically said we both know she's a strong woman, so what did I expect?"

Ken listened quietly and faced Scott.

"I told him he didn't understand. That it was worse than *Mommie Dearest*. He didn't even ask me any questions."

Scott sat and looked at Ken and waited for him to say something. He had shared enough and clearly proven the attempt at sharing had failed. Ken had to agree with him.

"Maybe he sensed you didn't want to talk about it," Ken said.

Scott puzzled on the possibility. "How could he sense that? I'm the one who brought it up."

"People pick up on things," Ken said. "You may have projected you didn't really want to get into it."

Scott paused. "It's possible."

He continued to sit and think. "I didn't."

"You can try again. Anytime."

Ken looked at Scott.

"You've been together for more than 10 years. It's obvious Francisco cares deeply for you. Otherwise, why would you still be together? You're so lucky to have someone."

Scott continued to listen.

"It's never too late to try again," Ken said. "You create your own future. You can share with him whenever you want."

"I'm not good at it," Scott said. "I just can't."

When the session ended, Scott left despondent.

Ken was acting strange. How could he not have realized the significance of the text message? He seemed uninterested and didn't really take Scott's side on anything. Was Ken getting bored with him? Was Scott lucky to have Francisco, because it was surprising anyone could tolerate Scott in the first place? He was bothered for days, but didn't tell Ken.

On Wednesday the following week, Scott's cell phone rang early while he was getting ready for work. It was Robert. What could he possibly want so early in the morning? It couldn't be good.

Scott sent the call into voice mail.

A minute later, he listened to the message, and learned that Ava had suffered a stroke the night before. She had collapsed in the living room, and was taken by ambulance to the hospital. It was serious.

Scott tentatively called Robert back. Ava was in the ICU and in critical condition, though it seemed she had stabilized. Robert was on the way to the hospital, and would call him later with more information. Scott didn't know what to do. If he went to visit, wouldn't he just be in the way? There wasn't anything anyone could do at this point, anyway. Maybe he could wait for the weekend to make the trip, because it was a bad time at work.

Scott decided he would talk to Ken about it at their session that evening.

As the day dragged on, he felt intense guilt. He was conflicted because he had been telling Ken about his childhood, and now — out of nowhere — his mother was gravely ill. It was like he had been bad-mouthing her. He wasn't even sure he wanted to visit, but knew he had to.

"The timing is unfortunate, given what we've been talking about," Ken said.

"I know," Scott said. "I'm feeling very angry toward her."

"That's okay," Ken said, "It's part of the process."

He sat silently and watched Scott.

"I've always felt sorry for her because she never met her father," Scott said. "Now, I also feel mad about it. How much she hurt me. Sometimes...."

Scott stopped and looked out the window beyond Ken's desk.

No one spoke for a moment.

"Where are you?" Ken asked quietly.

In another moment Scott continued.

"Sometimes, I think I hate her."

Scott looked as far away as possible to escape the eyes of Ken.

"She told me she hated me. And then came back and said she loved me because she had to." Scott spoke slowly, pausing after each sentence. "Only because she was my mother. She was *obligated* to love me. But she didn't *like* me. It's ironic, because now I love her. Because I have to. Because she's my mother. *But I don't like her.*"

There was silence, then Ken spoke.

"You are allowed to have multiple feelings toward your mother. It's a very complex relationship. Many people don't have only one set of feelings."

Scott looked at Ken, and tried to smile.

"That helps," Scott said.

"If you need or want to call me, we can do a phone session during your visit," Ken said.

The next day, Scott flew to Vermont and met Robert and Pamela at the hospital. The extent of damage from the stroke was not going to be clear for weeks — or perhaps even a year — but from indicators, Ava was able to communicate and doing okay. She was awake, and responding to doctors and physical therapists.

Scott sent Ken a text message and they agreed on a time to talk. Scott sat on a bench in a private spot outside the hospital and called him. Scott hated being home and the situation with Ava was worse than he had imagined. He had never been inside an ICU. Seeing Ava weak and in the bed was a horrible juxtaposition with the memories of childhood he had awakened of her as a giant towering over him.

They talked more about the concept of "multiple feelings." Scott found it very useful. It allowed him to compartmentalize the anger he felt to live alongside other feelings of love and concern.

He decided he would return to Vermont each month for the rest of the summer and into the fall, if necessary, to help. It wouldn't be fair to leave Robert and Pamela alone to deal with hospital visits and preparing meals for themselves. He wanted to offer Ava support, despite what was surfacing in therapy.

On Wednesday, Scott told Ken he would return to Vermont in two weeks, and was considering telling Pamela he was seeing a therapist. It was something he wanted to share only with her, but was afraid to state. Francisco was not going to be able to make the trip because of a work commitment.

Ken said it would be a perfect time to talk to Pamela.

"If I have a therapist, she's going to ask me, 'for what?'" Scott said.

"Then tell her."

"I can't."

Scott stopped talking and thought about what to say.

"What if she rejects my reason?"

"What reason?"

"The abuse. That what happened with my mother didn't happen. That I imagined it. That I am exaggerating things."

They sat silently.

"That it wasn't really that bad and I'm making it into a big deal," Scott said.

He continued to think.

"It would kill me if she said that," Scott said.

"You need to do this," Ken said.

"I want to try," Scott said. "It's so scary."

When the session ended and Scott walked home, he replayed it in his mind. He wanted to talk to Pamela. She had been a witness to at least some of the beatings. She was two years older than he, and would surely remember things. What would be so bad about mentioning he was seeing a therapist? If she acted strange about it, he would stop. If she seemed okay with it, he would offer more.

When Scott entered the apartment, Francisco greeted him with a hug.

"How was *terapista*?" Francisco asked.

"Good," Scott said. He hung up his jacket, and put away his work bag. *Please don't ask me anything specific.*

"Do you want a glass of wine?" Scott asked as he opened the refrigerator.

He always needed a glass or two after a session with Ken.

Scott liked to review everything they talked about. He studied the difficult parts. He decided no session was going to be complete if he didn't bring up at least one intense thing to talk about, one thing that made him really nervous. It was a new rule he made for himself. He liked the feeling of relief and accomplishment when he walked home after a difficult conversation. It meant something significant had been discussed.

Francisco watched *The Voice* across the room as Scott stood at the kitchen counter with the wine and wondered what to do about Pamela.

The next week, Scott left for Vermont. He called Pamela, and she invited him to visit Saturday afternoon in her backyard while Ava had rest time in the hospital. Scott was determined to talk to her. It would be like forcing himself to talk to Ken during a session. He would not feel satisfied that he had tried hard enough if he didn't dare tell Pamela about his therapy, and perhaps even the reason behind it. He wasn't sure exactly where it would lead, or what he hoped to accomplish. He would do it for Ken, because he trusted Ken's advice.

Scott drove to Pamela's house. Her sons were spending the afternoon with friends, and her husband was golfing. Scott and Pamela sat in the backyard, in teak wood chairs by the swimming pool. Scott grew nervous because he knew it was the perfect moment to talk in private. They spent almost an hour catching up on how work had been going and what trips they had planned. Now was the time. He had to do it.

"I want to share something with you," Scott said. "Something new I've been up to."

"Okay," Pamela said. She put down the magazine she had been leafing through.

"I've been seeing a therapist," Scott said. "Started in April."

"That's interesting. Do you like it?"

"I got lucky. I found a great doctor," Scott said. "I'm already learning a lot from him. It's only been four months."

"That's great," Pamela said.

Scott's heart pounded. He had to say it.

"I know it's not the best timing, but a lot of what I've been talking about with him is my relationship with Mom as a child."

"I would imagine so," Pamela said quietly.

Scott felt a wave of relief. Pamela not only accepted he was seeing a therapist, but concurred he had a right to do so. He was validated.

"Did you guys watch the fireworks by the lake this year?" Scott asked. He suddenly felt stupid for changing the subject.

"No. We could see them from here," Pamela said.

He had to force himself back to the conversation he had started.

"Do you still have memories of Mom from childhood?" Scott asked.

"Yes. But not many of them are good," Pamela said, and paused. "No, actually there were good times, but also lots of feelings of never being good enough. Not measuring up. Stuff like that."

"She beat me. A lot," Scott said.

"I know," Pamela said. "You got it the worst."

"My therapist is helping me with it," Scott said.

The door to the garage opened.

"Casey's home," Pamela said in a loud whisper. She seemed nervous.

"We'll talk more some other time," Scott said. "This was nice."

He didn't want to force the conversation or make it threatening.

Pamela got up to check on her son. Scott sat quietly and was relieved. He had never shared something so significant with Pamela, and it felt amazing. She'd even agreed with him. Scott silently thanked Ken. He was right.

Scott typed notes into his phone so he could accurately tell Ken about the conversation on Wednesday.

When they met, Scott told Ken the simple words from Pamela — "I would imagine so" — meant everything to him. It was an acknowledgment he felt he needed.

Scott returned to Vermont two weeks later. Ava was still in the ICU.

On Saturday afternoon, Scott and Pamela helped Robert with grocery shopping and straightening up the house. Scott was surprised by Pamela's attitude. She suddenly seemed bossy. Scott felt she talked down to him, like he was stupid, and he fired back a strong response. Why was she being so stern with him? They had just shared an important conversation two weeks ago.

On Wednesday, Scott told Ken about the exchange.

"She gave me orders," Scott said.

"How so?"

"She said she was putting me in charge of the plants."

"And?" Ken asked quietly.

"It's not her place to be the one assigning duties," Scott said.

Ken sat silently and looked at Scott.

"Who put her in charge?" Scott asked.

"It doesn't seem so unreasonable to me," Ken said.

"You don't think she sounded bossy?"

"No." He moved his head slowly and almost imperceptibly side to side.

Scott was confused and angry. Why was Ken taking her side? He had always been supportive but now he was turning on him.

"She might be feeling scared and a need to control the situation," Ken said.

Scott sat silently. He hadn't thought of that. Maybe she was simply fearful.

Was it possible he was actually the one being defensive? Obviously Ken thought so. It was very rare for Ken to blatantly disagree with him. There was something going on.

Scott thought about it on the walk home, and as he stood in the kitchen with a glass of wine and watched Francisco read his iPad. The more he thought about it, the more it made sense: he was himself defensive and reading the worst into the situation. It was a major realization. He felt attacked, but he could stop, step back, and examine if he were the one taking something the wrong way. It was possible to imagine Pamela might be as frightened or anxious as he was about Ava and taking care of Robert. It would be an acceptable excuse for her aggressive behavior. He could try to be more understanding instead of opting to immediately defend himself.

Scott told Ken about his realization at the next session.

A few weeks later, it was late September and Ava returned home from the hospital. She would have to continue physical therapy sessions for at least the rest of the year, but had escaped the stroke with remarkably little lasting damage. Scott went to visit.

With Ava in recovery, Robert had to assume responsibility for shopping, planning, and preparing meals. Scott unloaded the dishwasher, and set the table. As he stacked a pile of dishes to bring into the dining room, Robert walked into the kitchen behind him, and rested his hand on Scott's shoulder. He carried with him a small sample of the steak he was grilling outside on the patio.

"Here, try this," Robert said, and extended a fork with a morsel.

Scott's immediate reaction was annoyance. He was startled. Why did Robert need to touch him? He wasn't even hungry. It was only 5:30 and why was Robert already cooking dinner? Who eats so early, anyway? Country bumpkins, that's who.

Scott turned and saw the smile on his father's face. He tasted the sample.

"Wow, it's great," Scott said. "Thanks."

Robert looked pleased, and exited the kitchen to return to the grill.

Scott recognized he had just caught himself. His father was showing him love, and Scott's first, immediate reaction was to dismiss it. To be annoyed by it. To analyze and criticize it. Scott was startled by his realization. His father meant only to show him kindness, and Scott wanted no part of it. Why would that be his first reaction? How long had that been going on? He needed to tell Ken what he had just witnessed in himself.

On Wednesday, Scott told Ken it perhaps didn't sound like much, but to him it was a major realization. He caught himself in the kitchen. He did not want to accept love. He wasn't sure if he blocked it from just his parents, or from everyone. Maybe he didn't know how. It was something he had never even considered.

Ken listened intently. They continued to talk about the possibilities.

Scott wondered if the non-acceptance of love also extended to Francisco. Scott was able to show him love. *That* was allowed. But he did not apply significance to love offered in return. It was nice to hear, "I love you," but the words didn't particularly *mean* anything coming from someone else. It was like he lived within a force field, and could send love out, but none was allowed in.

"Tell this to Francisco," Ken said.

"I would never," Scott said. He was suddenly alarmed. *"Why would you even say that?"*

"To throw a snake at you," Ken said. "Exposure therapy."

"What's that?"

"A patient with a fear of heights gets better with repeated visits, little by little, to a higher floor," Ken said. "Over time, the fear loses its power."

Scott thought about it. So what was *he* afraid of?

"The idea of sharing anything personal like that really scares me."

"On a scale of one to ten?"

"I think a ten," Scott said. "My heart is pounding just thinking about doing it."

"First of all, Francisco is not a real snake," Ken said. "It's clear from everything you've told me about him."

Scott was silent and stared at the wall. He felt shame and couldn't face Ken.

"Like the way he texts you in the middle of the day that he misses you," Ken said. "And he likes to cuddle with you, even though you pull away."

Scott found it hard to focus and listen.

"It all suggests he really loves you," Ken said. "I bet he'd be very happy to get to know you even more. The parts of yourself you've been hiding."

Scott looked at Ken.

"The idea of it grosses me out. *Intimacy.* I hate that word. It sounds so weak. Pathetic," Scott said.

He felt he had to fight.

"I'm already telling you my secrets. That's hard enough. I'm not telling anyone else. That's what you're getting paid for."

"The aim is to help you stand on your own. To open you up to the people in your life," Ken said. "To create the kind of connection you feel in here in your real life. You can't just confide in me, and pull me into your cave with you."

"I don't dare. It won't work," Scott said, and sat quietly. He whispered: "I know myself."

In early October, Scott returned to Vermont. He brought three recipes with him that were his favorites to make for Francisco. On Saturday afternoon he told Ava and Robert he was going to prepare dinner for them to give them a break. He would do all of the preparation, cooking, table setting, and clean up. He wanted them just to relax. He gave them the choice of the three recipes, and they selected the honey mustard, pecan-crusted cod. He called to invite Pamela and her husband. They were happy to join. Pamela volunteered to bring a salad.

Scott was excited as he drove around town to get the ingredients. It felt good. He had never cooked for them ever before. It simply wasn't his role. He felt like everyone was bossy and somewhat territorial about the kitchen and grill, so he never tried to push his way in. They had no idea he could cook.

In early evening, he set the table to get that part out of the way.

Later, in the kitchen, Ava and Robert curiously and excitedly watched him as he dipped the cod in the honey mustard mixture, and then in the pecan and breadcrumb mixture, and arranged the fish on a large sheet pan.

When the fish finished cooking, he plated servings for each person, and brought them to the table. Everyone commented. Robert said it was the best fish he had ever had.

Scott felt an enormous surge of pride. He analyzed what he felt. It was a *connection* to his family. Something new. Cooking the meal, taking control, and forcing himself into the process had enabled him to do something nice for them and to observe the effect on them. He was actively showing love toward them, and it felt good. It was the first time he felt included, and not only an observer.

Later, when the dishes were cleaned and put away, Scott sat in the living room. Ken had told him to share more with Francisco. He knew it was something important to try to do. Scott wrote a note to Francisco and pushed send:

Thanks to my therapist, I am having the best visit ever with my family. It is the first time I have ever cooked for them.
(And the first time I have been allowed to cook for them because they are so bossy.) It's the first time I declared I am doing it and they all said it was amazing.
Francisco: *I'm so proud of you. Thanks for sharing this with me.*
Scott: *There's much more I should share with you. The therapist wants me to.*
Francisco: *Then please do!! I'm here for you and you know that.*

When Scott returned to New York, he told Ken about the dinner, and what it meant to him. He had an *impact* on his family. His presence mattered. He was valued. He wasn't only a wallflower to be tolerated, as he'd often previously felt. He had also shared his pride with Francisco in a text message. Scott told Ken that he'd taken his advice, and it worked. Francisco was very open and receptive to his sharing.

Over the next few weeks, Scott was fascinated with the idea that love *meant* something. It wasn't a one-way stream out. It also flowed back in. *That* was what gave the connected feeling. Also contentment. If he never allowed a stream in, he would remain isolated. Disconnected. It made sense.

Scott considered this a key realization. And in the weeks that followed, it led to an abrupt change in his sexual behavior. Why would he need to have multiple guys in order to feel approval and self-worth? He already had love from Francisco, if only he would believe it *meant* something. It wasn't an empty phrase.

If he concentrated on the flow back in he got from Francisco — and didn't shut it out — he would have no reason to have a "bar boyfriend" to reinforce the value he felt that he lacked. He was already valued and loved by Francisco. Scott was the one unwilling to accept it.

Scott returned to Vermont for Thanksgiving, and brought Francisco with him. Pamela cooked the turkey and all the rest, except for Scott's specialty: cheddar cheese and sage mashed potatoes.

Scott monitored himself carefully. He forced himself to observe and accept the small things his parents, Pamela, and Francisco did for him that showed love. He monitored when he felt alarmed and defensive. Was he reading the situation too harshly? Was he being too critical?

He continually forced himself to remember his main goal: whatever happened, whatever might make him nervous, the most important thing was simply to enjoy being a valued member of his family and to be loving and supportive, after a lifetime of hiding himself.

As his family milled about the room and readied for dessert, Scott needed to send Ken a text. Scott knew he wasn't supposed to send messages. But Ken had to know Scott felt his influence, even at the family dinner table. He didn't care about breaking the rules. This was more important.

Scott wanted Ken to know he loved him, but that would be impossible. So he would settle for gratitude. It was Thanksgiving, after all. Scott carefully composed his note and pushed send:

I am very thankful for the huge
positive effect you've had on my life.

A few moments later, Ken wrote back:

And I'm very thankful for being able to share
and learn alongside you. You are an amazing person!

Scott's eyes filled with quiet tears of joy. He swiveled away from the room to hide his face. Scott read Ken's response repeatedly, savoring each word.

At that exact moment he felt connected and content, as if a fog had lifted and he was experiencing the world, and all of its possibility, for the first time.

CHAPTER NINE
2014

The first week in January, Scott nervously sat across from Ken in his office. He had come to an important conclusion, and needed to share it.

Scott's foot twitched and he sat quietly, struggling to speak, staring toward the window beyond Ken's desk.

"What's up?" Ken asked as he watched him.

There was no way to escape. He had to summon the courage.

"I think I need to take a break from therapy," Scott said. "It's good timing. The start of a new year. A clean break."

"Why? What's going on?"

"So much has happened in the past few months. I need time to think."

"Elaborate."

"I need to review things myself. My realizations," Scott said. "I feel like I just woke up. Like Ebenezer Scrooge on Christmas morning when he wakes up and finds out there's still time. He didn't miss everything. I'm feeling things for the first time."

"A rebirth," Ken said.

"Yes. Exactly. That's how it feels," Scott said. "But, I know myself. If I don't study and review the reasons, I'll forget everything, and slip backwards again. I don't want to lose what I've gained."

Scott paused and Ken watched him.

"You don't know how much work it takes. How much I gotta force myself to watch what I'm doing and thinking. Like every minute of every day. The realizations want to fade away."

"Let's review them."

Scott gathered his thoughts.

"First, the idea that the abuse mattered. It had an impact. It wasn't just something sad in the faraway past."

Scott paused. "Then, the realization I can be the one who is defensive. When I get mad, it's not necessarily someone else's fault. I can think I got a dirty look. But actually the person's face might just look that way. Or maybe he wasn't even looking at me. Or maybe he was just thinking about his shitty job."

"Also, the idea that I dismiss love," Scott continued. "I don't like to accept it. Love means something — someone really likes you and cares about you and you are a part of their world. With my family, last fall was the first time I felt that way. Now, I feel included. I have a role to play. An impact on other people."

Scott stopped for a moment and stared away.

"I need to review these things, or I'll forget," Scott said. "I know myself. I need time to study what's happened."

"That's okay. It's fine if you want to take a break," Ken said. "But, why do you feel you need to be alone to review?"

"There's so much changing. I want to enjoy the new feeling I have and focus on it," Scott said. "I think I've already gotten everything out of therapy I want to."

"I think there's more we could do."

"I want to stop while I feel good about things."

"You've made remarkable progress in a short amount of time," Ken said.

"Thanks. I think so, too. I'm very happy about it."

"You can go even farther."

"I don't really want to." Scott stopped and looked at Ken. "I need time to think."

"Of course. Let's wait a week. Whatever you decide is fine."

When the session ended, Scott tried to figure out his own intentions as he walked home. Why did he think that continuing to study his breakthroughs and continuing with therapy were mutually exclusive? It didn't make sense. Why did he want to get away?

He cared about Ken and completely trusted him. He was elated with the new connection he felt with his family and Francisco. But Scott recognized he was still avoiding any kind of discussion in detail about what happened with his mother. Aside from one or two incidents, Ken actually knew very little about his childhood. Scott hadn't shared it. There was too much other stuff to talk about, like alarms and defensiveness.

It was clear Ken wanted to push intimacy on him, and Scott had no intention of complying. Scott simply didn't want it. Was that why he wanted to quit?

He knew how much he loved it when Ken gave him insight into things, like how moving by himself to NYC had meant something. It was a symptom of his need to run away from things, and also a search for safety. Sleeping with multiple partners had meant something. Not trusting people had meant something. It made him look for shreds of proof they didn't care about him, so he could get away first without getting hurt.

In light of these insights, it didn't seem running from Ken was the answer. Ken was key to helping Scott with the realization he had gone through his whole life not understanding how love worked and also that he was worthy of it. Scott was only now learning that *te amo* from Francisco was not a superficial declaration.

Scott felt he was on training wheels. Disconnection and depression were his previous states of normalcy — touchstones that brought comfort, despite their darkness, because of a lifetime of familiarity. He knew he could handle himself from behind their defensive barricade. But, certainly, he could explore and nurture the newly discovered states of connection and contentment while continuing with Ken. It made sense.

When he arrived home, Scott felt satisfied with his rationalization to continue therapy. But in doing so — if he was going to spend the money — he would have to resolve to tell Ken more about his childhood. Otherwise what would be the point? It was still a buried secret. He needed to come to grips with it, to see if sharing with Ken would have an effect. He didn't know what would be the outcome. He only knew he trusted Ken to figure it out with him.

On Friday, Scott received an email from the Vermont Youth Orchestra. He was going to delete the message, but noticed a call for former members to join an alumni orchestra to celebrate the 50th anniversary of the organization in May. Something resonated with him. He had stashed his violin in the top of a hallway closet and had considered giving it away, because of the potent memories it carried with it of his childhood. It stirred a deep sense of impotence, fear and low self-esteem. He felt it immediately if he even looked up at the black case. As if in a time capsule, he could revert back to the boy he was by touching the instrument. He didn't like the boy he found. Sad, lonely, afraid, weak.

Could he actually play with the orchestra for the reunion? He was sure he could practice and get back up to speed. He never forgot how to play. It would be only one piece, *Finlandia*, by Jean Sibelius, and he had played it a few times in the past. The alumni orchestra would play it as a special mid-concert feature of the current youth orchestra's final concert of the season.

He could anchor a trip to visit his parents around it, and invite them to the performance. It could be a fun activity for everyone. He was going to force himself to continue the momentum and try to forge a closer connection to his family. He would also be proud to pay tribute to the organization that had helped to give him a creative outlet, travel opportunities, support as a young musician and a friendship network as a student when he had desperately needed it.

He checked the date on his calendar. He could make the trip as a four-day weekend. There was no conflict. The job he had taken after grad school was in a technology niche, shielded from most of the politics he used to abhor. His department working on mobile apps was left to their own devices, literally. He filled out the questionnaire and replied that he would participate. They could count on him to travel to Vermont, attend the rehearsals and play in the concert.

Scott recognized his response was, in itself, a positive change. He never would have pushed himself forward in such a significant way in the past. Of that he was certain. He would have to tell Ken.

Scott got a step stool and took his violin down from the shelf in the closet. He brought it to his bedroom, placed it on the bed, and opened the case. The strings were tarnished and the pegs were loose. He would need to have it refurbished before he could begin to practice again. He searched the Internet and found a man on 57th Street who repaired string instruments. The next day he made an appointment and dropped off his violin.

Scott told Francisco about the concert and invited him to come with him to Vermont in May. He called Ava and Robert and told them to save the date. They were excited, and said they would also invite Pamela.

At his session with Ken on Wednesday, Scott told him about the orchestra, and also about his decision to continue with therapy. Ken smiled broadly.

Over the next several weeks, Scott and Ken talked about intimacy. Scott knew he didn't like it, want it, or even understand it, but would be willing to work toward trying to foster it with Francisco.

He recognized that his attraction to comic book superhero fights and TV show fisticuffs he developed in early childhood would never go away, and he would never know exactly what "normal" sexual attraction was supposed to be. He was an *Other*. A damaged anomaly, because of his childhood. Decades later, he was stuck in a pattern forged years before puberty.

Scott told Ken of an experiment he had conducted a few years past. He had met a guy who fit his definition of a perfect sexual specimen. A '10' for him erotically. An athletic, toned Ninja assassin. Over a period of months, the first three encounters were the best sex of his life. The fourth and fifth, less so, but still amazing. By the seventh, the guy was no longer a Ninja. He had become real. A friend. They never had sex again. Scott didn't want it.

And now he was trying to look at people as beings capable of — perhaps deserving of — intimacy. They weren't objects. They weren't fighting machines. But that realization led to a complete lack of sexual desire for any human at all. It was the opposite extreme of promiscuity. The primary things he found exciting were the comic book fist fights on Marvel.com and fight clips on YouTube. Scott wasn't sure the new situation was any better.

"Maybe it's just where you're at right now," Ken said.

He gave Scott a book to read called *The Erotic Mind*. Perhaps Scott could explore the idea there was no "normal" for sex. It was difficult and complicated for most people. He wasn't alone.

By the end of January, Scott wanted something concrete to help him absorb and accept his discovery that the abuse mattered, and had an impact upon his development. He often found himself ambivalent, questioning the idea that beatings from Ava had consequences beyond a scary childhood.

He told Ken he thought he could write a story about it, to try to explain to himself the trail of events that unfolded as he grew. He could use it as a reference when he found himself questioning the relevancy of seeking help, or questioning if there was really a lingering impact. Ken said it was an excellent idea — Scott could write random thoughts and memories, no matter how fragmented, and bring them to the next session.

Over the weekend, instead of random notes, Scott composed a two-page narrative that briefly summarized his childhood, and the subsequent impact on his self-esteem and perception of the world. It was the first time he had put anything on paper. He trembled as he wrote.

> *My grandfather killed himself which, it turns out, gravely impacted two generations of family members. Perhaps more to come. My mother never met her father. She was raised by her mother and 3 older brothers. I don't know specifics, but it wasn't pleasant or easy. My three uncles became alcoholics.... My earliest memory of being beaten by my mother was at five-years-old, but it might have been earlier. I don't have a way to be sure.... For a period*

of about six years, I lived in fear of beatings that were sometimes daily. The worst memories still upset me. I remember being lifted off the ground by the hair and shaken. And another time getting my face slammed into the corner of a book shelf. It gave me a scar I still have on my eyelid. I remember I had to lie to my friend that I got the injury by somehow hitting my face the edge of a soda can. Once after a beating I went into the bathroom and panicked when I rubbed my head and clumps of hair fell out onto the counter top.... My mother often sobbed loudly in the next room after a beating. This made it worse, because I felt guilty for making her so upset. I would sit and wait for the crying to stop.... I was blamed for the beatings because I was a very misbehaved child. I knocked over her favorite candy dish and it broke.... "This is how your sister is going to remember me," she shouted once, while I cowered on the floor after a beating. "Why are you are making me do this?".... I remember some mornings I was hit and had to stop crying before leaving to catch the school bus. It was normal for me to balance fear, shame and sadness with the everyday process of growing up and going to school. I steeled myself against anguish by retreating to an internal safety zone that blocked everything out until I was ready to emerge again.... I learned the world was a cruel place. I believed things were much more difficult than they actually were. When faced with an obstacle I gave up easily, because I assumed I was too stupid to figure it out.... I tested only average because I thought tests were designed to trick you. I could not concentrate or remain focused while teachers spoke and daydreamed through important dialog in movies and television shows. I played the violin very well as a member of an orchestra, and was concert master throughout high school. But in competitions where I was in the limelight of an audition, I would play far below my abilities, because I imagined what was required was unattainable and exceptionally, exponentially difficult. The critical attention of strangers terrified me.... I did not prepare for the SATs. I scored average and did not take them a second time. It was good enough.... It did not occur to me the abuse of my childhood had an effect on my life. But it had insidiously shaped the person I grew into.... I had very low self-esteem which also meant I didn't believe people liked me, or that I was worthy of being liked. I didn't properly learn to trust or accept love or friendship offered by others. I had no idea about this until just recently. I desired isolation.... But with isolation came depression.... It became normal to hide who I was and keep to myself.... To the outside world, I was aloof. Once people got to know me I cultivated different personae because I really didn't know who I was (I still don't).... I was into modern, pop-cultural stuff like new wave music. Relationships were mundane and boring, as were the trappings of the upper middle class, suburban model we were all supposed to desire. The punk rock persona I created fit me perfectly. Cold. Detached. Cynical. Modern. Alone.... By the end of my college career, I had many acquaintances, but few close friends. Junior year I had one intense, sexual relationship that I ended viciously after returning from summer break. This person had made the mistake of showing me true love, and I viewed it as weak, needy and pathetic. After that, I kept to myself and made plans to escape to where no one could find me. I moved alone to New York City two weeks after graduation from college.

Scott felt satisfied the narrative captured the essence of what he felt and proved to him that the effects from abuse did not end when the crying stopped. The abuse had a profound impact on the expectations he held for himself, and on his ability to trust situations or people. It impacted his performance at school, and at work. He couldn't take criticism. He never felt secure.

He never before had the insight to look at his progression as a child from an objective distance. It was a huge breakthrough to consider his life as a unified whole and write it down to see how things linked together. He was excited to share his discovery with Ken. He couldn't imagine daring to share the information with anyone else. They would know he was damaged.

First thing on Wednesday morning, Scott pulled the pages up on his computer at work and sent them to the printer. He rushed to retrieve the pages before anyone could stumble upon them sitting in the paper tray. He nonchalantly grabbed the two sheets, returned to his desk, and slipped them into his backpack.

That evening, he was more nervous than usual as he approached Ken's office. He felt scared and vulnerable, but eager to show Ken he had completed his homework.

"How are you?" Ken asked Scott as he sat in front of him.

"Fine. And you?"

Ken didn't respond. He smiled and looked at Scott.

"I wrote my story," Scott said. He stood, unzipped his backpack, and removed the papers. "It's short. I kept it on two pages."

Scott handed them to Ken. He sat back down and watched Ken as he read silently. Scott's foot twitched on the floor as he waited. What was Ken thinking?

"Did you tell me your grandfather killed himself?" Ken asked, as he continued to read.

"Of course," Scott said.

He started to feel sharing the story was a mistake. How could Ken have forgotten a detail like that? It had come up several times. Scott felt a sense of dread.

When he finished reading, Ken turned toward Scott.

"It's quite typical," he said.

The words pierced Scott like a torpedo. He didn't say anything.

"I thought you were going to write trauma memories," Ken said.

"I did. That's what I wrote."

"This is more like a story. A summary."

"That's how I wrote it. I'm a writer. Sorry if I made it into a story."

"Trauma memories are stored differently from regular memories," Ken said. "Like snippets in the brain that don't all fit together."

Scott was fully alarmed and furious. This was not unfolding at all like he expected. He could barely speak.

"I don't understand what you are saying."

"The story is very archetypal," Ken said. "Like it could be from a textbook."

"You think I made it up?" Scott asked.

He was trembling and refused to look at Ken.

"You think I copied it? I didn't. I can't believe you just said that."

"What I mean is, I have a lot of patients and your reaction to trauma is very in line with them," Ken said. "Very similar reactions. You are not unusual."

Scott stared out the window beyond Ken's gaze.

He was done talking. He would never share personal information ever again. It was a huge mistake, and he needed to get out of Ken's office. Unfortunately, he was stuck in the chair for another half hour, so he just sat. Maybe he could walk out. He could fake a stomach cramp or a migraine headache. He pondered which would be better.

"Where are you?" Ken asked.

After some time, Scott responded.

"Just thinking." He was not going to give Ken one shred of information.

Ken continued to speak. He said something about he was sorry, but didn't realize Scott felt strongly about the story because of the way he tossed the papers at him, or something like that. And something else about how he was taken by surprise because he was expecting something different, like a list or something specific. And something and something and something. Blah, blah, blah.

When the session finally ended, Scott quickly stood and grabbed his backpack. He walked out and for the first time didn't say goodbye. He purposefully left the "In Session" sign on the outside door knob without the courtesy of moving it inside. Ken could get up off his chair and do it himself. Scott was deep inside himself — barricaded — and hoped he signaled how thoroughly disgusted he was with the entire episode.

As he walked home, Scott had to pull himself together so he could communicate with Francisco without leaking out anything was wrong.

He decided he would simply compartmentalize the situation: He had stupidly decided to write the story, and then share it. Now he had learned his lesson. He would not be so stupid a second time. Not with Ken. Not with anyone. Problem solved.

He entered the apartment and Francisco asked him about *terapista*. Scott kissed him and said it was fine. He poured a glass of wine for both of them.

The next day, Scott felt worse. What had gone so terribly wrong? Ken's reaction had been very unusual and unlike him. Did he actually think he had copied the story from somewhere? What would be the point? Did Ken think telling him his story was typical was helpful? It certainly wasn't because it minimized his effort and signaled to Scott the story wasn't important. It was something mundane and no different from what everyone with some sort of a trauma background experienced.

Scott couldn't sleep well that night. The dissonance between the love he felt for Ken and the betrayal he felt after Ken read the story was too great.

When morning came, he couldn't stand it. He knew it was forbidden, but he had to text Ken or his whole weekend would be ruined. He couldn't wait for Wednesday's session while feeling so conflicted.

Scott typed a message from his office during lunch hour, and pressed send:

I can't believe you told me my story was mundane. Like I copied it from somewhere. I am so upset, I can't even sleep.

A moment later, Ken responded:

I think my words are being misheard.
I'm so sorry you are still upset!

Scott thought about what mattered most. He wrote:

I need to know you are still with me.

Ken quickly responded:

Isn't that obvious? I'm texting with you even though it is a dangerous boundary violation. Together we will work through this and we will both grow from it.

Scott liked Ken's response: *Okay. Thanks so much.*

Scott felt a wave of relief. Ken still cared about him. He could calm down.

As Scott approached Ken's office on Wednesday, he didn't know what to feel. Was he hurt or angry or was the whole prior session simply a big misunderstanding? He needed to make sense of it, and hoped Ken would deliver.

Scott hesitated before turning the corner to enter the office. He was very nervous, but there was no avoiding it.

"How are you?" Ken asked.

"Fine." Scott paused for a moment. "I'd like to talk about the last session. I'm still upset about the whole thing."

"I was wrong," Ken said. "I apologize for not handling it better."

Scott was surprised. He immediately felt lighter. It was another reason Scott knew he liked Ken so much: he wasn't perfect, and wasn't afraid to admit it.

"It's okay," Scott said.

"I completely misread the importance of that story to you," Ken said. "I was taken by surprise because I expected a list of trauma memories."

"I thought you'd have a lot of questions because there was new stuff you didn't know about," Scott said. "Instead, you were very blasé."

"Only because to me it was clear how your experience unfolded like so many other trauma patients," Ken said.

"What I wrote was painful and hard to live through," Scott said. "Your comment that it sounded just like other trauma cases made me feel like you were 'ho-hum' about it."

"I didn't express it correctly," Ken said. "My response was intended to make you feel validated and that you weren't all alone."

Scott sat quietly for a moment. He wanted more feedback.

"Your comment about the writing style made it sound like I didn't have trauma because those memories can't be written about cohesively," Scott said. "Or, implies that you think I made it up. Like I copied someone else's story."

"I didn't think that at all," Ken said. "I thought we had talked about you bringing in a specific list, so I was surprised with your generalized story. I really like the way you wrote it. I was just surprised. You left out specifics."

Scott paused to consider Ken's responses.

"It bugs me you didn't remember my grandfather killed himself. It came up multiple times. It's key to understand how my mother could have gotten so damaged. Check your notes."

"I know you mentioned it," Ken said. "At that moment, built into the story, it simply read as something new. I didn't forget."

Scott exhaled. He said quietly, "Okay. I feel better."

"Me too," Ken said. "We had a rupture. But you stuck with it and trusted we could work through it. You didn't trash the entire relationship over one disagreement. You can do the same thing with your real world relationships."

Scott smiled and was still. "Now, can we talk about the story?"

Ken laughed. "Of course. Tell me more about the punk rock thing. I had no idea."

When the session ended, Scott left fully confident he and Ken were back to normal. He liked the intensity of the honest communication. It made him feel very close to Ken, and now — a week later — he was proud to have shared his story. The rocky reception to the narrative was inconsequential. Misunderstandings and misreadings sometimes happened. It was good to learn he could handle it.

In the weeks that followed, Scott gathered his sheet music collection of concertos and old orchestral scores. With fresh strings, a new bridge, and a new sound post, his violin came back from the repair shop better than ever. Scott practiced every evening after work for the upcoming concert. It felt good to reclaim his violin from the upper reaches of the closet. It was no longer a sad symbol. Instead, he saw it as a new symbol of his desire to connect with the world around him.

He received notification of the seating chart for the alumni violin section via email. He would sit toward the back of the second violins.

It wasn't glamorous, but it was perfectly fine. He was honored to be playing at all.

He knew only one other person returning for the concert, the former concert-mistress of the orchestra. Scott had played in the first violin section several stands behind her and wondered if she would remember him after so many years.

He downloaded the second violin score for *Finlandia* and practiced it, sometimes playing along with full orchestra in the background from his Spotify collection. A few passages were difficult, but like the child he remembered, he got to a B-plus level with minimal effort.

In his sessions with Ken, Scott realized he'd still avoided sharing specifics about beating incidents from Ava. He didn't know exactly why, beyond the obvious fact they were painful to remember. He also doubted how talking about the abuse could possibly help. It would only dredge up memories that were perhaps best left buried.

Scott told Ken he sometimes got disconcerting flashback memories. A burnt-orange plastic clamp used to connect Hot Wheels track to a window ledge could suddenly pop into a memory and make him feel an overwhelming sense of panic. If he searched the Internet for the clamp, he could find the exact one. If he forced himself, he could remember racing cars down the track in the playroom. And then a beating would happen. And he would find himself lying on the floor with the clamp near his face and the track a tangled mess beneath him. Somehow, years later, the image of the clamp remained a potent reminder of something dark.

He could also trace his lifelong proclivity for daydreaming — or perhaps even disassociation — to its genesis in a small sandbox in his backyard where he would sit within its confines, playing with a truck, desperate to escape Ava's watchful glare through the kitchen window, knowing he was outdoors where for the moment he was safely out of reach.

"I know we haven't talked that much about specifics. About my mother," Scott told Ken at a later session. "I've only told you a few things. But, there's more."

"What can you share?" Ken asked quietly.

"The final beating. I remember it. The last time she did it," Scott said as his voice trailed off.

Scott sat with both hands gripped together in his lap. He looked toward the window, away from Ken's eyes as he spoke.

"It started the same as other beatings. I have no idea what I did," Scott said. He stopped briefly between sentences.

"I have almost no clear memory of what led to the beatings. Just flashes of chaos during the beatings themselves. Out of control. Watching the world spin around, sometimes upside down."

Scott looked quickly at Ken and then back to the window.

"Like, there is no clear trail of 'X' happened, which lead to 'Y'. Except for maybe two instances. I have a clear memory of breaking a red candy dish which led to a horrible beating. I was very young. Like five. And we replaced the dish, but somehow I managed to break it again and the beating happened again."

Scott closed his eyes.

"I remember another time in the kitchen. I hid my report card and got caught. The beating was awful. But for all the rest, I don't know exactly what I did that led to a beating. Just a feeling of extreme dread prior to an attack. The feeling of dread is separate from the beating itself, which is separate from the aftermath, which was sometimes worse. Lying on the floor. Waiting for her to stop crying and to come back in."

Scott looked quickly at Ken to see if he was listening. Ken sat quietly, attentive, leaning forward. Scott again closed his eyes.

"The final beating, I remember. I don't know what I did to start it. But I remember being dragged on the floor in the hallway between the kitchen and the TV room. I hated being dragged. On my back. Pulled forward by one arm. Knowing the beating would happen in the next room. Kicking to try to stop the advance down the hallway, but with nowhere to go. A helpless feeling."

"This time, I remember she dragged me to the center of the room. I stayed down on the floor and watched as she walked to the closet to get a belt. She grabbed one and came toward me. I tried to back away, but she picked me up and I remember a feeling of rage. I was older now. Like 10 or 11. And I screamed at her as loud as I could:

"What are you doing?

It's not that bad!

What I did is not that bad!

What are you doing?"

Scott paused. "I was old enough to figure out her punishment was too extreme for whatever I had done. I screamed at her and she put the belt down. She hung it back in the closet and left the room."

Scott looked at Ken.

"I finally stood up for myself and she stopped. She never hit me again."

Ken looked at Scott and smiled. They sat silently for a moment.

"Talking about this stirs up other stuff," Scott said.

"What do you mean?" Ken asked.

"Other things pop up. Memories. Flashes."

"Elaborate."

"Like with the Hot Wheels clamp."

"Trauma memories," Ken said. "Snippets of things."

"Yes."

"Maybe you can write them down."

Scott hesitated. "What good would that do?"

"You can take away their power by exposing them."

"I don't know if I can do it," Scott said. "I don't think I dare. You remember what happened the last time I wrote something."

Ken stood and went to his bookshelf. He took down a DVD of a movie and handed it to Scott.

"Watch this first."

Scott looked at the cover. The film was entitled *Trust. Second Acts in Young Lives*.

"The kids in this are incredible," Ken said. "You'll be inspired."

"What should I do?"

Chapter 9 / 2014

"Watch the film. Then go to a quiet place and just write whatever snippets you can dig up. Anything. They don't have to make sense. You don't have to write them neatly. Just dig. Let your mind wander. Take your time. Be kind to yourself."

When the session ended, Scott took the DVD, thanked Ken, and walked home. He thought about his homework. The timing was good because Francisco would be away for the weekend on a business trip.

On Friday night, Scott watched the film in the living room. It told the story of a theater group in Chicago made up of teenage actors who write and perform plays based on the true stories of the members. The main character dared to share her traumatic story, and in return gained overwhelming support and friendship from the group. Scott marveled at the girl's courage to open herself, and at the bonds that formed after she dared to trust. They didn't reject her or find her damaged. It was the exactly the opposite. She was a role model, an inspiration. Scott decided to use her example to force himself to write a memory list.

In the morning, Scott made coffee and sat at his computer. He closed his eyes, then opened them again each time he was ready to type. He realized he was shaking, but continued to write, forcing each memory fragment onto the page. Two hours later, he had a three-page list with 43 incidents recorded. He re-read the first three:

Grabbed by shirt and shaken so red turtle neck stretches out and later I have to try to make it look like its fine or I will be blamed....

Trapped on floor of bottom of closet with boots and shoes above my head. Want to get out, but don't dare to move....

In basement, by washing machine. She shoved my face into something awful. Stain in underwear.

Scott stopped reading and saved the document. He had written enough.

On Wednesday, Scott shared the memory listing. Ken told him had anyone known, he would have been taken into care by child welfare services until his mother could get help.

A few weeks later, Scott and Francisco traveled to Vermont for the alumni concert. Scott had rehearsals Saturday morning, and the concert was late Sunday afternoon. Scott planned a shrimp and pasta dish to make for everyone Saturday evening, and they would all go out to dinner Sunday after the concert.

At rehearsal Saturday morning, Scott stood near the back of the hall, watching the excited movements about the room as some musicians took their seats on stage and others continued to arrive. He noticed the one player he knew from years past, the former concert-mistress, Jessica. She flashed a big smile and excitedly waved. Scott turned around to see who she was greeting, but there was no one behind him. He was shocked it was him she was waving to. He smiled and waved back. How did Jessica recognize him? He was amazed. She was an important player and he was a nobody. She walked toward him and hugged him.

"It's so good to see you!" Jessica said.

"You too," Scott said. "I can't believe you remember me."

"Of course! I studied the list for names I knew. You look how I remember, just grown-up now. It's great you came back for the concert."

They continued to chat. She had remained in Vermont, played in local ensembles, and had many private music students. They made their way to the rehearsal stage with the other orchestra members. Jessica seemed to know everyone, and introduced Scott to other violinists as they took their seats.

The conductor took to the podium, and began the rehearsal. He explained *Finlandia* was composed to protest the increasing power and control of the Russian Empire over Finland. He coached the brass section to think of Vladimir Putin overtaking Crimea as they blasted the brash, menacing opening chords of the piece. Scott struggled with a few difficult passages, but he was fully prepared to play. His practice had paid off. Following Jessica's warm reception, Scott was already happy he had made the trip and felt connected to the universe.

After rehearsal, Scott and Francisco shopped for the ingredients they would need for dinner. They returned home, and spent the afternoon relaxing with Ava and Robert.

Ava's recovery was nearly complete, but Robert still shouldered more responsibility for meals and household maintenance than before her stroke. As the day progressed, Scott repeated his approach from October: he told his parents to enjoy the evening free from chores and he would take care of dinner. And like before, Scott found contentment as he watched himself contribute to his family's happiness.

The next day, Francisco took photos of Scott dressed in his tuxedo as he posed with Ava and Robert. They drove to the auditorium, and Pamela met them in front of the entry doors. Scott hugged them and left to join the orchestra for a quick rehearsal onstage before the concert. Scott agreed to find them all afterward.

When the time came for the alumni orchestra to take the stage, the performance unfolded for Scott as if in slow motion. He looked out at the audience from his spot near the back of the second violin section to try to find where his family was seated. He located their faces in the crowd, and they seemed to be looking for him, though he was hidden deep within the belly of the ensemble. As the brass section began the bombastic opening to *Finlandia*, Scott realized the initial darkness of the piece, followed by episodes of intense struggle — and ultimately soaring triumph — echoed what he was feeling. He played with as much prowess as he could muster. When the conductor motioned to the violins to attack the upper octaves of the concluding sequence even more vigorously — with everything they had — Scott played as powerfully as he could. He knew he would not be performing again. It was his final concert. But he was immeasurably grateful to be playing at all. The violin, and the memories packed with it, had come out of storage. He was climbing out of hiding. The concert — with Ava, Robert, Pamela, and Francisco in the audience — was proof to him the process had started. *He* had brought them there. *He* had an impact. *He* was capable of changing.

The instant the orchestra pushed off the final note, the audience cheered. Scott beamed and stood with the rest of the ensemble at the conductor's signal. Scott savored the moment and wanted to remember the feeling. He was proud.

As the applause tapered off and the orchestra members filed off stage, Scott made his way toward the exit. He heard someone call his name. He turned to look and saw Francisco, who had moved to the front of the audience to take Scott's photo. Scott stopped walking and paused to smile.

At his session on Wednesday, Scott told Ken about the concert. He unpacked a portable, wireless speaker from his backpack and streamed a recording of *Finlandia* so Ken could hear it with better sound than the built-in speakers on his office computer. Scott did his best to convey the experience. He showed Ken the photo Francisco took of him. Ken asked Scott to email it to him. Scott was surprised and happy Ken actually wanted a copy. Ken opened the photo on his computer screen.

"It shows a pride I haven't seen in you," Ken said. "It's on your face. Your highest self. It's going to play on the highlight reel in my mind. I'd even love to hang it so I can always remember what we've accomplished together."

Scott was quietly elated. He smiled and looked at the photo on Ken's screen.

In the months that followed, Scott focused on and reviewed everything he had learned. He found himself in a near constant state of analyzing interactions and thoughts many times each day. In the same way a person who remains skinny throughout life is highly aware of absolutely everything consumed over the course of a day, Scott realized he had to continually monitor his thinking patterns. There was continual pressure to fall back into old habits and return to his go-to state of anxiety and withdrawal. He caught himself many times a day needing to reassure himself that a raised voice or a perceived slight were very likely not threatening or aimed at him. He accepted that it would be a new way of life. It would be okay. He was learning to immediately sense an alarm, quickly parse it, and drain its power over him as soon as it was clear he was simply reacting with a learned, knee-jerk reaction embedded many years ago.

Ken told Scott people were social animals. They needed each other to survive. Animals banished from the pack died without social contact.

Ken's analogy resonated, and Scott recognized he needed to resist a strong impulse to push Francisco away whenever he showed Scott love. When his department at work got outsourced, Scott didn't want to go on Francisco's health insurance, because it would make him dependent and a charity case. Scott refused Ken's offer of a reduced fee until Scott was back on his feet financially.

"You've got people who love and care about you," Ken said. "But you think you are a charity. A charity boyfriend. A charity patient."

"I know he loves me," Scott said. "He shows me. But it's something I reject. I resist it."

"Tell this to him," Ken said.

"How? When?"

"Why don't you ask him to come to a session with you?"

Scott froze.

"I could never do that," he said. "I'm not here for couple's therapy."

"Sharing this part of your world with him would be a big step," Ken said.

Scott closed his eyes. "I need time to think."

For the next several weeks, Scott toyed with the idea. On some level, he wanted to share his therapy experience with Francisco. Meeting with Ken had become an important part of his life, and if he truly loved Francisco — which he did — he wanted Francisco to see the office he disappeared into each Wednesday evening. It made sense.

But something about the idea terrified him. He couldn't put his finger on exactly what, because, rationally, he recognized there was nothing particularly scary about it. So what was so frightening? Perhaps it was the utter intimacy of the act. It was completely out of character for Scott to step up and assertively share anything so personal. As his report card so many years ago had noted, his assertiveness needed improvement. Surely he was ready now, no? His assertiveness preparing the dinner had worked. His assertiveness preparing for the concert and spearheading a family outing around it had left him surging with pride. All of Ken's suggestions in the past had been for the best. Scott would try again.

"Do you ever wonder about what I do with *terapista*?" Scott asked Francisco one night before dinner.

"Of course," Francisco answered.

"Do you want to come to a session with me?" Scott asked. His heart pounded. Could he do this?

"To talk about what? Me?" Francisco asked.

"No. Just to show you where I go. To share it with you," Scott said. "I'd like you to meet my therapist, Ken. He's very nice. He tells me it's important for me to share things."

"Okay. When?"

"This Wednesday?"

Francisco checked his phone calendar and said okay. Scott exhaled and forced himself to act nonchalant. But inside he was nervous. He feared that it would be like starting a war. He had no idea how it would turn out, but once started, it would be impossible to simply apologize, admit a mistake, and go back to how things were.

On Wednesday he agreed to meet Francisco in the street outside Ken's office, so they could go up together.

"Don't know why I'm so nervous," Scott told Francisco as he greeted him.

"Nervous? Don't be," Francisco said. He seemed completely at ease. The contrast between Scott's incipient panic and Francisco's apparent calmness unsettled Scott further.

Scott opened the front doors and took Francisco to the security desk, where they both signed in. They got in the elevator, and Scott led Francisco to Ken's office door. At this point, Scott was going completely on auto-pilot, forcing himself forward because there was no way out, but already removed from the situation mentally. Scott looked around the corner into Ken's office, and caught his eye.

"Hi Ken. Want you to meet Francisco," Scott said as they entered Ken's office. Scott tried to project confidence and calm, though his heart was pounding.

Ken extended his hand to Francisco. "It's great to meet you."

Francisco sat in the chair that usually held Scott's backpack. Scott placed the 'In Session' sign on the knob and closed the door. As he listened to Ken and Francisco make small talk, Scott felt alienated. The entire dynamic he had come to expect in the room was now completely different. He felt like the outsider. Ken and Francisco were already getting along famously, politely laughing. At what, Scott didn't know. He didn't hear.

When the introductions stopped, Ken looked at Scott with an expectant look on his face that forced him to speak.

"We thought it'd be nice for you to come to a session," Scott said, looking at Francisco. "Ken's been pushing for it."

Each word was an effort to force out. He heard his voice, but it was as if from a distance. Like someone else was saying it.

"Okay, that's cool," Francisco said.

Ken looked at Scott. It was clear Scott didn't know what to say.

"What is the goal?" Ken asked.

Scott paused. "I'm trying to share more."

"That's great," Francisco said. "I'd love that."

Scott stared at the window beyond Ken's head. "It's hard for me to do it."

No one spoke for a moment. Scott felt the silence was incredibly awkward, but he couldn't make words come out.

"And why do you think that is?" Ken asked Scott.

Scott couldn't believe how horribly the session was unfolding. He looked at the clock and only two or three or five minutes had passed. They both stared at him.

"I think it's because of the way I grew up," Scott said. "The childhood."

Scott looked away from both of them. Was Ken going to push the abuse topic? There was absolutely no way he was going to talk about it, right now, in front of Francisco. He had to change the subject.

"Even sometimes with friends, I don't like to share," Scott managed to say.

Francisco jumped in. "I know. There are many times when they ask you about yourself or your career and you act like you are being attacked."

Francisco looked at Ken as he spoke, and Ken nodded with approval. It was as if Francisco was telling on him.

"Like it happened with Karla last week," Francisco continued. "She asked a simple question and you sounded snippy in your answer. Defensive."

Ken smiled and Scott thought he looked pleased as a peacock. He had the proof he knew existed. Scott had to defend himself.

"That's because many times people are being snobby," Scott said. "All they care about is sizing you up to see if you are worthy of their time. If your job is good enough."

"He does it a lot," Francisco said to Ken.

Francisco continued to elaborate and Scott was terrified. He glanced back at the clock. What he instinctively feared would be awful had come to pass. Ken and Francisco were openly discussing him. Tag-teaming him. It was two against one, like an intervention. He felt completely blindsided by Ken. Scott didn't feel protected and safe. He felt scrutinized and under attack. Ken seemed to like Francisco even more than him. And why wouldn't he? There was nothing not to like about Francisco. Scott had to get out of there. The hands on the clock moved so slowly.

Scott managed to say more throughout the session that made it seem like he was a part of the conversation, but he wasn't really there. When the time finally came to a close, Ken thanked Francisco for coming and said he hoped he would come again. Scott cringed. It would never happen. He would make sure of it. As they left the office, Scott gave Ken a dirty look, but wasn't certain it came through.

Outside, as they walked home, Scott tried to act nonchalant.

"How did you like it?" Scott asked.

"Loved it," Francisco answered. "Ken's really cool."

"I thought it was a nightmare," Scott said.

"Really? You seemed okay."

"I wasn't. It was really hard for me. Felt like I was the crazy one, and you two were backing each other up."

"I'm sorry," Francisco said.

"But I'm glad you came. You got to see where I go every week. You got to meet Ken."

At his session a week later, Scott closed the door to Ken's office and collapsed in the chair.

"We need to talk about last week," Scott said.

"Okay. Tell me about it," Ken said.

"It was horrible. Worse than I expected."

"Elaborate."

"I was unaware how I would react with Francisco here in your office with me. It was a whole different feeling. I was accustomed to your full attention. But, it felt like I was the mental patient and both of you were analyzing me. You were on the same side as Francisco. It was strange sharing you with him. I wasn't prepared for it."

"I'm sorry you felt that way," Ken said. "Had I known, I would have done more to moderate that."

Scott paused before he spoke. "But I'm glad he came with me. At least I tried to show him."

"It was a huge step."

"It proves to me there's something wrong with me. With intimacy. Sharing."

"You'll get better at it," Ken said. "Little by little. Starting in here."

Scott gathered his thoughts. "There are things I'll only tell you. Private things."

"You also have to share with Francisco," Ken said.

"That's bullshit," Scott said.

Ken listened intently.

"What's the point of having a therapist if in reality people are just supposed to share everything with their partner, anyway? Why does your field even exist? Why are therapists even needed, if it's just so easy to share with someone — anyone — else? Some things cannot be shared with anyone else, because they're too difficult to talk about, and too profound for the other person to know how to react."

Scott stared at Ken and waited for him to speak.

"I agree with you," Ken said. "You changed my mind."

His response reinforced to Scott why he cared so much for him. Ken was flexible. He didn't think he had all the answers. He admitted to making mistakes. But in the process, he gained the trust that enabled Scott to open to him in the first place. To begin his journey out of hiding.

Ken had become a brother, partner, and father figure all in one. He was all of them, and none of them. Someone unique and difficult to define, with a special status. Calling to mind his name in a stressful situation brought calm and clarity. Scott's sole regret was the gnawing reality Ken would be gone forever when therapy was ended. To never see Ken again would be unacceptable. But continuing to see him would be unsustainable. Scott avoided thinking about it.

In the months that followed, Scott continued to process his feelings about his mother. He wondered if he needed to forgive her. But there was nothing to forgive, and Ava wasn't asking for it. Rather, the abuse was something he had to move on from because she never knew the corrosive damage that was inside her from the suicide of her father. She thought the pain had to be stoically faced, alone and without any help. Seeking a therapist was seen as weak and an unnecessary indulgence. Her family didn't want to face, or even talk about, the suicide. It was something to be erased. Except its pernicious influence lived on through actions. Had Ava known what was happening inside, Scott reasoned, she never would have beaten him to the point of producing life-long consequences. She'd damaged him without ever knowing it, silently driven by the ghost of her father.

But for Scott, the way forward was inclusion and connection. With both his parents. Scott doubted Robert knew about the extent of the beatings because they usually happened during the work day. Even now, after Ava's stroke, Robert saw his role as protecting her at all costs. He'd taken care of her since they'd begun dating in college, when Robert had learned about her fatherless childhood.

Scott wondered about Pamela. It seemed her approach to parenting intentionally ran counter to Ava's approach. Through the years, Pamela coddled and attempted to overly protect her children from all manner of potential threats. But her efforts to control were not without consequence. At the Thanksgiving dinner table her youngest son exploded in front of everyone: "Mom, I see you watching me with that eagle eye. Stop it." Was it normal teenage angst or something deeper? Scott didn't know. But he saw a link. He knew Pamela had been there with him as a child, hiding inside her room, listening.

Scott assessed how he felt about his life. The songs playing on repeat in his head used to be the most crushingly poignant parts of orchestral works, like the morning after the storm at the end of *Night on Bald Mountain* by Mussorgsky. But now the overbearing sadness had dissipated. He rarely bottomed out. A nervous reaction didn't take over and completely ruin things. He could often control the alarm.

Scott vowed to write about his experience. It would help him to learn and to release things he had only shared with Ken. It would serve as a reference that his childhood had consequences. He still needed hard proof of it. He had been unable to add it up before he met Ken. Now it made sense in a linear way. For the first time, he could piece his life together as a sequential whole. He could follow how his grandfather's suicide had impacted three generations of his family.

Scott was no longer ashamed of the abuse. It wasn't his fault.

He would put it all in a book. He would share it with Francisco. It would be a big step toward a new life lived with authenticity and intimacy.

Fifteen months later, he finished a first draft.

Marriage between people of the same sex was now legal. A possibility. Scott wanted Francisco to know everything.

It was the best he could do. Scott hoped it was good enough.

AUTHOR'S AFTERWORD

The final chapters of *Grandson of a Ghost* describe the psychotherapy sessions that inspired me to write the book. I never could have done it — nor could I have sustained the effort — without the encouragement and continuing emotional support of my therapist.

All characters in the book have fictionalized names, and I write under a pen name to protect the privacy of my family. But the book is dedicated to Jacob Ham, Ph.D., a real-life person. And it's not much of a stretch to conclude the psychotherapist in the book — a character named Ken — is based on Jacob and the last two chapters are based on our sessions together.

I still didn't understand how pulling memories up to the surface could possibly help matters. In fact, in the short run, digging deep made me feel much worse. At times I resented digging. But Jacob explained to me that exposing memories to the light of the present day would — over time — lessen their power over me. Exposing them would allow me to file the memories away properly, instead of feeling a vague, vast pit of pain inside that I felt forbidden to access, but at the same time fueled my feelings of low self-esteem, shame, sadness and the need to hide myself.

I was fascinated by the idea that life unfolds in a sequence like falling dominoes. My childhood impacted future events because of the way I grew to perceive the world as a threatening place where I was defective — much worse than other kids — and I needed to be constantly on guard to protect myself. Abuse from a primary caregiver in turn made everything in the world very scary.

This now makes sense to me, but I wanted to put words on paper to cement the idea and have something to use as a permanent reference to keep me pushing forward. I outlined the book in sequence so that I could literally follow the narrative as it unfolded. That meant starting when the abuse began, the most difficult memories first. Jacob suggested I save the first chapters for later, so I could work up to them with some momentum. But I wanted to know if I could actually face and record the pain. The whole project would collapse if I couldn't. I needed to know.

The first chapter took months to write. I trembled at the keyboard while typing. I found it particularly difficult because I had to imagine and create the mindset of my mother and how she could have been plausibly driven to beat her child. Often stories never attempt to explain the reasons behind the perpetrator's actions. Jacob and I would discuss the portrayal of my mother often. He observed I was taking care to not portray her as a one-dimensional monster. But was I going too far to justify her actions? I didn't know, but it was the only way I could complete the chapter. I had to have a reason she did it. The story would be too painful without one.

The second chapter was somewhat easier to record because I was old enough as a character to have my own thoughts and motivations. I could wrest the perspective of the story away from my mother, and work with stronger real-life recollections because my character was now age 10 instead of 5. In sessions, I told Jacob how I found myself switching to "detached reporter mode," focusing on an accurate description of the narrative, instead of reliving the scenes as a reader or participant. The technique helped to remove me from the keyboard, but I still trembled. I had to text Jacob a few times while writing for moral support. A no-no, I know, but he tolerated my process. When I finished a chapter, I would send it to him to discuss at our next session. I paid a small, symbolic honorarium fee for his time to read.

As the chapter-writing process unfolded, Jacob told me I was mining deeply into crevices — much deeper than I would have been able to dig talking face to face because of the amount of time I spent at home: typing, reflecting and recording minute details. Extracting buried memories. Finding new relevancy in past actions long forgotten because now I had greater self-awareness.

We continued the cycle of my sending a chapter, followed by discussion. At first I attempted to just sit in our sessions, trying to make Jacob recount to me what he found interesting about the newly uncovered material. Things I had never shared. I wanted to test him so I could be sure he had read it, and didn't simply skim it. But he quickly caught on and turned the conversation to how I felt about writing it, what revelations surfaced, or what were the difficult parts. In between new chapter completions, we talked about other areas of my life: work, parents, partner. Sometimes real life would reflect or mimic events in the book, such as my avoidance of confrontations at work. The book started to become illustrative and educational.

I took special care in recounting the last two chapters. The prior chapters each cover time periods of three, five or even 13 years. But the final two chapters each cover only one. They serve as a record for me — and I hope as a general guide for others — of how Jacob was able to reach me and pull me out of hiding. How, working together, he got me to forge a connection with the world.

For that, I will always be grateful.

For that, I've dedicated the book to him.

Scott Depalma

www.ingramcontent.com/pod-product-compliance
Lightning Source LLC
Chambersburg PA
CBHW021121300426
44113CB00006B/245